C. E. LE MASSENA

Galli-Curci's

Life

Of Song

An
Opera Classics Book

Monitor Book Company, Inc.
PUBLISHERS

International Standard Book No.: 0-917734-00-9

Library of Congress Catalog Card No.: 76-46603

The author gratefully acknowledges his indebtedness to

MME. GALLI-CURCI for authorization and approval of this work;

HOMER SAMUELS for valuable assistance in supplying data and material, also for reading the manuscript and for suggestive modifications;

LAWRENCE EVANS and JACK SALTER for willing and helpful co-operation, for full access to their records, for supplying photographs, etc.;

DR. ARNOLD H. KEGEL for his personal account of the operation for goiter.

Acknowledgment is made to William Seward, Director of Operatic Archives, for furnishing the photographs in this book and for the facsimile signature of Galli-Curci on the front cover.

Publisher's Preface

Amelita Galli-Curci died on November 26, 1963, at the age of 81. She had retired from the opera and concert stages some years earlier and was living quietly and contentedly in La Jolla, California, devoting herself to painting, reading, occult philosophy, and preparing herself "for the exodus—The Great Adventure!"

This book, first published in 1945, has been re-issued in its original form to acquaint a new generation of music lovers with this "singing sorceress," and has also been brought up to date with a "Final Cycle" and an exclusive interview with Galli-Curci by William Seward, director of Operatic Archives.

Amelita Galli-Curci won triumphs and established herself as the most remarkable soprano of her day and generation by the magic of her glorious voice. Her singing will continue to live in the hearts of multitudes of music lovers the world over.

Contents

CYCLE OF
ANTECEDENCE

PRIOR TO 1889

"*Although brains may not be
universal, the heart is.*"

—GALLI-CURCI

Hereditary Background

E IS COUNTED superior who, during life, is able to record a single outstanding achievement or, in some miraculous manner, gain ascendancy over others even for a time. But what shall be said of one who, before the age of thirty-one, attains the pinnacle of fame and retains that place against all comers for years ahead! A genius? Yes, and more—a personality and an art of such rare kind and quality that, in combination, can create an exalted position for the fortunate possessor.

That one individual could make such conspicuously brilliant debuts at leading opera-houses in great world centers and, during thirty years (1906-1936) continuously and uninterruptedly give over one thousand performances and attract audiences which, in the aggregate, probably constitute the largest number any singer has ever faced, is a feat probably unprecedented in the annals of musical art; while the sums paid into box-offices, augmented by phonograph record sales, would run into several million dollars. No wonder H. C. Lahee characterized Galli-Curci as "undoubtedly the most popular singer of this day."

For such an unusual happening there is, of course, a cause—one whose sources extend back into an historic past and which the following narrative aims to trace and show thereby how the hand of fate mystically directs courses and fashions destinies; yet, there are four fundamental assets that must be present to guarantee a successful art career: *Family*—artistic temperament directly through inheritance or indirectly through individual endowment. *Environment*—esthetic development during early years. *Talent*—vital factor

1

of achievement without which distinction is impossible. Nationality —birth in a country with an outstanding cultural antecedent.

There is no adequate pictorial preface to a career of one whose life is music corporeally personified. At best, a picture can portray nothing but an outward view. What lies behind those mobile features and vitalizes them into being is not so much as hinted at in surface delineation. Look at any photographic reproduction of the subject of this record. Note every detail, consider every phase, then say if therefrom you can mentally retrace the life which it is sponsor for, or visualize its teeming episodes, reconstruct the past, reanimate the silent, impenetrable exterior until it becomes a living picture. Linger a moment longer over this very striking likeness, this charming figure resembling some rare Italian work of art.

Upon that finely-rounded face we can perceive no indication of what, when animated, the countenance discloses; nor does the reposeful manner express, in any way, the gentle, sympathetic range of highly-sensitized emotions, or show the graciousness, magnetic charm and gaiety of spirit of its original. Behind that apparent simplicity of mien all else is veiled—the spiritual, the erudite, the artistic pulse—and the woman? She is nowhere to be seen.

The continuity of a distinguished artist's life divides itself naturally into a series of cycles, the number depending upon the distinctive episodical situations involved leading, one by one, from the initial plan and purpose to the eventful crowning of a glorious career.

Oswald Spengler claims that history is a series of "cultures" in story form which bloom in different eras in different places according to destiny and corresponding to human lives—"culture" being taken for that inner symbolism which holds certain peoples together in certain parts of the world. "Art is an organism, not a system," according to his theory, and each art-genius is the chosen means of expression of that art. A history of music, then, is an impossibility since music is cyclic, each cycle being different and complete; hence, history can be continuous only through a series of "cultures" (cycles), chronologically linked, but never finished. Biography conforms also to this formula. Every life that has contributed to the world's welfare bears backward into the past and forward into the future with ante-natal influences determining and post-mortem influences projecting the particular kind of contribution made by any single individual, such influences applying both *pro* and *con* according to the nature and the scope of each and every cycle.

We cannot comprehend a life if we consider only its functioning period. We cannot comprehend a song unless we know the story of the singer and of the art that singer glorifies, unless we evaluate the relationship between the years of that existence and the years gone by. Galli-Curci's life did not begin the day of her birth, for the precise number of years of any individual existence is but a tiny portion of that continuity of which every individual is a part. The Galli-Curci "Life of Song" is cyclic—encompassing the past, the present, and the future of those activities with which she has been identified. Great lives exert influence for good long after they have ceased to be. The art of Raphael cannot be shut up in a time-span bounded by 1493-1520, nor that of Schubert by 1797-1828, nor that of Darwin by 1809-1882, nor that of Washington by 1732-1799, nor that of Wagner by 1813-1883, nor that of Christ by the days of Herod and of Pilate.

In every cycle man appears to have a two-fold aim—to find himself and to find his sphere—a combination that makes for consummate felicity. So the drama of life is just a spectacle of the struggle for existence and the survival of the fit.

In physical existence, the chief end is self-preservation and extension through reproduction, accomplished by an onward, unending march through many involved, but well-defined, cycles covering all phases of activity: creation, origin of evolution, advent of man, prehistoric operations, dawn of civilization, culture and education, discovery and invention, esthetic consciousness and religion, Christ, the New World, the Middle Ages, the Renaissance, the Modern World, and then—the Future with myriads of uncreated masterworks.

If one be of a mind to argue as to the chief end of art, he becomes enmeshed within a mass of staunch conflicting views; yet one thing is glaringly irrefutable—every artist worthy the name dreams of beauty in color, stone, and sound, and strives unceasingly to imprison it. Few fashion their lives independently because of the omnipotent "if," and Galli-Curci is no exception. *If* she had not been trained as a pianist; *if* her family had not needed financial assistance which she could render by giving lessons; *if* she had not possessed a voice; *if* she had not taken the advice of a great musician; *if* she had not listened to the birds and studied them; *if* she had not taken fate by the hand; *if* . . . she might have been . . . but why conjecture? That she recognized the "ifs" and bent them to her purpose and her will is all we need to know.

When we speak of Italy a flood of memories is unloosed covering a vast historical arena and extending far back into the past, perhaps even to the Garden of Eden which some Biblical scholars believe occupied the valley now filled with the Mediterranean Sea, so that Adam and Eve may have dwelt upon the very slopes of that fertile peninsula designated by geographers as Italy. Many familiar names crowd upon us for recognition, names that have reverberated around the world and shine as stars in so glorious a firmament!

With so rare a heritage and so excellent a prestige, it is no small honor to have been born Italian.

CYCLE OF
AWAKENING

1889-1906

"Anyone who will pay the price
can succeed."

—GALLI-CURCI

Cycle of Awakening

OVEMBER 18, 1889—an important date. Milan, on this particular calendar day, was pursuing its customary routine of business, art, and pleasure, but on the Via Oriani the usual household duties were interrupted because of the unceremonious visit of the proverbial stork, who deposited a female infant into the otherwise quiescent home of Enrico Galli, whose wife was Enrichetta Bellisoni, niece of Countess de Luna of Cadiz. The new arrival was christened Amelita, and shortly after the ceremonious event the Galli household returned to normalcy. It was a bright, sunny day, free of the usual November fog, which caused the composer Celega to remark: "*She was born on a sunbeam—she will become great.*" The parents had longed for an artist child and, as a good omen, placed a golden star over the infant's cradle.

This home was one of culture and refinement. Signor Galli was a prosperous man of business, Signora Galli a woman of unusual attainments, with a regal background gained, prior to her marriage, in temperamental Spain. The child's paternal grandfather had been an opera conductor and her grandmother, Carlotta Rota-Galli, an opera singer of high standing; thus, the environment was conducive to artistic growth and esthetic progress should the offspring show any trend toward cultural education. When a year old, Amelita was able not only to remember her mother's lullabies and airs, but could sing certain strains quite completely in time and tune with a high, clear voice. At the age of five, she began the study of piano earnestly, having disclosed a liking for the instrument during the previous pair of years by endeavoring to pick out on the keyboard, as an aid to

7

As a small girl (on lap of woman in front seat), in Milan, 1884-1885

Four-year-old Amelita

her singing, tunes she was familiar with, though scarcely tall enough to see the digits. Practice with an object was very different from experiment and she recalls the childish rebelliousness against the routine drudgery of earnest effort, though unaware that fingers must be trained to fashion music when bones and muscles are soft and pliable. Signora Galli always sat beside her daughter during the morning's practice from 6:30 to 8:00, explaining, and guiding the little mind and hands so as to make them like the work and comprehend the music they struggled to produce—a period enhanced by story-telling as an aid to that desired end.

At the age of seven, Amelita was taken to a performance of *The Huguenots* and thereby initiated into the demesne of grand opera. The child, however, was more interested in the ballet than in the singing and, upon returning home, tried to make her dolls dance rather than perform like prima donnas. By some strange psychic intuition, she sensed the relationship between the physical and the spiritual worlds. Unconsciously, she tried to grasp some of its mysterious significance through a closer contact with her inanimate playthings, which suddenly became real playmates. She endowed them with psychic vitality and they served her purpose well.

Amelita attended the International Institute for six years (1895-1901) and the Liceo Alessandro Manzoni for four years (1901-1905). The former was under German management, which meant thoroughness and industrious application, not only to the prescribed courses but to modern languages. The student therefore became conversant with German, French and English, acquiring facility in reading, writing and speaking these languages. This, with her acquired command of Italian and Spanish, gave her unusual linguistic culture.

At the same time she was receiving private piano instruction from Vincenzo Appiani, professor at the Royal Conservatory of Music. Amelita did not try to play the big, exhausting piano works because of her frail physique, but developed an excellent technic and touch through the less trying media of Chopin, Bach and Schumann. Of course, the opera scores she played and knew. In addition to this work, she studied theory and counterpoint as an adjunct to her piano course, attended concerts and opera, and so built up a splendid musical foundation, further strengthened through her daily association with musicians and other cultured folk, not the least of whom were the members of her own family. At the age of sixteen, therefore, Amelita was not only a thorough technical, but an erudite, musician. Always a thinker, she developed the habit of analyzing everything from the music she played to the problems they involved and applied the best principles thereof to her own use, a method that served her well throughout her whole career.

The elder brother, Giuseppe, two years her senior, was also making fast progress as a pianist and, at this time, counted a finer player than his sister who, not to be outdone by a boy, set out to catch up and pass him, if industry and determination were the means of doing so. For several years there was no interruption to this schedule. The second brother, Enrico, four years her junior, showed signs of possessing an excellent tenor voice but his preference was for the guitar, upon which instrument he became a skilled performer. Each member of the family now seemed set upon the road leading to a successful metier, although the young men applied themselves to business as the main vocation. Their childhood days were happy days, which fact unquestionably contributed to the molding of that blithesome disposition and serenity of demeanor so characteristic of Amelita's personality. Of those early days, Christmas was the happiest of all. If you wish to see the love-light flash in her eyes, lead the lady's memories back to Christmas-time in Milan when she was a child basking in the land of dreams. She will tell you that preparation for the grand event began months ahead leading up to the climax on the festal day with a family dinner and a candle-lit tree. The three children were equal factors in the celebration with parents and grandparents, who always attended these gay gatherings.

Amelita, Giuseppe and Enrico were not merely to be seen and not heard. They had individual parts to play and were expected to contribute their share to the entertainment after the dinner. As with other children, the night before was anything but one of sleep. Drowsy eyes scanned the outside darkness under a canopy of cold, blinking stars, hoping to catch a glimpse of the expected Christ-child, or of the angel host, or perhaps of Kris Kringle's sleigh; and, while Lita's vigils were unproductive her faith never wavered, because with the morning's sun came answers to her prayers.

Not alone she watched—that would have been too fearsome—her favorite doll, hugged tightly to the beating bosom, kept her company. Other dolls adorned the little household over which she presided, but this particular one was never displaced in her affections. Headless, with arms discolored and some fingers missing, an ungainly sight, yet full of charm for her—the charm begat by long familiarity and first love. It was this pair that, with the first flush of dawn and all the house hushed in silent slumber, stealthily stole downstairs to investigate and get the first Christmas thrill.

Sometimes the streets lay under a cloak of snow and roofs gleamed as if freshly painted white. Gardens seemed like huge frosted cakes and trees as if transplanted directly from Santa's land. Christmas is therefore peculiarly hallowed to Galli-Curci, whose career has compelled her to pass the festal day in divers places. From 1910 to 1920 every Christmas was spent upon the opera stage where, in the quietude of her dressing-room, sweet visions of the past, buried deep in memory, would arise to invest her tone, later in the evening, with an unusual mellow tenderness.

Children were taken to the cathedral on Christmas morn, its myriad pinnacles and statues glistening in the brilliant touch of Phoebus' rays upon the gleaming flakes of snow and outlined against the cloudless sky of blue. Within, the marble pavement was aglow with jeweled light—not gifts of the people, but the gifts of nature—a scintillating array of sunlit articles clothed in multi-colored garments of light filtering through stained-glass windows. Two antiphonal organs pealed forth joyous music tempered with anthems from a hundred boyish throats. The sanctuary was ablaze with light and, in the distance, the altar proclaiming the very presence of the Holy One to receive, as little Amelita thought, her thanks and adoration.

Christmas dinner was the crowning glory of the eventful day. At eight o'clock the joy of joys began. First, grandfather and grandmother, arm in arm; then father and mother, likewise united; and finally the children, hardly able to keep in line due to their excited eagerness. Ah, such a mother had they! Each had the privilege of naming a favorite dish for the menu. Amelita's was always chocolate with whipped cream. But once when she set a mechanical donkey spinning around the table, her special *entré* fared none too well, for the toy sped true and straight to the dish and wrought havoc to the contents by its unmannerly behavior.

The supreme rapture, however, was reserved for the aftermath—the family program, of which the most applauded number was grandmother's contribution. So perfect was her vocal method that, at three score years and ten, she could thrill her home audience as she had done her opera audience in years gone by. Her singing of "Una voce poco fa" from Rossini's *Il Barbiere di Siviglia*, was, according to Amelita, something never to be forgotten, and especially with grandfather, almost eighty, playing the accompaniment in grandiose style and manner. During the golden days of their life of art, he had conducted performances in which she had sung. Her girlish beauty and lovely voice had inspired ardor in his soul—his manly, gay personality and his fine musicianship had kindled a response in her receptive heart. And how they adored their grandchildren! It was only natural that these young folk should hold them in deepest reverence, and what passed from those beloved lips was accepted as the sacred truth.

Amelita's part was to play a piece and sing a song, which meant preparation. She acknowledges that her mind was more upon the undertaking than upon the music. Memorizing the words was a more difficult task than learning the music and perfecting the finger work. After her rendition of the prescribed song, her reward was a smile from the erstwhile prima donna and words of heartfelt encouragement. "Bene, bene, mia cara!" she would exclaim. "Perhaps some day you may be a better singer than I ever was." Perhaps! To be better than grandmother was impossible—to be as good, a not-too-easy goal to reach. The mere remembrance of the dear old lady's singing of "Qui la voce," from Bellini's *I Puritani*, in operatic fashion, still echoed in her ears, while the lovely quality of tone and pathos with which she invested the aria haunted her continually. Dreams and visions of a golden future! But there was her father, who had a greater interest in instrumental than in vocal music and weighed matters, whether of trade or art, in the financial scale; and her mother, who looked askance at any vocation leading to public stage appearances. It was neither the approval of her grandparents nor the disapproval of her parents that proved the influential factor in deciding her future course, but the playing of the famous Italian pianist, Ferruccio Busoni. After hearing him Amelita realized the utter futility of becoming such a player, her hands and strength precluding any such attainment. She went home after the concert, more sad than glad, subconsciously feeling that success for her as a pianist was impossible. Figuratively, she must have given up the idea then and there—a fortunate turn, since it paved the way for a coming *tour-de-force.*

Another juvenile characteristic peculiar to Amelita was a predilection for weaving napkin-rings with artistic wreathing thereon of the "Merry Christmas" motto. As this was the only thing she liked to do and the only thing she could do in the line of fancy-work, she kept the stock well supplied. Her breathless happiness, however, centered upon the building of her little Town of Bethlehem—a charming custom laden with tender sentiment and sublime associations. From colored pasteboard pictures, tiny houses were cut out and set up in a bed of moss, each held in place by a cardboard prop. In the center of the group was a sanctuary of laurel and evergreen entwined to represent the cradle of the Holy Babe—not perhaps as perfect in detail as the modern cut-out forms, but nevertheless sufficient for the purpose, as childish imagination is equal to any fancied suggestion and not perturbed by inharmonious discrepancies.

Until she grew up, her Holy City seemed the real abode of Christ with the radiant light on His golden curls and pure-white garment, the tiny outstretched hands offering everything she had wished and prayed for. Her devotions were thus fraught with additional fervor because there was so much she wanted. This, however, does not imply any inordinate degree of selfishness; indeed, there was much consideration of those less fortunate, for in a certain place stood a sack into which was deposited, from time to time, all sorts of things to be sent to orphans at Christmas, in which project Amelita took special interest.

There is no such thing as a Galli-Curci tantrum, for the little lady got rid of her last at the age of eight when, with thumb in mouth facing a wall and flowing tears to mar the usual smiling countenance, she realized the futility of petulant obstinacy. According to her own remembered version, Papa Galli was the direct cause of her conversion. A strict disciplinarian, he discountenanced ordinary childish modes of showing opposition to parental dictums; hence the children soon understood that stubbornness served no purpose and that tantrums were a waste of energy, more effectively applied to work. This new attitude of mind gave her control of temperament as an asset for acting, and that is an achievement of great worth. "Self control is the finest thing in life," avows this shrewd philosopher. "No one can stand the wear and tear of temperament, the artist least of all." Those of more sturdy stock might expect one Italian born to "blow up" occasionally so as to be in phase with that racial propensity, but no! "The Italian people are supposed to explode, but it is only the untrained peasants who let their emotions get the upper hand. We of the north have temperaments, of course, but from generations of Austrian supremacy we have learned to hold ourselves in check. Calm and unfeeling persons, on the other hand, are cabbages." In a word, the life-task of Galli-Curci has been to take the temper out of temperament and apply it more effectively; for, while temperament controlled is an engine that will drive one to success, temperament tempered with temper will as certainly destroy.

Amelita was strongly impressionable. Light, tinted glass, silks, flowers, sunsets—everything possessing color aroused her deepest interest. Stage performances held her rigid. At La Scala Opera House she would slip to the chair-edge and sit immovable and tense, as with beating pulse she became engrossed in the spectacle and tried to absorb everything she saw and heard. From six to sixteen she attended constantly, so grew familiar with all the standard operas. After each performance she would hurry home to re-act it all with her brothers, who served as supers for the self-appointed prima donna, who must have astonished them with her spontaneous outbursts, her sparkling high notes, her grandiose cadenzas, with improvised flute obbligato, and her dramatic windmill gestures. The finale was always tragically imposing, with the entire cast assassinated, the instrument of destruction being the large kitchen knife purloined by the elder brother.

At the age of twelve, her imagination had reached the point where it began to function outwardly. No longer was she satisfied with home productions. She began to build castles-in-the-air which assumed the shapes of opera houses with magnificent stages and georgeous settings. Comparisons, too, provided exercise for the rapidly expanding brain. She would link together the names of Amelita Galli and Adelina Patti, because both had an equal number of letters—a coincidence which she accepted as a beneficial omen. She believed in her star—the star of heredity which shines along a path for generations of music-minded people to stop, at last, over the cradle of an artist-to-be. Such precocious mentality had to be served also along other lines. At school, her best-liked studies were such as stirred imagination—history, geography, geology, botany, zoology—subjects that told of things accomplished, of adventure and discovery.

She was fascinated by books that described birds and animals and their modes of life; by flowers, which were actual personalities to her and utilized sometimes in operatic games. Fairy stories kept her alert, yet sobered by intelligent reading of biography. For science she had no relish, but revelled in classic poetry, always read in the original, from which she learned the rhythmic flow of words, though she could not always understand their mystifying meaning.

These make-believe enactments were productive in that they planted seeds of ambitious rectitude. Even while playing etudes she would sing the melodies and often became irritated at the lack of true legato in the instrument which stubbornly refused to respond to her caressing touch. Thus was developed a sense of music appreciation that fostered a desire to master the complete science of vocal art. It also proved that art was more direct and free coming from within oneself immediately instead of having to pass through an instrument. She became alive to the fact that singing was a surer mode of contact with auditors than piano, violin or orchestra, which are intermediary agencies.

This urge to find herself increased steadily, manifesting itself finally in 1905 when at the conservatory contests she won the gold medal prize for piano, and, though but a maid of sixteen, was tendered a position as professor which she accepted, and prepared to make playing and teaching life's vocation. But that was not to be —the cards of fate read otherwise. Her real vocation had not yet been revealed, nor had she herself any consciousness of what the future held in trust for her, or of what influences were directly bearing upon that future from the past. Since nationality by birth in a country with an outstanding cultural antecedent is the first fundamental asset to a career, those Italian-born enjoy a beneficial preponderance of this native inheritance. Italy is the melting-pot of eras, ages and epochs embracing people, lives and arts, yet it is not the birth-right of every Italian to have a voice. Singing is a natural, spontaneous expression of this people; however, natural singing is not always good singing, proper singing, artistic singing. Like many another girl, Amelita sang at work and at play but wished to do more—to express herself in song—but how? Little Italian boys, it is said, dream of being great tenors, little girls of being coloratura sopranos, and so her dream proved a most perplexing problem to which she now addressed herself. In the midst of this gigantic riddle-solving process, the Galli home in 1903 was brought low by sorrow, and to Amelita in particular, through the death of the beloved grandfather, who had been a fortifying bulwark guarding the budding talent of this destined child; yet, with grandmother to encourage and advise, she could still march upward toward that far-distant peak on which her eyes were covetously fixed—almost enshrouded in a maze of uncertainty and doubt.

Mascagni's Dictum

In 1890 the Milan music publisher, Sonzogno, offered a prize for the best one-act opera. The time was short—six weeks—the need most pressing for a certain young, unknown composer of twenty-six with the will to work and the ability to achieve. He bent to his task with such devotion and such skill that, when the jury met to consider the seventy-three manuscripts submitted, their judgment was unanimous and the award of $600 was bestowed upon *Cavalleria Rusticano*, by one Pietro Mascagni of Leghorn, a former student at Milan's conservatory.

The success of this bold adventurer was hailed with utmost delight at the Galli residence, wherein the youth was always welcome as a friend and enjoyed intimate relationship with the groups of artists and musicians which continually gathered there.

Amelita grew up under the Mascagni influence and encouragement. The composer, as before, was a frequent visitor and often paused to hear her play and comment upon her work. So passed the years—until one day that same inexorable hand reached forth again and placed it gently upon the head of this unsuspecting maid—and thereby dedicated her to art anew, but in another sphere which henceforth should prove the rightful one. It was in the year 1905 when, one day, Mascagni dropped in to call at the Galli home. Perhaps the musician, now a middleaged man of forty-one, and disappointed over his inability to give the world another *chef d'oeuvre*, was in a philosophic mood; at any rate, this evening was to prove momentous for Amelita. As was his custom at these impromptu visits, Mascagni devoted the time to discoursing upon favorite themes—for he was an engaging talker, a profound thinker, and well-informed on topics of every kind—and to playing opera scores. Being a fine pianist and a facile reader, his renditions always stirred the Galli family, which constituted the admiring audience. On this occasion Bellini's *I Puritani* was the opera chosen for exposition. As the soprano arias were reached, Amelita would sing them, to the delight of the little audience who, at the conclusion of the performance, mingled compliments for their charming vocalist with those for the brilliant musician.

But Mascagni was thinking of something else. He turned to the sixteen-year-old girl and launched out upon a subject that caused astonishment to his auditors. He would spare her the irony, the pain of failure which had been his. He would lead her into fields of beauty and of happiness. At the end of his eloquent speech, he broke into a peroration that startled all because of its trend and significance.

"Lita," he began, "there are many good pianists, but the good singers—they are few. You play no better than hundreds of others."

He paused a moment as the girl's hands grew cold and words froze upon her lips. She could only stare bewilderedly at the speaker.

"But," he continued, "with your voice—well, I wonder!"

"Maestro! I do not understand . . ."

"You will be a great artist—not a pianist—a *singer*."

"But I have very little voice."

"You have the quality—quite unusual—and that is the one requisite for singing. One can study all one's life and never be a singer unless the voice is there."

"You really think I have a voice?"

"I assure you that you have a voice—a wonderful voice."

"Then I'll try."

Mascagni did not compose another *Cavalleria*, but he was instrumental in giving to the world a most accomplished vocalist, perhaps the most accomplished vocalist, the most universally popular singer of her day.

Message of the Birds

Such is the mystery of life that some inconsequential thing or circumstance may turn a course or chart another route more certain than any skilled astrologer. In the present case, it was a bird—a pretty nightingale—that began to sing, and such was the ardor of its song, such the spontaneity, such the sweetness of those untutored tones, such the gamut of their message and the fluency of their execution as to charge the very atmosphere with new vitality and loveliness. Involuntarily, unconscious of surroundings, indifferent to human auditors or applause, it sang—sang for the joy of singing under the impulse of a feeling too strong to be denied.

There was, however, a single auditor to that impromptu recital delivered from nature's concert hall—a listener who heard with illuminated countenance and abated breath. As still and white as any statue freshly chiseled, this unseen audience of one imbibed the message of the pretty warbler. Amelita felt within herself the growing pains of art's desire and heard the silent call of an awakening soul to be set free in song. Poor little bird! So innocently, so unknowingly did you become the instrument of fate and take upon yourself the fixing of a life career. Having published its song of love upon the circumambiant air, the bird flew upward into higher spaces, there hoping to find some feathered listener with ears attuned unto so rapturous a wooing.

Glorious little bird! Perhaps you fluttered away to die, yet never to be forgotten, for over your unmarked grave there hovers an invisible epitaph: "My song was not in vain—it lives in her who gave it to the world."

For a moment, Amelita—no doubt concealed behind a window curtain—remained immovable, then turned to the piano which she had left clandestinely to hear the extempore music from without. Her fingers, deftly skilled in digital dexterity, moved o'er the keyboard automatically. The trickling tones of a Chopin etude came forth with speed and clarity, albeit the player's thoughts were not engaged with interpretation, but centered on a welling castle-in-the-air. *To sing like that!* No prima donna, however, has been able to match the tempestuous song of this unschooled vocalist whose matchless melody soars by day and night with no other purpose than to please some other bird—capable of warbling twenty seconds without pause for breath, the sound of which in favorable weather fills a mile of space and with a variety of mode, melodic line, embellishment and expression far lovelier and more astonishing than any human aptitude.

Suddenly she stopped, then, apprehensively in timid utterance, began to sing as nearly imitative of the bird's song as she could. So easily came the tones, so pure in quality, so even in quantity, so true to pitch, as to inspire confidence, whereon the youthful vocalist indulged in further trial of her ability accompanied by improvised harmonies upon the piano. The test ended, Amelita commenced a monolog, since it gave audible expression to a feeling indicative of what was foreordained to be.

Long before man became a part of life evolution, before birds sang, insects were engaged in supplying an antediluvian world with strange sounds which, in time, were supplemented by the warblings of the feathered throngs and finally transformed into an art by man, who discovered therein a new and beautiful world—the world of song. Why should not a finely-touched and thoughtful signorina find entrance into that same world through its first vocalists—the birds?

Tone is not the primary desideratum in bird song, but technic. Warblers belong to the coterie of troubadours, not of musicians. Homo sapiens can learn from them concerning precision, correct intervals and tone clarity; especially the coloraturas may reap benefits from close observance of bird utterances. The theme may be simple but the execution will be flawless, likewise that surety of breath and consummated confidence would prove beneficial for any singer's study. To birds singing is play; to humans, it is work.

If birds can sing, then so could she—for had she not a similar equipment? Aye, she had more—intelligence, also poets and composers to fashion things for her to sing. What a world—the world of song! Hers for the taking, hers for the asking, hers for the rest of time. No regrets should mar her future, no sorrows warp the years to come, no memories of what might have been or left undone. To sing and be forgotten like the bird—that was the saddest thing of all.

Her being became charged with enthusiasm. Energy was revitalized. Moods gave way to visions, impressions expanded into desires, ideas begat determinations. She scanned the future, then cast her horoscope more accurately than any seer. From that moment, her real character, hitherto dormant, burst forth and instantly became the compelling force that was henceforth to lift her above the earth into the spiritual sphere; and the goal? Supremacy!

In this new determination Amelita received no encouragement from her parents. Her father's attitude was founded on the illogical premise that it would be foolish to abandon an art, already mastered and producing income, for something uncertain and experimental. Her mother also feared the influences of public stage-life and cautioned her daughter against any hurried action. In spite of parental opposition, Amelita continued to devote herself to investigating the situation. She had discovered that she had a singer's throat and that the legato flow which she had been unable to extract from the piano was now at her command, hence singing appealed more strongly because of this uninterrupted flow of melody, and the little voice responded nobly by demonstrating its superiority over the hands as a majestic music-maker. Thus she strove to solve the problem for herself.

Her mentality distinguished between sentiment to be expressed by local music and by instrumental music as the embodiment thereof. She therefore had to remodel her entire scheme of things. Her yearning was for a future in which she would be the purveyor of gladness through song and, to do that, she must be true to the cause by being an artist, not a pretender. If she joined the coterie of those who made singing a business, then she would fail as a singer. When she faced the momentous decision, she asked herself: "*What is the greatest thing in life? Would I die if I became dumb or voiceless? Would it be the prime tragedy of my existence to be told that I had no voice—that I was idly dreaming?*" Self-analysis was, then, the first requisite. She knew she wanted to sing because she could not resist the impulse that arose from her gladsome soul. She never thought of being a prima donna, of making a fortune, of thrilling big audiences—those matters bothered her not at all. She had to decide whether the thing she wanted to do, and loved to do, was to sing.

The Greatest Joy

Having determined that her greatest joy was to sing, sing she would even at the risk of antagonizing everyone. She interviewed two teachers of voice and acquainted herself with their methods as disclosed in pupils' exhibitions, after which she deemed it safer to teach herself. Self-instruction! A hazardous undertaking, yet the only way for her. There were several means of procedure. She could follow the method of Francesco Lamperti, among whose famous pupils were Campanini and Sembrich; she could adopt the studies of Giuseppe Concone, the composer of technical vocal works; she could accept the formula of Manuel P. R. Garcia, the distinguished Spanish vocal teacher—son of the famous tenor, brother of Malibran and Viardot, and teacher of Jenny Lind; or she could use the plan of Lilli Lehmann, who had published the important *Meine Gesang-kunst* and her autobiography. The final decision centered upon a Garcia-Lehmann combination. The former could teach her how to produce a pure tone, the latter how to know the *feel* of tone sensation.

Her next consideration was the line of song to follow. Of one thing she was certain—it would be opera, grand opera. She would sing in opera-houses, big, famous opera-houses. She would sing big, famous roles. She would match her art with that of any other singer, past or present—but she must work, toil, study, think. What roles should she sing? There were many from which to choose, many with which she was familiar, yet only certain ones would fit her particular style and capabilities. Grandmother had explained them to her, had interpreted them for her—had even sung the principal soprano arias during those precious formative days when Amelita played the piano part of the vocal scores and hummed the melodies in unison.

But now she must choose one and master it, then enlist grandmother to polish off the roughness. For this endeavor she had ample time because, not being like other girls, she did not play games and had put away the dolls which had served her so well as ballerinas for her operas in miniature. Her preparation was completely scanned. She would read Shakespeare and Goethe in addition to Italian writers. She would busy her hands with fashioning some nice bit of embroidery while conning her words and music. One secret she had—she liked to be a tomboy on occasion; but even that must stop now. She was to be a singer, therefore she must begin to weave the web of the artist-life which requires all things to work in harmony with that rigid formula.

It is natural for birds to fly, for dogs to bark, for cats to purr, for frogs to croak, for stars to shine, for fish to swim, for flowers to bloom, for trees to bud, for grass to grow, for ships to sail, for fires to burn—everything according to its natural inclination and individual preference. So with man. He is happiest who follows his especial bent and gives the urge within him unhampered sway. Amelita expressed this eloquently when she declared, "My greatest joy is to sing!"

There were many intimate consultations and confidences between the elder and the younger actors in this preliminary scene. Perhaps one dialogue might have progressed somewhat along such a line as this:

Grandmother	You must know, my child, that it is something to be a Milanese—an honor to be Italian born.
Amelita	Yes, I know, but that is not enough.
Grandmother	Not enough?
Amelita	While it is an honor to be an Italian, it is more to be a great Italian.
Grandmother	You are right. See, then, that you be great, for mediocrity, particularly in opera, will not suffice. There is room at the top only for the few—the very few.
Amelita	I shall be one of the few and more—I shall be the greatest of Milanese singers.
Grandmother	Don't foget Grisi.
Amelita	But I must surpass even Grisi.
Grandmother	That will be difficult. She was a marvelous artist.
Amelita	Were there no other famous singers of Milan?
Grandmother	None—those who have served our city well unfortunately were those who came from other parts.
Amelita	But Italians, nevertheless.
Grandmother	Of course—who can sing with them?

Amelita	But why was that? Why had we to import singers? Had we no teachers, no voices, no institutions to train our own talent?
Grandmother	La, la la! We had no urge or need to develop either schools or singers. Strangers came to build Milan, foreign painters, foreign sculptors to beautify her— even our noble cathedral was designed by a German.
Amelita	Were there none here to do that work?
Grandmother	It seems not. The Renaissance is still preserved, but the Milan of Lodovico has vanished forever—only fragments remain as ghosts to remind us of a magnificent cinquecento era which wanted painting, architecture, sculpture, poetry, music, and masquerade. It is because of this gorgeous past that ours is still the queen city of our realm. You know the adage, "Milano la grande, Venezia la ricca, Genova la superba, Bologna la grassia, Firenze la bella, Padova la dotta, Ravenna l'antica, Roma la santa." (Milan the grand, Venice the rich, Genoa the superb, Bologna the fat, Florence the beautiful, Padua the learned, Ravenna the old, Rome the holy.)

Gilda

Amelita perhaps walked from the Via Oriani to the Via Giuseppe Verdi, then to the Piazza della Scala. Arriving there, she may have cast a furtive glance upon the Teatro alla Scala facing the square through which she passed so often. It was not the exterior of the building that her outer eyes beheld, but the interior that her inner eyes visualized. She saw herself upon that stage enacting the role of . . . what?

Verdi! Italy's operatic idol! The girl's eyes must have dilated as she received the flash of inspiration and, with that flash, her artistic soul burst into flower. Verdi! Yes, she would sing Verdi. Her breath came in quick, spasmodic spurts as she hastily scanned the immortal heroines of the master's scores—Elvira, Violetta, Leonora, Amelia, Aida, Desdemona, Luisa, Gilda . . . *Gilda!* The name started within her a sympathetic vibration that set her heart on fire. Gilda! Yes, her first role would be Gilda, because the music fitted her voice best. Aglow with throbbing enthusiasm, how she must have hurried home to tell grandmother of her decision—they together to transform a pianist into the vocal embodiment of another being.

But, alas! that was not to be, for ere the year was out, the beloved soul was called from earth, leaving a great void in the family circle, particularly so for the little singer who depended so much upon the aid that would be hers no more. Her path chosen, her goal set, the girl's chief object was to become, not a singer, but an extraordinary singer, and to accomplish that end, no professional teachers of voice would have a part. She would teach herself and triumph. She had the proper background, the right environment, the intuition, the will, the knowledge, the motivating force, and the birds. Two pretty warblers were purchased to instruct her in the art of tone production and facility of execution. None can wonder at Amelita's choice—a life of romance and of song—her wish, her need, her world.

But at this crucial period an adverse tide set in to check temporarily the onward march. Financial reverses beset the father's business, necessitating a change in domicile as well as style. Economic pressure compelled two radical modifications in the Galli family. *Pater familias*, without ado, packed his bag and departed for the Argentine, which loomed alluringly before his saddened eyes, there to retrieve, if possible, his lost estate. This condition was responsible for the daughter making a profession of her music and turning her pianistic talent to immediate commercial ends. Her brothers were able to assist in thwarting the many threats of penury, while the girl added her small fees from teaching—privately and at the conservatory. This outside work necessitated her going to the homes of her pupils and, anxious not to deplete her tiny store of hard-earned liras, Amelita walked to and from her several destinations, thereby expending more on shoe repairs than transportation might have cost. In this way, the four were able to make the ends of their family string hold together until fortune's wheel had made its turn and permitted the sons to follow their father to South America.

With the old home abandoned, a new one had to be found. This was soon done—in a queer, narrow street where Amelita found refuge wherein to combat the world and create a pleasant waiting-place for Mother Galli. The two schooled themselves to happiness in those four small, low-ceilinged rooms on the topmost floor, linked together by a dark hallway with a kitchen hitched on as an after-thought in the form of an L. The main apartment was a combina-tion studio and living-room. Here Amelita devoted two thirty-minute periods a day to the piano and another double period to the voice. Finally, the diningroom was moved from the kitchen to the larger space, thereby forming a triad of industry. Some of the pupils were older than their teacher and very serious, such unnatural virtue resulting only in the complete eradication of their names, faces and personalities—the usual fate of good little girls who never set the world aflame or make history memorable. It is the adventurous little girls who do that—girls who think and do things and go contrari-wise to normalcy, the fear of which holds most adolescents from developing individuality in time to serve some worthy end. To be different—that is the problem that confronts youth everywhere and holds talent in a leash.

Amelita was no ordinary miss, for even during these formative years a decided inordinateness was manifest in almost every act and thought. She became a good teacher because of this appositeness which permitted her to infuse personality into work and, having learned how to instruct others, she found a way to teach herself. The dusty phrase "Poets are born, not made" applies also to vocal-ists. A singer is never made but often unmade. No teacher can give a pupil, except artificially, power of discernment, judgment, tone sense, pitch accuracy, shading, resonance, and brains, nor can esthetic appreciation be implanted in a dull-minded scholar. A parrot can mimic but he could never become artistic. Good teachers may perfect and develop talent, but inject the germ of genius, never.

For two years Amelita toiled with technic so as to secure smoothly-articulated and full-flowing tones. At the opera she noted how others sang and often recalled her grandmother's admonition *never to force a tone.* The usually prescribed vocal exercises were eschewed, for they seemed a waste of time. She did not need knowledge so much as drill on special weaknesses. Preparing a repertory and perfecting voice production demands a lot of time—so much that none is left for anything not needed. Natural fluency and coloratura were already hers, hence she could apply herself to the practice of such vocalises as would iron out whatever irregularities there were in her scale continuity. A simple formula from middle C to the octave above, with breath after every four-tone group, served for general use, which was augmented with rapid work extending from low A to F above high C. This was the daily routine to be sung until the full scale was cleared of blemish and with the high tones true and pure; for, claims this self-teacher, "if one wishes to sing E in public, one must be able to sing F in private." Another important exercise was the trill on C and D of the staff.

Preparedness! That was her aim and that, she knew, constituted the basis of success, for when opportunity knocks, such as are prepared are accepted. This conviction grew into a faith to serve her ever after, for of this unusual woman's characteristics none is more outstanding than her ability to recognize opportunity, seize it and turn it to account.

Between piano lessons, and practicing, she read books on singing and applied such principles as attracted her to her own work. Difficult? Very, for she had to decide what to do and what not to do. Dangerous? Very, for she had to proceed slowly and with much care in order to be sure, in order to be right. She had a keen sense of judgment and discrimination, otherwise the effort might have proved a blind, perhaps a fatal one. She reasoned, searched, discovered. "That is why I know it," she asserted later. "I know exactly what I am about when I sing. I know what muscles I use and in what condition they should be. I know what parts of the anatomy are called into action and why."

Nature gave her a voice and a sound constitution. The first she developed, the second she preserved. The first was built on work;

the second on correct living, regular hours, exercise and fresh air with a healthy state of mind and a belief in spiritual forces. She knew also that, as no two voices are alike, each must be subjected to the kind of treatment best suited to its needs. Much of her vocal knowledge was acquired by listening, which disclosed to her what was good, what bad—one to be adopted, one to be avoided. The principles established in those early years and the constant application of them throughout a quarter of a century have proven the soundness of her reasoning and the correctness of her method, which included morning vocalises after taking draughts of fresh air from an open window, no matter what the weather. Contrary to the practices of most singers, she followed the Garcia rule of keeping the diaphragm elastic to support the breath so that the tones might always be produced with ease.

Another fallacy she always avoided—that of singing loud against a large orchestra, especially when in the hands of a temperamental conductor, usually compelling tone forcing by means of a tight throat. She never resorted to such extravagances, for she could form a pure, clear tone, the placement and quality of which is such as to carry farther than one formed contrariwise. That kind of tone soars and floats to the uppermost parts of any hall. Her favorite songster is the nightingale because he uses mixed vowels. Some birds have harsh tones—mere quacks—because they open their mouths too far; but the "King of Song" uses a lovely, dark, covered tone, the kind that reaches the heart—the most exquisite quality of all. Little wonder that she found her feathered friends greater teachers than those of human kind.

CYCLE OF TESTING

1906-1910

"I sing my songs to appeal to the heart."

—GALLI-CURCI

Amelita Galli, when she made her debut in Trani in 1906

Call to Trani

N THE SUMMERTIME of 1906 Amelita went often to the public gardens, where she sat and listened to the band concerts while pondering upon the *Rigoletto* score.

Gilda, she knew, was a stock part for singers of every grade because it offered many and diversified opportunities, and a favorite role for illustrious vocalists. That she could master the music she believed—the high notes and the embellishments were mere vocal bagatelles.

Characterization was not so easy—that presented mental delineations to tax the power of any actress. Yet the magnitude of the task did not appall this confident youngster, who thereby showed a natural fitness for operatic activities. The first hurdle having been taken gallantly, the second loomed ahead formidably. Where, when ready, would she present her embodiment? How secure a trial? Still another difficulty confronted her. Mother Galli was horrified by the thought of one so young going on the stage. But the daughter's philosophic view was the sounder. "*Why fear evil which is everywhere? When one is filled with the grandeur of art, one has little time for the low things of life.*"

In the fall, Dame Fortune appeared with succor for the aspiring vocalist. At a private musicale, Amelita was invited to sing. It happened that a certain orchestra conductor was present, and was so impressed by her rendition of the "Caro Nome" as to warrant his assistance. He thought he might help her to an engagement for the Lyric Carnival Season at Trani, as the manager of the opera, Voghera, a friend of his, was in Milan looking for an inexpensive singer. Next day, there was a conference at the Galli home and

Amelita was duly enrolled for three months, during which period she was to sing ten performances of Gilda and receive therefore three hundred lira—about $60 at the time. So filled with joy was she that industry was only added pleasure. So eagerly did she apply herself to her task that the entire role was mastered in eight days, after which began the working out of action, interpretation, and delivery.

Acceptance of the invitation was not without risk, but no hazard ever begat fear in the bosom of Amelita Galli. She knew that opera publics in southern Italy were music-wise, very critical and insistent on full value for their money. She knew also that a first performance failure meant blighting the career she had already planned and pictured mentally. But timidity was never a Galli trait, and had no place in the dreams and aspirations of this youthful shaper of her self-determined career. While letter-perfect as to the music which Gilda has to sing and familiar with the opera as a whole, she assumed no risk through unpreparedness, therefore undertook to learn the entire score.

For the needed stage technic and the physical interpretation of the role, she depended on her own abilities to see her through; yet, long before the scheduled time for the performance, Amelita had so absorbed Gilda's personality that she could become Gilda as soon as she began to sing. Having accepted the engagement on confident nerve, it was her aim to fortify that nerve with artistic surety, while the liras she would receive during the three months of eye-teeth cutting tended to puff her up, for novice debuts were usually paid for, not contracted.

Milan she knew to be the center toward which singers gravitate in search of opportunity, yet she had no wish to try her fledgling wings at home. She saw singers come and go. She realized that competition was keen. She had been told that one must run the gauntlet between managers, conductors, critics, editors, and "sharks" looking for "minnows." Real talent, she observed, faced a struggle for existence—as true in art as in nature. Therefore, she must test herself quietly in another place. Trani offered this test.

The Italians know their opera and they inherit love for music and crave artistic environment. Italians must have their spaghetti and their opera. They will go without food in order to hear a favorite singer or a popular work. Italy is as familiar with Verdi's melodies as with "O Sole Mio" and "Funiculi, Funicula."

Verdi tunes! Urchins whistle them, venders hum them, boatmen sing them, housewives croon them, hand-organs grind them, orchestras play them, children practice them, old men dream them, artists glorify them, and gallant swains coo them beneath the windows of their enamoratas with mandolin and guitar, while the masses bask in the mellifluously laden atmosphere of the haunting Verdian melodies.

At the time of Amelita's advent into the operatic arena, the stage was dominated by the big four—Verdi, Donizetti, Bellini, and Rossini. As her sphere lay within this enchanted circle, the roles she ought to prepare against the time when opportunity might beckon her on should be the popular favorites from these composers; therefore, as a basis for repertory, she would select from them. In the operatic performances she had attended, this careful listener noted a general tendency on the part of singers to lay the emphasis on vocalization to the neglect of dramatic portrayal. Characters were molded in a fixed groove under the guise of that misused term "tradition." If singing be all, then why join them? If locale be without significance, then why scenery and costumes? Why act, if there be nothing to impart thereby? She could understand the stress laid upon brilliance and beautiful vocal art, but not why every other element had to be sacrificed and be subordinate thereto. The explanation of this paradox lies in the fact that Italy was musically absorbed in melody. The popular demand was for sweet tunes and vocal pyrotechnics, so composers catered to this whim. Patrons wished for nothing higher than to be entertained by ear-tickling tunes, hence there arose a group of skillful singers whose vocal facility disguised their dramatic weaknesses.

Thus it seemed a precarious undertaking for one without experience to beard the Verdian lion in his own specific den. Throughout the summer she thought and toiled and polished. Before mirrors she scrutinized facial aspects, and in the privacy of her studio enacted the dramatic episodes. The manner in which she acquired the necessary technic is her own secret; that she did acquire it was fully demonstrated when she made her initial bow.

Little did Amelita think that in going to Trani she would be going into two outstanding life events—marriage and career. So, unmindful of all save the coming debut, at the approach of winter Amelita and her mother went to the little "white town" on the Adriatic, proud of her twelfth-century cathedral and her "Moscato di Trani" wine. The Turenum of the ancients could boast of but a small population, but they were lovers of opera and had their own opera-house.

Debut as Gilda

Thrift and economy were the only passports that Amelita and her mother could use in order to subsist on the singer's puny income. Forty cents a day for rooms and forty cents for food enabled them to live like gentlewomen, if not like princesses, during the period of their stay.

Then came Christmas Day—a day long to be remembered, for it severed fond home ties through the passing of the actors, one by one. With a new vocation demanding all her time, a new era dawned, a new cycle began. The morrow would bring the long-hoped-for opportunity. How the hours dragged! But the reward was big—worth all it cost in time, in effort, in study, in preparation, in anxiety. With that day, the wheels of fate started to turn. With that performance began the journey skyward.

For that debut she had no limousine, no taxi, no carriage drawn by prancing steeds or opera enthusiasts to displace them and escort the prima donna to the opera-house. Amelita walked, with her mother, in the rain—two adventuring women huddled under a big umbrella. Was debut ever more inauspicious! The dressing-room—what a sight it was! The table littered with a heterogeneous mass of make-up articles; chairs, pegs and hangers laden with costumes, one of which Amelita had to choose, for she had none of her own. Her slim figure was almost lost in the mass of material comprising Gilda's dress, but numerous huge safety-pins and a mother's dexterous fingers finally averted a caricature. With little make-up skill, two bright red spots upon the cheeks served well enough, though much too low for natural effect.

The audience would show perhaps slight interest in the beauty-spots or ill-fitting drapery—they came to hear an opera and pass upon a voice; so, if that voice conformed to their stern standards of artistic fitness, minor details could be overlooked. The stage presented only barrenness and bewildering confusion. Though a soiled, drab curtain and bleak canvases in rank disorder are not conducive to esthetic stimulation, there radiates none the less a glamor and a whetting of artistic appetite that those who witness a performance from the other side can never comprehend. The lure of stage, the thrill of footlights, the atmosphere of performance life, the inspiration of delighting auditors, of receiving plaudits, of being *Somebody*—these are joys unknown to all save such as have actual acquaintance with them.

Now the stage is set. The auditorium lights are dimmed. The footlights flash. The orchestra begins the overture—the curtain rises. What an audience!—in gala mood and in festive spirit. Women beautifully gowned and jewelled. Men in evening dress, others in galleries informally clad. Family parties, old friends meeting upon a common ground. Rich and poor, old and young—the whole town represented in that mixed assemblage gathered by a common impulse—to spend Christmastime in festive fashion—listening to a favorite opera, maybe with some misgivings because of the unknown Gilda.

Italians are fairly disposed toward a new singer, willing to let her show the kind of stuff she is made of. If the debutante makes good, she is accepted; if she fails to please, she is immediately apprised of the fact in no uncertain way. The untried singer, on this occasion, realized that the test hour had arrived, yet she was cool and calm, unperturbed. Her mind was on the part, fortified by the knowledge that she was prepared, so nothing mattered but to do her best.

At last, she was singing—doing what she had longed to do, what she loved best to do. Now she was giving out her message of joy and rapture in heart and voice. Her "Caro Nome" went straight to her audience like a dart. It did not have time to be surprised or stunned, to think or analyze—but broke spontaneously and tumultuously into a great demonstration of approval. Her triumph was complete. The unknown singer at the beginning of the opera was an acclaimed artist at the end. The miracle had happened. Amelita Galli, in one short half hour of Act I, had been transformed from a *Nobody* into a *Somebody*, and at the end of the performance was the subject for headlines in the press and the object of conversation in music circles. Trani had discovered an operatic marvel and Italy had presented another prima donna to the world.

"When I heard the orchestra begin," she recalls, "it was like attending a great feast, or a young girl's first dance—all joy. Discomforts and disorders were forgotten in the thought that *I was to sing.*"

Recalls after each act vouched for her acceptance by Trani music-lovers, and that is a notable achievement for a beginner, since in Italian opera-houses there are two kinds of demonstrations—"*Bravo!*" and "*Boo!*"—the one expressive of approval, the other of contempt, each accompanied by explosive manifestations in the customary Latin manner. With the pronouncement of that verdict, the singer stands or falls. It is the *ultima dictum.* It is the *vox populi* that determines whether a singer shall go forward or retire. According to the customs of the house, the successful singer offers an extra number between the second and third acts, Galli giving the *Lucia* "Mad Scene."

The conductor was Giovanni Colucci, the tenor Fatarini, the baritone Riboldi, the contralto Paelli, the basso Baldi.

The night's success proved momentous with respect to Amelita's future. In the dressing-room, when all was over, a happy mother took an elated daughter in her arms and whispered, "*Lita, you have chosen wisely.*" Precious-sounding words, for they conveyed a change in the maternal mind which heretofore had been opposed to a stage career for this frail flower of her heart who, having become a budding rose, ought not to be denied its full development.

The little Milanese soprano proved a happy choice for Manager Voghera, for she not only captured highest honors at performances but won notable commendation from the press—highly important flashlights upon these initial appearances.

When the copious reviews are analyzed, an amazing agreement with respect to certain factors is obvious; viz., voice of beautiful quality, pure intonation, technical facility, extensive scale range even throughout, surety and dependability, ability to stir enthusiasm, power to win ovations, capacity to capture honors, affability and modesty.

Yes, Amelita Galli was born to sing, but, like thousands of others who were born to sing, she might have been like them—lost in the folds of oblivion—if that were all. She, however, had the essential accessories that go to make a career of song. She had the vision, the courage, the determination to advance. And more—she had the inspirational, intellectual, industrial urge to make herself a factor in the singing world. No more idealistic singer ever lived, but her idealism was the glamour that surrounded a well-grounded art and knit it into a perfect thing.

Romance

In that audience at the Teatro Communale on December 26, 1906, was the Marchése Carlo Curci and his two sons, Luigi and Gennaro. The latter, then a lad of eighteen, was a music student at the Academy of St. Cecilia in Rome and was at Trani to pass the opera festival with his family. The performance was a worthy one in their opinion, with the new soprano showing a remarkable talent, so much so that Signor Curci turned to Gennaro and said, "Write down the name of this young singer. In due season, she will be celebrated." Never did prophet of yore speak more discerningly.

Luigi, at this time, was making some repairs upon the pictures in a church which Signorina Galli expressed a desire to see, having become acquainted with the Curcis, and thereby began a romance. During her stay in Trani, the painter offered to make a portrait of the lady and there were several sittings, but the work was never finished, as the two were more interested in their personal affairs. When Easter came and the Trani season ended, Amelita went to Rome with a letter to Morichini, director of the Costanzi Theatre, from a prominent singer of Milan. Fortified by her recent success, she secured an audition, and after singing "Caro Nome" with Conductor Ferrari at the piano, she evidently convinced the impresario as to her fitness, for he offered her a contract for the 1908 season at the rate of $6.25 a performance, which, considering that Caruso began with a $2 fee, was not disproportionate.

Gennaro was engaged to play piano in an orchestra that accompanied a Passion film. Associated with this production was a mediocre singer who was to sing an "Ave Maria." One night, when Amelita happened to be behind scenes, this singer became ill, and without ado the young Costanzi soprano substituted, to the great satisfaction of everyone. In the meantime, Luigi, who had become Marchése di Simeri, came to Rome to continue his wooing, and when Amelita departed again in May for Milan, she was affianced to him. On reaching home, an unexpected oasis in the form of another engagement greeted her. A rich, elderly Frenchman, then visiting Milan, liked the way the little Amelita sang old folk songs and engaged her to sing at his residence in Pisa where he amused himself with private musicales given by a violinist, cellist and pianist from the Pisa Conservatory. Her share in the entertainment was to render old Italian songs to improvised accompaniments by the other artists.

Costanzi Debut

The summer and the autumn soon passed and, with their passing, loomed the Costanzi debut which was to prove the first real step upward of the Parnassian climb. Mother and daughter took an apartment and established themselves therein for the winter, while the latter prepared the role of Bettina in Bizet's *Don Procopio*, in which she would be presented to the Roman public in the spring.

Rome could not do other than exert a tremendous charm upon one of Amelita's constitutional impressionability. Hours in the Vatican and galleries, enchanting rambles among the Forum's ruins to revive the history of a celebrated era, absorbing the fascinating side of the ancient capital's life, associations with people, famous and otherwise. Though extremely poor—not permitting themselves so much as a hotel room on so meager a salary—mother and daughter were happy in their little suite, where they received a continuous stream of callers who were entertained with tea and talk as delightfully as if in a regal suite. There came "wonderful visitors," as Amelita called them—poets, painters, musicians, composers, singers, writers, managers—for mother was well known in Rome as in Milan, and daughter had made a brilliant debut, hence they were worth knowing.

April came at last and on the 20th, the Costanzi premiere of *Don Procopio* under the conductorship of Leopoldo Mugnone with this cast:

Bettina..............................Amelita Galli-Curci
Eufemia................................Ida Bergamasco
Odoardo...............................Alberto Dardani
Ednesto..............................Giuseppe de Luca
Don Procopio.......................Federico Carbonetti
Don Andronico.........................Bernardo Berardi
Pasquino..............................Giuseppe Gironi

The performance of the little work was received cordially and the youthful debutante won a pronounced success in a part that afforded an opportunity to show her cleverness in comedy acting as well as in delicate singing.

Marriage

During the Rome season Amelita Galli became the Marchésa di Simeri, having married Luigi Curci on February 24, 1908, and in order to maintain both names, she adopted the hyphenation Galli-Curci. The season ended, Mama Curci returned to Milan, the bride and groom to partake of a belated honeymoon in the Briganza mountain district of Como. During the summer much time was given over to more serious diversion than to lovemaking, for the young artist had work ahead, completing the roles of Lucia and Violetta for the fall, when she would go to Egypt under the Voghera management, also preparing Adina, Rosina, Amina for the future.

Originality has ever been the basis of Galli-Curci's winsome personality which has been so strongly contributory to her outstanding

position, not only as an artist, but as a woman. At the very outstart
of her career, she had her own ideas and opinions. Prima donnas'
ways, if not conformative to the end planned, were taboo. During
this period of restful study she found that the accepted cadenzas
were unsuited to her, and therefore wrote her own coloratura embellishments. A bold innovation, but not disagreeable to the staid
opera-lover or unacceptable by the conductor. Being a musician and
a vocalist, she knew what to do and what not to do, hence the
interpolation of her own cadenzas proved both a novelty and a
blessing.

Many of the old-time librettists were obsessed with the idea that
an operatic heroine must be either insane or a victim of seduction.
The singer who enters the field, especially the coloratura field, has
to accommodate herself to this incongruous supposition. Building
up her own repertory, Galli-Curci seemed almost fated to appear in
parts of this genre, inasmuch as operas most suitable to her style
were woven about a hypothetical character. For such highly florid
music as the arias these operas offered, one was not supposed to
concern oneself with characterization or interpretation—singing was
the principal thing, nothing else mattered.

Two roles so diversely different from that of Gilda opened a new
vent of thought, a new phase of analysis, although Lucia and
Violetta are less lucid as types than Gilda. While the three characters are subjected to musical treatment for the benefit of smooth
vocalists, and while the dramatic incidents are such as to cause a
stock singer little concern so long as she can vocalize the written
notes and make routine gestures, the singer who is also an artist
can differentiate between them, dramatically and musically. Only
occasionally are these spectacular arias sung other than as a vocal
show, an opportunity for the prima donna to advance down stage
and fire her rocket at the audience as if it were a concert number,
while her associates take statuesque positions and become a supple-
mentary background audience. But at the first digest of a score
Galli-Curci, apprehending the association of words and music, proposed not to divorce that association. Her natural sense of balance
and proportion would not permit her to do otherwise. Though audi-

ences did insist on forcing her, after certain arias, to interrupt the continuity, she never considered an opera aria as something injected into the scene for applause purposes; rather did she prefer to receive applause at the end of acts.

Her study of Lucia was conducted along quite different lines from what her study of Gilda had been, because Lucia requires another kind of treatment. Donizetti and Verdi, while representatives of the same school, are at variance in musical thought and craftsmanship. The former never rose out of his musical atmosphere —that of beautiful melodic phrases for the singers—whereas the latter felt dramatically and much of his melody is couched in that idiom. The *Rigoletto* quartet, while dramatically intense, is also melodiously intense. The *Lucia* sextet, which ought to have been dramatically intense, is merely musically intense.

Violetta presents still another phase of Verdian treatment, hence needing individual characterization. If there be a coloratura role requiring an artistic portrayal, it is that of *Traviata's* heroine, which demands fine singing, subtle psychology, bodily grace, and high interpretive ability, else the part becomes stereotype. Not every fine singer can make this role vital, but Galli-Curci saw the need of bestowing special care upon its preparation. Voice she had, also grace, mentality, power of analyzation and insight. Her portrayal of Gilda disclosed these assets, but with Lucia and Violetta that composite talent must be broadened perceptibly; indeed, so considerate was she of the propriety of appropriateness as to make a careful diagnosis of Violetta's malady; yet, not content with her own conception of the last scene, she consulted a noted tuberculosis specialist as to the manner in which the disease would be manifest in final consumptive hours. She learned the correct use of hands to correspond with the jerky gestures and incessant fidgeting so characteristic of the disease. She was cautioned against coughing, as in the concluding stages of consumption there are only stabbing pains in the lungs; therefore Amelita omitted the usual cough and, instead, clutched her chest as if to mitigate the distress thereby.

Even in the early cycle, Galli-Curci always conformed to national customs and dress, which she studied with meticulous pride so that she might accommodate the stage picture, accurate as to every motion, as to vocal authenticity. Because she paid exemplary attention to details, singing became a joy rather than a task and that joy was communicated to her auditors.

The ripening prima donna returned to Milan from whence, in the fall, she and her husband entrained for Naples to take passage for Alexandria, where she was to appear with a company under the direction of Voghera, with Guerriri as conductor. The 1908-09 season thus opened auspiciously. It provided two new opportunities —to sing in another country and to try out a pair of new roles.

Egypt

As the steamer pointed her nose southwest into the bluish waters of the Mediterranean, Galli-Curci experienced a pleasurable sensation—that of setting foot upon an unknown trail, the end of which she could neither visualize nor speculate upon. She knew only that she had launched forth upon an operatic course and proposed to follow it until her port was reached though it took a lifetime to do it.

The Alexandria debut was made in what was becoming our artist's "war-horse"—*Rigoletto*—in the interpretation of which she had as associates the tenor Nadal, the baritone Sante, the contralto Liviabella, the basso Perin. The production was under the direction of Mo Manno, and presented at the new Teatro Alhambra.

The first appearance outside her own country provided an excellent test for the young artist, and that she met the test successfully was affirmed by the enthusiastic reviews of her performance, all acclaiming her a "first-rank" artist and assigning her to a position "high among illustrious singers."

But Fate, alas! seems often jealous of a too-easily earned success, hence places a check upon over-rapid advancement. At this particular point she deemed the time favorable for another test in adversity. Before the company had completed its schedule, a mighty hurricane that swept the sea from end to end and from shore to shore, bore down on Alexandria to uproot property and lay waste the land. With the opera-house *hors de combat*, everyone faced financial ruin and *La Galli* found herself in a foreign land, with no

means of collecting her unearned salary. She might have been forced
to return home but for an unexpected engagement. Manager Adolfo
Bracale, who was giving a season of opera in Cairo and was in need
of a Gilda, had gone to Alexandria to hear what Voghera had in
hand and so impressed was he with the young soprano that he
offered her 300 lira each for six *Rigoletto* performances, a sum
which, at that particular moment, seemed like golden manna
dropped from Heaven. So, instead of looking for some convenient
way to regain the shores of Italy, the Marchése and Marchésa di
Simeri departed for the older and more southern metropolis of that
ancient land of mystery and amazement.

Cairo, situated at the apex of the Nile delta, is famed for its fine
opera-house, where on December 24, 1871, the premiere of *Aida*,
composed by Verdi on commission of Khedive Ismail Pasha for the
inauguration of the Théâtre Khedival, was given.

From the stage the glare of dazzling footlights forms an impenetrable wall so, until the act had closed, Galli-Curci had no
knowledge of her audience, the first glimpse of which, outside the
curtain, disclosed a multitude of red fezes scattered profusely among
the parquet seats. The box occupants were screened by elaborate
grilles through the ornate openings of which gazed lustrous female
eyes, shrouded in white veils that gleamed faintly behind the barriers. The Khedive, inveterate music-lover, was a nightly visitor.
Many foreigners in occidental dress with English predominating,
gave contrast to the brilliant uniforms and splendidly attired women
in the unscreened seats.

To be domiciled in a big hotel amid luxurious surroundings, with
servants, good food, hot water, fresh linen and soft beds, was a
welcome luxury. She recalled those first nights away from home
when she tried to transform the dingy spaces of her room with
pictures and photographs pinned upon faded walls and, when she
had an extra lira, would add some flowers to offset the drab carpet
and antique furniture. It was in those trying days that Galli-Curci
gained an insight into life that made for self-mastery. She uncovered,
too, a secret of paramount significance: "The less you see and hear
and talk, the better"—which wisdom she applied to what she saw

and heard and said during the ensuing years. Another important discovery was this—"A mother is the only perfectly safe confidant in this world. To be a great mother is next to being a great opera singer. When you go away to make the career, take your mother with you. She is the only human being who has your interest at heart all the time and before all else."

Italian Tour

The year 1909 brought engagements in Italy—Palermo in the spring with Rigoletto, Traviata, and a first Elisir d'Amore. It may appear odd that, in the land of Bellini, Galli-Curci did not appear in one of this master's operas, but the fact is that she was not as yet ready to sing either Sonnambula or Puritani. In the autumn, during the carnival, Galli-Curci sang one Rigoletto in Ravenna and three in Livorno (Leghorn). With 1910 began the spring season at Ravenna with six performances of Traviata and nine of Lucia (first times in this role), also one Rigoletto in Pola. In many of these performances, extras were necessary—not the customary encores, but additional numbers, the "Proch Variations" proving one of the most popular. Critical opinions were of the same laudatory sort as elsewhere, bestowing unstinted praise for the elegance and ease of her singing, as well as for her sympathetic and graceful treatment of the roles. "Galli-Curci is such a singer as to well merit the name of diva, because she calls to mind the virtuosa of another period," said Il Foro Romagnolo of Ravenna. This was exactly her aim and wish —to carry on the art of singing as established by her illustrious predecessors.

CYCLE OF
ADVANCEMENT

1910-1915

"Art is a glimpse of the beyond. We are mediums between the spiritual and the physical worlds."

—GALLI-CURCI

South America

ALLI-CURCI'S THOUGHTS were now centered upon her 1910 South American trip as a member of an opera company directed by Mugnone and including the popular Neapolitan soprano Clasenti, also De Luca, Didur, Stracciari, Anselmi, Zenatello, Agostinelli, Mardones and Smirnoff.

Arriving at Buenos Aires in the spring, there was the hurly-burly of getting settled, then rehearsals, but now came the frost to nip the bud. Surprise and disappointment greeted her when she was assigned to sing only minor parts, an arrangement of which she had had no previous knowledge, having taken it for granted that she would sing her repertory of leading roles as she had done continuously from the start. But the contract of the prima donna allotted all such leads to her and she was not the sort of person to relinquish any, particularly to a younger and a better singer. To augment this embarrassment, Galli-Curci had no other prospect ahead for months to come. Throughout the season no change developed other than some well-directed taunts and slights which the pseudo-second soprano pretended not to see or hear.

Argentina proved attractive to the young artist in many ways. Her father, who went there when she was a child, had since died and the family never saw him again. This country, she discovered, while musically abreast of the times, was weak in orchestral concerts and individual recitals. Grand opera was the cultural amusement of a highly-artistic people, with the hub of activity established at the Colón Theatre. In this celebrated opera-house, performances were regarded as functions of distinction. Audiences, while quiet listeners,

As Gilda in Rigoletto, *Act 1, 1910*

As Violetta, in Traviata, *Act 3, 1910*

were most expressive of their love for opera and there were few late arrivals. The applause after favorite arias was warm but there was none at the star's entrance, appreciation being reserved for the end of the scene. Devotees demanded the best singers and newest sensations of the vocal world, but Galli-Curci was not to grace the boards of this house until 1915. The 1910 performances were given at the Teatro de la Opera, those of 1912 at the Coliséo.

Contacting this quality of audience, Galli-Curci was inspired to her best in spite of the fact that she had no chance to present herself in her best parts. Nevertheless, her work merited the approval of manager and public, and so became a stepping-stone to a favorable outcome.

The little artist proved a good waiter and a believer in ultimate success, therefore she adopted the policy of watchful patience. With no alternative, she submitted to the inevitable, and in her little hotel room she indulged in pleasant reveries of past achievements and of future hopes.

Rigoletto night arrived. An hour before curtain-time, the selfish prima donna reported illness. In wild excitement, the manager appealed to his second soprano. Could she sing Gilda without rehearsal? She could. Would she sing it? She would. The audience expressed annoyance in the change of cast by rattling programs, by murmurings, by other signs of disapproval at the absence of La Clasenti. They had never heard the little singer from Milan in a leading role, yet with the "Caro Nome" that audience began to listen most attentively—first, in silence; then, after the entrancing trills and roulades of sparkling brilliancy, with cheers and calls. Three times she had to sing the aria, and lo! hope was fulfilled.

> "Galli-Curci revealed the exquisite singer and an art of great talent."—*Patria degli Italiani.*
> "Galli-Curci measured up to her prestige, indisputably, on her way to a grand future."—*La Argentina.*
> "She proved a revelation, and received an ovation in which all participated."—*Urgonif.*

The Buenos Aires engagement finished, the company moved across the river to Montevideo with *Rigoletto* billed for early presentation and Clasenti announced to sing Gilda, but the illness of Galli-Curci's petty associate had developed into pneumonia, which forced her from the cast for a considerable time, at the end of which she found herself not only supplanted by another who had captured public fancy, but with a cancelled contract. Thus our dainty artist became leading soprano of the company; thus was deserving patience and dependability rewarded; thus was selfishness and egregious egotism punished. There was also a first-time *Barber of Seville* and a first-time *Pagliacci*, with Galli-Curci singing the roles of Rosina and Nedda.

The Montevideo reviews continued the same line of praise:

> "The audience really was conquered by her *Caro Nome*, which was an expression of equisite style and sentiment. When she repeated the aria, the applause reached delirium. Her interpretation of Gilda seemed insuperable."—*El Diario Español.*

> "A triumph for Galli-Curci. The applause and the bravos burst forth enthusiastically and the exquisite singer was obliged to repeat the famous romanza, which was sung with extraordinary purity, and received another ovation."
> —*La Tribuna Popolar.*

There were several different expressions assigned by reviewers to the quality and type of voice possessed by the artist. In Spain it was called "lirico-leggero," sometimes specified as "ligero" or "ligera." The Italian word is "leggiero"—literally "light of calibre" but not thin or weak, as distinct from lyric and dramatic. This type is not to be confused with "coloratura," which is not a degree of vocal strength but a term to express display of vocal skill. "Coloratura" may be employed by both lyric and light voices. Galli-Curci's voice was also described as "soprano lirico," meaning "limpid." The voice, at this time, had not as yet come into its full powers, hence the variance. At a later date, however, it developed fine lyric quality, so that she qualified as both lyric and coloratura.

Milan Debut

The long voyage back to Italy brought our little prima donna in time for an autumn appearance in *Rigoletto* at Trieste. "Particularly was Galli-Curci sublime," said *L'Osservatore Triestino*, and there were many more similar comments.

Evidently the enormous successes of the twenty-year-old prima donna aroused attention in her home city, for without further ado Manager Oreste Poli dispatched a letter to Galli-Curci requesting her appearance in Milan at the fall Dal Verme carnival season, featuring her in *Lucia*, and to demonstrate that she deserved her popularity in the role of Gilda, a special *Rigoletto* was arranged for Milan music-lovers.

La Scala meanwhile was preparing a revival of *Sonnambula*, so, with professional business sagacity, our singer called upon Director Mingardi with a view to making her debut in this opera at that house—but to no purpose, as the lead had been assigned to Rosina Storchio; however, he offered her the little part of Lisa. Galli-Curci, with an unforgettable withering smile, replied, "Dear Mingardi, don't forget this—I shall never put my feet again in this theatre," and she never did. Milan, however, was to hear its own prima donna often, but not at La Scala.

The Milan press found in this product of its own municipality a personality and an art worthy of highest praise:

> "She raised enthusiasm during and after the *Mad Scene*, was forced to repeat the cadenza. She sings with exactness, fine intuition of the Donizetti style, fluent agility, and most pointed silver-toned notes, on an equalized scale."—*La Perseveranza.*
> "She is blessed with a grand voice."—*Il Secolo.*

San Carlo

After Rome and Milan, Naples is next in numerical importance. Scarcely do we think of Naples other than picturesquely, romantically, passionately; therefore we are surprised to find it encompassed by steel mills, ship yards, locomotive works, engine, glass, glove, perfume, cotton, wool, linen and silk factories, with wine, brandy, dried fruits, nuts, paper and hemp industries in juxtaposition with guitars, mandolins, songs and music, and the San Carlo opera-house —the largest in Italy.

Receiving a call for the 1911 spring season, considered one of the most important in the kingdom, Galli-Curci selected *Sonnambula* for the debut. The music fitted her vocal style admirably, while the role was sympathetically suitable to her interpretative qualifications; for the opera has ever been a puissant vehicle for singers of top quality, arias such as "Come per me sereno," "O Mio dolor," "Ah, non credea," and "Ah, non giunge" demanding pure and tender vocal exposition.

That she accomplished the feat of impressing a San Carlo audience in three performances of the opera is vouched for by the reviews:

> "She has no ordinary knowledge of *bel canto* art, she possesses
> a perfect acquaintance with histrionic expression."
> —Don Marzio.

After Naples there were three *Rigoletto* performances at Modena and one at Parma, also a recital at the residence of Marchésa Manara, followed by a respite until the spring of 1912 with another *Rigoletto* at San Remo, over by Nice in the Riviera.

During these interurban visits Galli-Curci met with some queer experiences. While no public disclaimer was ever discharged against her, she recalls having witnessed its operation on several occasions. At Parma, where she was a guest of the local company, a number of baritones were tried out in the role of Escamillo, but all collapsed on the high E which occurs several times in the "Toreador Song"— a vocal red flag that incites yells of rage accompanied by a shower of pennies on the stage—most ignominious of declarations—and sundry other wrathful tributes as hurling vegetables, smashing furniture amid a storm of vocal outcries both wonderful and varied. No other signal was necessary to impress upon such unfortunate singers the advisability of leaving by the quickest route. Finally, a mediocre vocalist, because he was able to howl out his high E's with great sonority, was immediately accepted with wild acclaim to become a fixture for the balance of the season.

South American Tour

In the summer of 1912 Galli-Curci began a second trip to South

America as prima donna in the roles of Gilda and Rosina. She was also to sing Walter in *La Wally* by Catalani and Oscar in *Il Ballo in Maschera* by Verdi. Always the conscientious artist, Galli-Curci gave to the smaller roles the same careful consideration as to the larger, hence won praise for the excellence of her interpretations as well as for her delivery of the music. It was with Gilda and Rosina, however, that she gathered richest laurels, arousing journalistic trumpet-blasts and creating furores among audiences; indeed, the columns of exalted praise became a tedium because of their gushing volubility and apparent uncontrolled fervidity:

> "The audience, with a unanimous ovation, demanded a *Caro Nome* encore, which Galli-Curci rendered with such exquisite consummation as to surprise the auditors, who had no knowledge of ever before having listened to an artist of such power."
> —*Il Giornale d'Italia*, Buenos Aires.

> "The success of this singing-actress was complete, one of those successes that can and should be made insuperable."
> —*L'Italiano*, Buenos Aires.

The tour covered Buenos Aires, Rosario, Rio, São Paulo, Montevideo, and Santiago. Performances in Buenos Aires were under the direction of Gino Marinuzzi and given at the Coliséo; those in Río at the Teatro Municipál, in Montevideo at the Teatro Solis, in Rosario at the Teatro la Opera, in Santiago at the Teatro Municipál, at São Paulo at the Teatro Municipál. Regarding her first performance of Micaela in *Carmen* in Montevideo, a role which she had learned on this tour, reviews stated that she sang the music brilliantly and sweetly, with technical facility, for all of which she received the most sincere applause of the evening. Strange to some perhaps that she never sang the part again, for it must have fitted her quite admirably; but, like other roles discarded for some sufficient reason, this, too, was dropped, no doubt because of its limited vocal opportunities—truly no prima donna vehicle.

Now came the journey over the Andes to Santiago, Chile. Nothing outside the usual repertory presented in the usual way characterized this short visit, which brought the tour to a successful close; then the return voyage to Italy, where another supreme opportunity awaited the aspiring songstress.

For the autumn there were ten guest engagements at Turin (five *Sonnambula*, three *Traviata*, two *Rigoletto*), and later in the season, at Mantua, six *Rigoletto*—all preliminary to the ten performances of *Rigoletto* at Rome during carnival season. Our now-famed artist, at last secure in her position as a premier interpreter of *bel canto* opera, was in constant demand and the Costanzi management, ever alert, fell into line to secure the popular prima donna.

Gilda at Costanzi

This significant event, which caps the Galli-Curci early operatic ventures, is chronicled as January 19, 1913—a first appearance at this house in a leading role—significant because the one in which she had begun her opera career in Trani and had been so eminently successful in portraying elsewhere. Many Gildas had come and gone at the Costanzi. Many notable singers had trod that historic stage. It was therefore no small achievement for this young and self-schooled singer, just past the age of twenty-three to have gained the topmost rank—in itself a monumental victory. The first performance was honored by the presence of Queen Eléna and an audience of Roman culture.

> "Galli-Curci returns a finished artist, presenting a method of singing impeccable and perfect, enriched by all the finesses, modulation and blend that permit her to sing most deliciously, mastering the most arduous difficulties throughout an extensive range. She put in evidence all the riches of her marvelous throat-staccati alternating with trills and flute-like tones wonderfully executed—produced upon the subjugated audience real and intense pleasure manifested in clamorous applause. When Gilda closed the cadenza with a high E natural, true, sure and clear, she evoked an enthusiastic and interminable ovation."
>
> —*Vita Teatrale.*

> "Galli-Curci in the part of Gilda was sublime. Her voice, ever fresh, ever sweet, ever paradisiacal, gave off the most intimate filament of the heart and the public, truly affected, was ravished by such perfection, such art, such sentiment. The trills, warbles,

middle-tones, the clear emission, the richness of her art, enhanced by the Galli-Curci spirit, gave an illusion more of a
dream than of a theatre."—*Il Mondo dell'Arte.*

"She is a finished artist with a perfect method of singing. Her
voice has a silver-toned quality, clear and of astonishing intonation."—*Alfredo Vandini.*

Catania and Puritani

Another outstanding appearance was at Catania, where Galli-
Curci was engaged to sing the role of Elvira, in seven performances
of *I Puritani* during August, 1913.

To successfully face a Catanian audience in the Teatro Massimo
Bellini requires assurance born of experience and art born of genius
—two qualities possessed by our artist that hitherto had never failed
her. Due to complete mastery of self and voice, nervousness and
stage-fright were to her unknown. Large audiences, cultured audiences, critical audiences, temperamental audiences, even when she
was singing a first-time part, neither upset her equilibrium nor disturbed her state of mind. Self possession was her guard as well as
her anchor. Singing with artists of bigger reputations never dis-
heartened her but, contrariwise, spurred her to greater endeavor.
She knew what she could do, what she was expected to do, and her
business was to do that—not merely well, but superlatively well—
better, if possible, than had been done before. She feared none,
hence courted no favors. She won her honors single-handed and
compelled recognition by the very potency of her art and the
glamour of her personality.

To sing Elvira for the first time, in the Bellini city, would have
stimulated most sopranos to an abnormal degree of nervous excitement. Not so the intrepid Galli-Curci who, with bottled nerves,
infallible surety of voice and memory, utilized each of the seven
performances to climb upward toward the summit of imperishable
fame. At each appearance before a crowded house our young artist
was warmly greeted and received. It was, according to her own statement, "a joy to sing for these people because they have a consanguineous trace of the Moorish which shows itself in their sad
songs and proud characters. Their behavior at the opera, though

tempered by Latin temperament, is admirably held in check, therefore less versatile in modes of expression but nevertheless positive." The commentators conferred upon her most complimentary titles and regarded her performances as examples of supremest art. They called her a virtuosa of the first order; likened her trills to those of the nightingale; stated that she executed technical difficulties with utmost skill, sang with perfect intonation and astonishing agility; credited her with a voice of luscious quality and an art of highest polish. One called her a very queen of *bel canto*; another closed his critique with this special line—"Salve, illustre artista!" A third wrote: "The grand artist added new leaves to the magnificent crown of glory which already adorns her," and a fourth summed up her success in a single word, *"Triunfo!"*

As a tribute to the composer, to the city, and to the art to which both contributed so mightily, Galli-Curci visited the cathedral and placed a sheaf of golden berries upon Bellini's tomb—"exquisite homage from a great servant to a great creative genius." (*La Sicilia.*)

To grace the August season at Ostend, Belgium, the Kursaal management engaged the Milanese soprano whose name was now reaching out beyond the confines of Italy to distant music centers, therein creating a desire to hear an artist the grandeur of whose singing was heralded among connoisseurs of vocal art and followers of operatic moves. Engaged for two concerts, her popularity became so pronounced that she was requested to give a third for the accommodation of such as could not attend the first and second. Her engaging personality and beguiling style of art begat an avalanche of critical tributes couched in the elegant language of the French, yet re-echoing the encomiums elsewhere bestowed.

Five *Barber of Seville* performances in Trieste followed, then back to Milan to sing a special *Sonnambula* at Dal Verme with a new and brilliant young tenor, Tito Schipa, with Ettore Panizza conducting. In this production the local-born soprano again ascended to heights of brilliancy and impressive vocal art with which to compel more extolling paragraphs to augment the many already amassed, of which even a casual perusal would suffice to satisfy any skeptic of the fact that here was a singer unanimously recognized as a vocalist of extraordinary competence whom all the world is pleased to honor and applaud.

Madrid

Under clouds of approaching war, the 1913-14 season looked none too hopeful, yet it afforded Galli-Curci one of the most resplendent chapters in her career—a first season in Madrid. At this particular period of its history, the Spanish capital was grounded in traditions of ancient chivalry and romance. Practiced at court with all pomp and formality, the etiquette was most rigid, stately and spectacular, yet within the royal family relationships were of charming simplicity. The opera house, Teatro Real, one of the finest in the world, had witnessed performances of important works by famous singers for generations. It was practically the natal place of Patti, whose mother gave her birth shortly after singing on that very stage. The advent of Galli-Curci into this demesne was at a time of colorful environment, therefore to be viewed in the light of that splendid period.

As Amina in *Sonnambula* our artist made her debut November 25, 1913, which event was honored by the presence of the King and Queen and the Infanta Isabél, who occupied the royal box. Press reports were lengthy and of adulatory grandiloquence, the applause enthusiastically bestowed. "The audience rose to its feet and shouted admiration and content until their voices became hoarse and weary." (*El Imparcial.*)

On December 20 Galli-Curci sang Elvira in *Puritani*, with Alessandro Bonci as Arturo. The reception accorded the little prima donna was similar to that of the previous occasion, which critical comments can be expressed best in the chief caption words: *Triunfo! Ovación! Admiración! Suceso! Perfecta! Bravisimo! Aplaudido! Entusiasmo! Qué Belleza! Qué Poesía! Qué Idilio!*

Rigoletto followed on the 25th—another Christmas on the stage. "The Caro Nome reached to Heaven!" "Premier among Gildas!" etc., etc. Perhaps the spirit of Verdi hovered about the Real upon that anniversary night; or perhaps the presence of Their Majesties with Princes and Princesses and a magnificent audience in a dazzling flood of illumination, was the compelling force to rouse the singer to inspired effort.

A Palace Recital

Among the high spots of this Madrid season was the recital at the Royal Palace. The day previous, Galli-Curci had received a request invitation to appear at the function given by the King to solemnize the patron saint of his august spouse, an honor which, of course, received immediate acceptance. The banquet was attended by members and relatives of the Royal Family, their courtiers and maids-of-honor, ministers and other persons of distinction, including the colonel and officers of Victoria Eugenia's regiment, who had made a hurried journey from Valencia for the occasion. At nine-thirty the assemblage moved into the Salon Gasparini where Galli-Curci and Viglione-Borghese gave a joint program, the former singing the "Bell Song" from *Lakmé*, two songs, and the *Rigoletto* duet with the baritone. According to custom, the artists received embossed souvenirs and were recipients of many compliments, notably from Their Majesties and the Queen Mother, María Cristina, with whom the ingratiating soprano established a warm and lasting friendship.

The mere recording of this event is *per se* inconsequential without the glamorous historic background of the Spanish Court, into which Galli-Curci fitted as perfectly as any figure on a Watteau canvas. From her Spanish mother she inherited the Castilian flare for picturesquesness, while the fascinating witchery of Italian art was hers also—a combination that enabled her to fuse her personality into the composite of the court. Individuality of person and of dress made her distinctively prominent in any company. A simple, winsome manner clothed her with a graciousness that charmed kings and queens, princes and peasants as well as musicians and dilettanti.

Galli-Curci describes her visit to the palace thus: "I knew that I could not compete with others in the matter of dress, so wore a simple frock, and I had no jewels to put on. A wonderful scene greeted me when I reached the royal abode. Queen Victoria was ablaze with diamonds and precious stones. The Queen Mother was in black, set off with a rope of black pearls around her neck that reached to the floor. The court ladies were attired sumptuously but, in my modest white dress, I challenged no comparisons. Yet, the welcome I received and the reception accorded after singing made me feel, after all, there were better things in life than clothes and jewels. I tried to look well on the stage, so sacrificed my everyday dress to that end."

After singing at the palace, the custom of serving tea in the private apartments prevailed, and none may sit in the presence of the Queen without permission. The Infanta Isabél, however, tactfully circumvented the decree by saying to Galli-Curci: "You have been singing and need to rest—so you and I will both sit down." The King came in to greet the singer and conversed intelligently on music though himself no connoisseur. Private appearances, while *en rigeur*, were less formal than functions of state. Only the family and royal ladies attended the former, all attired with simple elegance; but at the latter, given in the great music-room, modeled like a concert-hall with an adjoining room for artists, gowns and jewels knew no limit in extravagance, with low-cut bodices literally gem-encrusted and ropes of pearls extending to the floor. This first visit to Madrid prepared the way for a second the following year, for our artist had won the approval of the opera audiences as well as the friendship of the royal family.

To begin the 1914 New Year, on January 16 Galli-Curci participated in an operatic benefit for the Madrid Press Association. This program consisted of opera acts and an operetta, *Molinos de Viento* (Wind-Mills), in Italian. The composer led the orchestra, and the favorite artist proved herself as inimitable in light operetta as in heavier works, singing and acting with bewitching grace and finish.

Huguenots served to disclose more Galli-Curci talent in the role of Marguerite of Valois. There was another *Rigoletto* with Mario Sammarco in the title part, then a first *Barber of Seville* with this noted baritone as Figaro.

"In the music-lesson scene the enthusiasm rose to madness. The audience with one accord rose in a mad delirium with cries of *Bravo! Bravíssimo! That's how to sing! Insuperable artist!* while the handclapping seemed like a wild tornado. It was one of the greatest triumphs and will be registered permanently in the annals of the Royal Theatre."—*La Correspondencia Militar.*

Later in the month Galli-Curci participated in a concert given by the Dowager Countess of Hoyos, which was attended by Doña Isabél, Doña Luisa, and Don Carlos. Invitations were extended only to the most notable of the feminine aristocracy which formed the index of the royal opera list. Before the musical entertainment tea was served in rooms graced by the wives of ambassadors and maids-of-honor in gorgeous toilettes, ropes of rubies, and diamond insignias of office. In the meantime, a piano was placed in one of the lovers' corners, covered with a rich antique cloth bordered in pale colored silk. On various divans and chairs sat the guests.

In the second part of the program appeared Galli-Curci, dressed in a spangled white gown, with hair a little curled, which gave an aspect of the Directoire epoch. Of her numbers, the "Shadow Song" from *Dinorah* absolutely subjugated her auditors. After the affair the singer received a pretty note from the Marquésa de Vinent, expressing appreciation of her art in behalf of the Infantas Isabél and Luisa and the Infante Don Carlos.

At last the inevitable farewell, in order that Galli-Curci might have time to reach St. Petersburg for operatic engagements there in March. All the papers carried headlines, "Farewell to Galli-Curci."

"Señores, el delirio!" began one review; "I have no remembrance of witnessing so spectacular an ovation, so sensitive, so colossal, as that last night lavished upon the eminent diva Galli-Curci."—*La Tribuna.*

Russia, 1914

Exigency appeared to be the source from which engagements emanated, for no sooner had she finished one than another sprang up. Now it was for a long land journey to Russia with a company headed for the capital city to present an Italian repertory. This experience was of value, since it tended to further broaden her outlook. She had felt the cold of northern Italy and of South America, but found no frigidity like that in Russia. Audiences, enveloped in copious furs and wearing high goloshes, arrived looking more like

Russian bears than Russian people. Then as butterflies emerging from chrysalises, the gorgeous toilettes were disclosed—Parisian gowns, sparkling gems, alabaster complexions, gleaming eyes, aristocratic grace, exquisite taste—furnishing a fascinating pageant in the foyer and a scintillating picture in the auditorium; a music-loving assemblage steeped in brilliancy, hospitality and pleasure but not in wisdom, which mass of beauty, wealth and art was a few years later to be swept away by the revolutionary avalanche that buried Russian culture with the Russian empire.

These appearances during March were delightful episodes to Galli-Curci, for she was cordially received and appreciated, the flowers alone sent to her representing more perhaps than her fee because coming from such great distances—violets from Parma and roses from Palermo. One of the most gracious customs of former Russian opera was calling out, at the end of the performance, the name of the singer who had pleased best—an honor frequently bestowed upon the little lady from Milan. Due to her outstanding success she was invited to sing at the Imperial Opera, which had its own company but none the less could afford to make a bid for extra popularity by presenting a distinguished guest.

Observing audiences formed, as usual, one of her nightly pastimes. While the Italian and Spanish are, according to her estimate, the most boisterous in displaying pleasure or displeasure, the charm of their appreciation, the enthusiasm and musical understanding are rich rewards to the singer who merits their artistic approbation. In Leningrad (then St. Petersburg), demonstrations were of a more peaceful nature, yet intelligently and sincerely bestowed.

The Russians, for a considerable period, have been musically important, contributing many of the world's finest examples of art through the masterworks of her composers. Opera was one of the chief forms of entertainment of this gifted people, and one counted his career incomplete without an appearance in at least one of the chief music centers of the domain. Strange, however, was the interurban jealousy of Moscow and St. Petersburg, the former school dominated by Tschaikowsky and Scriabin, the latter by Rimsky-

Korsakoff, Moussorgsky, Borodin and Cui. Rivalry between this pair of capitals was of such keenness as to preclude success in one if made in the other. Hence, Galli-Curci was not asked to sing in Moscow, though undoubtedly the music-lovers of that city would have flocked to hear her had the opportunity been provided them.

Returning to Italy, Galli-Curci rested until early April, when more engagements called her to activity—a series of performances at Barcelona, under the musical direction of Gaetano Bavagnoli. *Sonnambula* was the opening opera, then *Barber of Seville*, *Lucia*, and a final honor evening for the favorite prima donna, who appeared in the first and third acts of *Sonnambula* and the second act of *Puritani*, with added numbers which she was ever called upon to contribute.

As to her popularity, the laudations of the press attest convincingly.

> "For those who attended the opera last night for the first time, it was a revelation. It was a complete and overwhelming triumph to the singer's pure and noble art. Her voice, secure in all its range, is of the purest timbre and of extraordinary pliability. She is a prodigy, the absolute mistress of her voice."
> —*La Tribuna.*

> "To have heard so marvelous a singer as Galli-Curci, Bellini himself would have applauded her until his hands burned."
> —*El Progreso.*

The 4th of June witnessed the inaugural of the renovated Teatro Carcano, Milan. After Mozart's pretty operetta *Bastien and Bastienne* by the local company, Galli-Curci sang the *Lakmé* "Bell Song" with orchestra, which was followed by *L'Amico Fritz* directed by its composer, Mascagni. On August 27 she was in Brescia for a *Barber of Seville*, Ferrari of the Costanzi conducting. *Traviata* followed on the 15th of September.

Galli-Curci participated in the gala performance of the *Barber* at the Carcano, Milan, on October 16, with Tito Ruffo, Luigi Mancinelli conducting, the event being a "festival of art organized by the *Artist's Journal.*" Another *Barber* at Bologna on the 29th

with Ruffo; a repetition, on November 4, as a farewell to her, led
to the December appearances at Bari, *Traviata* with Schipa and
another *Barber*.

La Muérta Resuscitada

Now dawned the crucial period of Galli-Curci's life—the 1915
season, which was to climax so unexpectedly, so unpremeditatedly.
With no apprehension that this setting forth to Barcelona en route
to Madrid would prove a farewell to Italy, a goodbye to the past, a
step toward the Valhalla of renown and to an almost tragic conclusion to her career, and engrossed with happy thoughts of new
awaiting triumphs, she reached the largest city of the Kingdom, not
to tarry there for singing, but merely en passant. Perhaps she had
a mind to pass a day or two in such a salubrious environment, but
her arrival served only as a prelude to a bitter tale of woe.

In the shade of the Aesir's sacred ash, so we are told, sit three
Norns weaving human destinies. As in the Prologue to *Die Götter-
dämmerung*, while in the act of passing it back and forth, the frail
thread end snaps inaudibly between their twining fingers and the
tragedy of fate begins. Just as Galli-Curci seemed to have attained
the object most desired, just as she seemed to have gained her
premier position in the vocal world, just as she seemed to be smoothly coursing on the wave of popularity—that delicate, invisible fila-
ment which binds the finite to the infinite became, with unwarned
suddenness, hard-drawn almost to the point of severance.

Engaged for the early 1915 season at Madrid, Galli-Curci proceeded to the Spanish capital via Barcelona where, as if beset by
some dastard, lurking foe, she fell victim to an illness as strange as
it was dire, as fearsome as it was bewildering. Doctors were sorely
puzzled but finally diagnosed her malady as typhus, yet could not
understand the swiftness of its smiting. No doubt the mystery lay
in the fact that Barcelona had been visited by a typhus epidemic in
the autumn previous and that Galli-Curci imbibed some flitting
germs the spring before when there as opera guest. Eager to fulfill
her duty, she must have started from Milan with an incipient fever
which broke into a raging temperature at Barcelona where, though

impatient to reach Madrid, she was forced to bed. Reports were transmitted by telephone to Madrid and from day to day proved gravely pessimistic. Her life, in serious danger, hung on each passing breath. Doctors, with furrowed brows, watched that frail, prostrate form gripped in a typhus stupor for six pain-racked weeks as the patient lay between life and death, while Madrid's opera management was torn with anxious apprehension, for upon her appearance depended the season's anticipated success.

Through a miracle of God, which man can neither comprehend nor analyze; through a marvelous vitality, perhaps through an indomitable will and indefatigable courage, Galli-Curci conquered the disease and soon after was able to be moved to a sanitorium near Madrid for convalescence. In the city of the famous Philips it was the custom to give two series of operas. The first had passed without the charming prima donna; the second was at hand. Because of the continued announcement of her inability to sing, subscriptions had been few, box-office sales practically nil. The manager, however, perhaps hoping for another miracle, called upon the invalid a week after the lifting of the quarantine, with an unparalleled result.

"Can't you *possibly* sing?" asked the impresario with pleading emphasis.

"Yes, I can *sing*," replied the prima donna, "but I can't *stand*."

"Then *I* am ruined," he moaned. "*Opera* is ruined! *All* is ruined!"

"Alas! I would gladly sing if my legs would only hold me."

"Dios! I shall lose *everything!*"

"And I— for I have counted on this engagement to pay my debts."

"Muy bien! There is nothing left for me but a bullet in the head."

"Wait! I have an idea—I *will* sing."

"Magnífico! But how?"

"I will sing from a wheel-chair."

"Grandísimo! You are an angel!"

When the little singer, in a wheel-chair, was rolled upon the stage on the evening of February 16, in the second scene of the *Barber*, holding a bouquet of flowers bound with the national colors pre-

sented by an Infanta, a hurricane of shouts beset her. Vocally she
was in fine form and won an instantaneous ovation with "Una voce
poco fa." Between scenes she was fed strong meat jelly and cham-
pagne, and only the excitement kept her from collapsing. The effort,
however, instead of causing a relapse, set her on the road to recovery.
The day after she was able to take a short walk, and on the 18th
received an audience with the King and Queen-mother, who felici-
tated the singer upon her recovery and return to activity.

Reverting to that "death recovery" appearance, it is recorded that
the audience did not cease applauding the brave singer who, however, declined the many encore calls because of fatigue, conserving
her strength which had been subjected to a great emotional strain.
Fortunately the disease had not affected the vocal organism. Infanta
Doña Isabél sent from her box to Galli-Curci compliments and
praise, with an invitation to sing at the palace as soon as she felt
able. The composite headline of the press was *Gran Triunfo de la
Galli-Curci*; the paragraphs, a veritable explosion of superlatives.

> "She sang the 'Una voce poco fa' with such perfection and
> masterful delineation of the diffifficult passages that the ap-
> plause broke out again at the end and continued for fully five
> minutes, interrupting the opera, and from then on the enthusi-
> asm kept on increasing. The entire opera was sung in perfect
> style, befitting a star who today occupies a premier position in
> her art. She has obtained the supreme gift which God, from
> time to time, bestows upon humans, viz., *immortality*."
>
> —*El Mundo.*

So the Madrid season was saved and Galli-Curci became the idol
of the city, leaving an unforgettable record, the royal family bestowing honors and affectionate kindness upon her.

On February 24 she sang at the opera house in the third act of
the *Barber*, interpolating several Spanish songs to her own piano
accompaniment after the regular lesson numbers. On the 26th the
royal family was convoked in the apartments of Maria Cristina for
afternoon tea and to hear an intimate concert by Galli-Curci.
Traviata on March 7 was followed by another concert given in
honor of the royal family at the palace by the Infanta Doña Isabél

on March 25. At the conclusion of the concert the hostess presented to Galli-Curci a brooch of precious stones.

The Child of Fate

Galli-Curci was a child of fate. Every move of her career was guided seemingly by some invisible force without premeditation, in the most sudden and unexpected manner. Again, at this particular moment, when the next immediate step lay eastward toward Italy, the wheel of fate spun around once more to change, not only the direction of her course, but the trend of her future activities.

Just at this decisive instant there came a contract with a money draft from the Colón management in Buenos Aires for the opera season; so without ado Amelita, Luigi and Gennaro set out for the Canary Islands, there to rest and fully recuperate before proceeding to South America for a third season, which proved an open sesame to an unimaginative reality.

The people of Teneriff knew of Galli-Curci's tremendous popularity in Madrid. They knew also that having the diva in their own city would constitute an opportunity for them to seize upon that circumstance with invitations to favor them with at least one occasion to listen to her voice. Four concerts therefore were arranged in conjunction with the Renacimiento String Quartet under the auspices of the Sociedád Filarmónica, given during the early part of May. This island in the sea where appreciation was as keen and candid as on the mainland, though not so favored with respect to visits from artists of international repute, bestowed upon its visitor a glittering array of praise and, as a tribute to the distinguished artist, a tea was given in her honor by prominent ladies of the city. The Municipal Band participated in the affair, and Galli-Curci, graciously accepting the pressing invitations, contributed several vocal numbers. At the final concert the pleasure of the audience was subtly shown in a shower of rose petals which fluttered from above the stage until they had formed a bed of fragrant blossoms ankle deep about the singer's feet. After that a caged canary, flower-wreathed, was slowly let down before her eyes, and finally a flock of white-winged doves flew from the gallery, each bearing a mottoed card, with several of the boldest alighting on the shoulders of the smiling recitalist. The Teneriffs truly have an expressive word for hospitality—*Enchantment*. On leaving for her ocean journey, Galli-Curci was presented with a tropical bird which sang to her throughout the voyage.

Sailing westward unknowingly to enter a new cycle of existence —artistic, domestic and national—there were many recollections of bygone days indelibly impressed upon the mind of our prima donna, some of an amusing character. There are tricks in every trade, even in opera. On one occasion, after Galli-Curci and the tenor had responded to numerous curtain-calls, he whispered to her engagingly, "Now you go out alone." Sensing his trick, by means of which he would be entitled to do likewise and get full benefit of his paid claque and thereby remain indefinitely before the curtain, she replied "No, thank you. I make my reputation while the curtain is up, not while it is down."

Another experience that Galli-Curci recalls was that concerning a black kitten—not a bad omen in this case, though forcing a trying situation. When singing Violetta in one of the smaller cities, the little animal strayed nonchalantly upon the stage and went directly toward the singer, who turned aside the impending comedy, when it was least needed, by moving slowly in the direction of the playful creature. Then tipping her full crinoline skirts and dropping them over the black body, she slid along, one foot before the other, still singing, until she reached the wings; then, with a gentle shove, sent the unwelcome visitor into the waiting hands of a man crouching to receive it.

It seems appropriate to close this cycle with another sidelight on the character of this remarkable woman about to step across the threshold, facing a garden of utopian splendor and fame.

From now on her innate aptness for the theatre, hitherto only embryonic in its prominence, begins to flare forth conspicuously and potently. Certain of God's creatures have the capacity to hold the spotlight—they can't help doing so because it is their nature. Like Sirius among stars, the rose among flowers, the oak among trees, the eagle among birds, the lion among animals, the diamond among gems, so certain individuals know how to dramatize themselves—an unstudied, involuntary accomplishment effected without premeditation or exertion. One of these is Galli-Curci, in whom such talent functioned to a very high degree. She never sought publicity—publicity sought her. Not until she adopted America as her home did she endorse the commercializing of her art and then only upon the strictest lines of truth and honesty. Her position of eminence in Italy, Spain, and South America was gained through earnest effort applied to genuine talent—a combination of voice and personality that beguiled the eye, enravished the ear. As the future scenes begin to unfold, this undefinable precedence trait summarily summoned her to leadership and made her, in whatsoever company she found herself, the center of attraction. This innate aptitude became stronger, more decisive through maturation until its maximum potentiality had been attained.

CYCLE OF
TRANSITION

1915-1916

"I have no favorite song. Everything I sing is my favorite."

—GALLI-CURCI

South America Again

 FUNDAMENTAL TRAIT of every distinguished artist is self-control. Appearing for the first time before the fastidious audience at the principal opera-house in Buenos Aires should have been sufficient to cause a fluttering of nerves, an accentuated ventricular movement of the heart. Intense excitement, too, might expectantly arise to discompose the calm demeanor of our artist when she learned that her chief associate in her *Lucia* debut would be the great Caruso, then at the height of his fame. But that circumstance neither disturbed her equanimity nor lessened her self-assurance. Galli-Curci was not the flustering type of singer. The hoped-for opportunity had arrived; she would make the best of it. That she did so is vouchsafed in the press reports of that notable event, which took place on June 27, 1915.

"Outstanding Triumph for Galli-Curci and Caruso." "Galli-Curci is one of the rarest among singers." "She was the heroine of the evening." So read the headlines.

Flowers and invitations poured in, but most of the latter she could not accept, for singing had first call upon her time and energy, and she had two new rôles to rehearse for early presentation—Sophie in Richard Strauss' *Rosenkavalier* and Ophelia in Ambroise Thomas' *Hamlet*. This third visit to the Argentine capital was important and imposing because of the distinction which the engagement carried and of the eminence which association with Caruso brought our singer. This appearance with the world's most famous tenor was highly significant, as it foreshadowed three events in which the pair were to be subsequently allied: first, their meeting in New York, a year hence; second, making Victor records that were to link their names and voices together forever; third, her engagement by the Metropolitan Opera Company and, after Caruso's death, her opening of the season—an honor always his.

LUCIA DI LAMMERMOOR

Cast:

Lord Enrico Ashton . . . . Giuseppe Danise
Miss Lucia, su hermana . . . . Amelita Galli-Curci
Sir Edgardo di Ravenswood . . . . Enrico Caruso
Lord Arturo Bucklaw . . . . Luigi Nardi
Raimondo Bidebent . . . . Bernardo Berardi
Alisa, Doncella de Lucia . . . . G. Torelli
Normanno . . . . N. N.
Director de Orquesta . . . . Giuseppe Sturani

Although she was never privileged to sing again with Caruso on the operatic stage, the single opportunity in Buenos Aires was of monumental worth, for it eventually lifted her to an eminence quite on a par with his. Ships pass in the night, usually to make no durable contact; human beings, too, pass in life, often to make a prophetic contact, involuntary or otherwise. Such is the anomaly of existence. These two *Lucia* performances with Caruso in 1915 proved to be the handwriting on the wall for Galli-Curci.

Traviata, on June 29, brought Galli-Curci before the Colón clientele in the rôle of Violetta. Of this performance the Buenos Aires *Herald* said:

> "That so long as there are voices like Galli-Curci's crowds will flock to hear the time-worn melodies of the florid operas was clearly demonstrated when Donizettian trills and roulades held all listeners spellbound. Her trills and cadenzas were astonishing in their bird-like purity, and clearly proved her right to be classed with the most prominent singers of the coloratura school."

Ever responsive to appeals of a worthy nature, Galli-Curci appeared at the Coliséo on July 5 in a benefit in behalf of a hospital for wounded in France sponsored by the Polytechnic School of Paris. Concert numbers were contributed by Galli-Curci, Caruso and others.

July 17, the *Barber of Seville* with Tedeschi and Ruffo; August 1, *Rigoletto* with Hipolito Lázaro and Ruffo. Press comment on these performances followed the same line as those previously quoted—lengthy, laudatory, positive. One of the most gracious acts of any prima donna was that of Galli-Curci when she surrendered her right to the part of Gilda in favor of the Argentine soprano, Soler, in which to make her debut. Answering the request of the management, she replied: "Most cheerfully I relinquish the part, for one needs experience during the first steps of a career and it gives me much gratitude not to obstruct the road, in the slightest, at the beginning."

July 30 brought a debut as Sophie in the *Rosenkavalier* with Rosa Raisa. A festival of music on August 3, under the auspices of the Association of Critics, was given at the Colón, the program consisting of the second act of the *Rosenkavalier*, with the regular opera cast, an instrumental and vocal concert directed by Marinuzzi, Act I of *Pagliacci* with Caruso and Ruffo.

August 9 proved another red-letter night, for it provided an opportunity for Galli-Curci to disclose still another phase of her seemingly illimitable art—Ophelia in *Hamlet*, Ruffo singing the title rôle. There was much praise in the press for her work in the delineation of the character as well as for her rendition of the music.

A second *Lucia* with Caruso, with additional performances of the *Rosenkavalier* and *Hamlet*, brought the season to a close, but not the activities of the company which, under the Colón management, participated in a tour covering Montevideo, Río, and São Paulo. The opening performance on August 15 at the Teatro Solis was *Barber of Seville* with Galli-Curci, Ruffo and Tedeschi; *Rigoletto*, with Galli-Curci, Lázaro and Bernardi was also presented. The repertory further included *Lucia* and *Hamlet*. This tour concluded, a number of the artists were still eager to extend the schedule; that being impossible, another tour was arranged through Bonacchi &

Co., affiliated with the Colón management. The Grand Italian
Lyric Company, featuring Galli-Curci and Lázaro, began in October. The musical director was Ricardo Dellera of La Scala, Milan.

An interesting name on the prospectus of the *Grande Compagnia
Lirica Italiana* was Prof. Luigi Curci, artistic director. The Marchése
di Simeri, hitherto inconspicuously submerged under the glory of
his celebrated wife, now emerges from his obscurity in a new capacity. The announcement further stated that thirty-five orchestra
professors and a chorus of thirty from La Scala, Milan, with splendid
scenery from Buenos Aires opera houses, would augment the individual vocal units and thus insure highest artistic productions in
keeping with Colón tradition. The itinerary covered the same territory as the previous tour with the addition of Porto Alegre, 1400
miles north of Río, where late in November the enterprise wound
up its business with a substantial profit.

The Call to Cuba

That invisible, irresistible force that directs the courses of certain
individuals along the path of life in accordance with correct principles and rightful purpose, always operating strongly and strangely
for Galli-Curci's guidance, now exerted a vigorous and irrepressible
pull in a new direction. If our singer had not been a darling of the
gods—hence the recipient of such beneficial boon—in all probability
she would have returned straightway to Italy, there to continue her
operatic endeavors until the effulgence of her art should arrest the
attention of some American impresario and induce him to secure
her appearance in the United States. But that return to Italy was not
to be, for seemingly out of the very air came an offer by cable from
the "Gran Compañía de Opera Italiana Silignardi" for the early
1916 Havana season.

With no other prospect in view, this engagement, though necessitating a shift in plans, offered two adventures of tempting entertainment—that of singing in another operatic center of musical
importance and a journey home via the New York route.

The contract completed, the three Curcis sailed from Buenos

Aires in December, arriving in New York the middle of January. Galli-Curci at once sent a dispatch to the Diário de la Marina to the effect that she had arrived and, before leaving for Havana, wished to extend her salutations to the authorities, the press, and the public. The contemplated Teatro Payret season seems to have been abandoned, for on that same day Manager Bracale forwarded from New York to Teatro Nacionál the names of artists leaving for Havana via steamer from Tampa, Florida, that of Galli-Curci heading the list. The telegram stated that the company would not be able to leave before the 20th, as it would not be possible to free Galli-Curci and assemble the equipment earlier. The opening performance was to be scheduled for the first week in February.

Salve Habana!

Here was delight for the inquiring mind of Galli-Curci. Cubans, she found out quickly, love music—their own and the imported kind. They are particularly responsive to opera, famous singers and instrumentalists.

The grand season of opera, under the management of Bracale & Company, began February 3, Galli-Curci making her debut in *Lucia*. Artistically the season loomed auspiciously, but one *contretemps*, unavoidable as well as immaterial, contibuted to what might have been a very embarrassing situation if Galli-Curci had not been the supreme artist, able to quell any show of splenic temper.

The opening had been postponed two days for any one of numerous reasons incident to the establishment of an opera company in a distant city for a series of performances, yet this slight delay was provocative of a most unusual sort of dissatisfaction on the part of a certain opera cult, the minds of whom had been prejudiced and who resorted to a very discourteous and ignoble means of retaliation which, according to Conde Kostia (La Lucha) eminated from "anger and disgust." But whatever the cause, his account stated that Galli-Curci's entrance was met by a "hostile silence" which the reviewer called "a most silly form of rudeness, an example of indifference that originated perhaps in the eclipse of the Tuesday

On her arrival in the United States, 1916

Amelita Galli-Curci, the Remarkable Italian Soprano Who Early This Season Came to America Unheralded—Now, Whenever Her Name Is Announced for a Performance with the Chicago Opera Company, the "Standing Room Only" Sign Is Hung Up

As Elvira, in I Puritani, *Chicago, 1916*

As Lucia, in Lucia di Lammermoor, *Act 1, Chicago, 1916*

As Juliette, in Romeo & Juliette, *Act 1, 1916*

As Gilda in Rigoletto, *Act 4, 1916*

promise." "I am not inclined," said he, "to hold any tenderness for the moral narrowness of our so-called social elite who seemed to have lost all enthusiasm and all high aspirations . . . and one of the manifestations of this unhealthy condition showed in the inexcusable coldness toward such an artist as Galli-Curci." This view was also that of other leading critics, the aggregate opinion being that the third day of the second month of the sixteenth year of the twentieth century was a glorious date, inasmuch as it marked the debut of Galli-Curci in Havana.

Despite this injustice, the artist did not vacillate in exhibiting all the grandeur of her sumptuous song. Unperturbed by the silent greeting, she set herself to work a miracle. There might have been another singer somewhere in the world able to accomplish what Galli-Curci did that night. There may be recorded somewhere in the chronicles of operatic art a feat of equal magnitude, a victory of relative scope; but no general on an ill-omened battlefield so completely grasped the situation and, with rare judgment and skillful tactics, so thoroughly vanquished an enemy and subjugated a hostile host as did Galli-Curci on that eventful evening.

"Attention!" cries the critic. "In a wild conflict, with a luminous sword of genius, the exalted intellectual and vocal power of this phenomenal artist entered into the souls of the audience who, humbled by the enthusiasm and magnetized by the glorious cascades of notes that fell upon them, burst forth tumultuously at the end of the *Mad Scene*. Nor was the singing all. Galli-Curci turned from the traditions followed by all other interpreters, who made of the sorrowful Lucia a figure of mechanical nonsense. The singer reached the highest flights of art." Under the rays of that vocal sun, the audience actually forgot its ill-humor to participate in the ovation.

Then came *Traviata*, *Sonnambula*, *Puritani*, *Hamlet*, *Rigoletto*, and *Huguenots*, in which our singer added to her popularity. Havana capitulated—once again Galli-Curci demonstrated her superlative powers as a singer, as an actress, as an interpreter, as a woman of gentleness and charm, graciousness personified—fascinating and irresistible.

"Galli-Curci is a great singer. She is quite entitled to the premiership of light sopranos and to the appellation *diva*."
—*Cuba Herald*.

"She was incomparable and was received with ecstasy and enthusiasm. A prodigy of true art, a perfect artist. There were tears in many eyes, shouts of *Bravo*, heartpants and emotion."
—*El Triunfo*.

For this Havana performance the name of Gennaro Curci appears on the program. That Amelita's brother-in-law was a basso, as well as an accompanist, had not hitherto been disclosed.

With the season completed, the company moved southward to Cienfuegos for a triad of operas, then to Campagüey, in the center of the island, for a similar set—*Puritani, Lucia* and *Rigoletto* being used in each series. This brought the calendar up to the end of March.

Central America

The opera-giving business was so manifestly good that a continuation of the activity was deemed advisable, so a tour of Central and North America was planned under the direction of A. G. Tinoco and Company. The prospectus sheet was a marvel of publicity ingenuity, carrying a succession of Spanish superlatives calculated to induce large purchases of advance tickets. A repertory of twenty-nine operas was listed, and the names of four artists prominently displayed, Galli-Curci being featured as "The Premier Light Soprano of the World"; Mario Valle, baritone; Gennaro Curci, basso; and Amadeo Ferrer, musical director.

The opening date was announced for April 29. The company went to Central America and enjoyed much success, especially in Guatemala, where the prima donna won additional plaudits and laurels. Everywhere natives showed real affection for the singer and attended her performances in large numbers.

Cognizant of the fact that one must show what one can do before others are convinced of one's ability, Galli-Curci considered these last appearances as tests. "It is the only way," said she, "as the great public is the judge from whose verdict there is no appeal—it is final, whether for or against, and brings either happiness or despair. The public is much the same everywhere and reacts about the same to singing. Everything centers on the fundamental principle of appeal. When I stay close to my audience, the musical appeal is strong, for sincerity is the supreme factor of success."

Our artist, now firmly set in opera's groove, seemed headed for the prescribed life of Italian singers—the round of chain opera houses in a repertory of standard rôles and if, perchance, an American manager should hear her, she might some day sing in that mystic land of wealth and opportunity. Her present sphere was a prescribed circuit that European impresarios controlled, and once entrenched therein, one soon becomes a routinary pawn unless fortune snatches her away. In spite of artistic success and prestige won, Galli-Curci's future, at this time, was truly hazy, if not obscure; but worry and anxiety are two mischievous imps that never paused on the shoulders of the Milanese singer to whisper doleful words of pessimism into ears attuned to nature's sweetest harmonies.

After the past year's activities it seems incredible that her brilliant achievements should have passed unrecognized in the United States. The fact that she was an operatic nomad, singing in various opera houses in numerous cities with divers associates and under different managements, no doubt mitigated against the spread of her fame and popularity outside the particular countries where her name was known and honored, her work heard and appreciated. Had she been the established favorite of some famous theatre, she might have reached sooner the plane where she rightfully belonged and eventually gained through fortune, rather than through design. She had a living to earn, hence was compelled to fill such engagements as came her way. Hers was not to choose but to accept. Fortune's gate, however, always swung open at her approach, and to crown the year 1916 appropriately, she was ushered into the land of her dreams— America!

CYCLE OF
ACHIEVEMENT

1916-1920

"Unless I put my whole heart
and soul into a piece, I cannot
do justice to it or to the audience."

America!

AGAIN the Statue of Liberty's extended torch seemed to give a specific welcome to three passengers aboard that steamer making its way through a network of river traffic toward the pier. No doubt the Marchése di Simeri was explosively eloquent when the skyscrapers of Manhattan rose mysteriously out of the very waters to grow taller and slimmer as the ship approached the island. His wife, however, was not thinking in terms of stone and steel, but in terms of future opportunity—wondering if the New World perhaps held something for her. Friends, the year before in Buenos Aires, had expatiated upon the wonders of the United States and upon its greatest city— told her of the two big opera companies, of the celebrated artists, of the enormous fees, of the universal love for operatic fare—which awoke in this opportunist a wish to behold such grandeur and to participate in the thrills which it invoked.

Amelita's eyes were on the showy shores, but no doubt she saw beyond them—to the stage of an opera house with herself as Gilda or Lucia and with the great Caruso. Dreams! She had been told that Americans accepted, applauded, demanded artists of international repute. What chance, then, had she, unknown, friendless and poor? True, she had won praise in Italy, Spain, Egypt, Russia, Cuba and South America, but what of that, if she were a negative quantity in a land of stars? There were no reporters to meet her on arrival, no camera man imploring a pose or two, not one friendly countenance to greet her. Alone, they watched the docking. Alone, they marched down the gangway. Alone, they drove to the hotel. The little

With first husband, Luigi Curci, Chicago, 1916-1918

As Dinorah (her favorite role), in Dinorah, *Chicago, 1917*

As Violetta, in Traviata, *Act 4, 1917*

De Luca, Caruso, Bada, Galli-Curci, Perini and Egener, after recording of "Lucia Sextette," Camden, N.J., January 25, 1917.

At time of her debut in New York, January, 1918

As Norina in Don Pasquale, *Act 1, Chicago, 1919*

Dresden china singer entertained no fantastic hopes and would have been skeptical of even a suggestion that before her loomed an epochal day in the chronology of musical art. She would have dismissed as nonsense any such thought. Little did she think that just fifty-three days from this inconspicuous arrival she would make a conspicuous debut and arouse a city to such uncontrolled enthusiasm as to cause her name to be written in letters of fire upon the nation's sky.

Could she have visualized those coming years, well might she have questioned her sanity. Such castles-in-the-air were for fools and jesters—she declined to indulge in any such idle pleasantry as building them.

In New York her knowledge of English was of value, for it enabled her to understand Americans. By whatever psychological process impressions grow into fixtures we know not, but Galli-Curci's first contact with the United States proved so potential as to create in her mind a desire to become one of our indomitable race. "These are the people of my ideas!" she exclaimed. "I would live and die among them if I could!"

The only public announcement of so insignificant an arrival was the following inconspicuous item in the New York *Times* on September 27, 1916:

> "Mme. Amelita Galli-Curci, the Italian coloratura soprano, who in private life is the Marchesa Curci, arrived yesterday on the Ward Line steamship "Havana" from Cuba, where she has been singing on a concert tour. She sang the leading roles at the Colon Theatre, Buenos Aires, last season with Enrico Caruso and has come here to join the Boston National Opera Company."

The writer of course did not know that the singer's correct title was Marchésa di Simeri, that she had been singing in opera—not on a concert tour—or that she had come to New York to embark for Italy, not to sing with the Boston Opera Company. The important fact is that she reached New York one day after Campanini—the impresario of the Chicago Opera Company—a circumstance of almost predestined significance.

In 1916 the population of New York City approximated five million, with an enormous additional influx of suburbanites and transients, making a grand total of perhaps six or seven million human units swarming to and fro, like busy bees, each intent upon his particular individual task. The chance of meeting, in this scurrying, cummingling multitude, any one person was so obviously infinitesimal as to preclude its possibility; yet it happened, for the hand of fate brought Galli-Curci face to face with William Thorner.

Friends of a previous year in Italy, Thorner had first heard her sing in Catania, Sicily, and recalled the interest he had taken in the budding prima donna—so much so that he secured from her authority to represent her interests in America. The New York vocal teacher introduced her to Campanini and to Caruso, who of course remembered her from the two *Lucia* performances in Buenos Aires. As a result, Thorner induced Campanini to give Galli-Curci a trial, which he agreed to do with a two-performance contract at $300 each. Six hundred dollars was a very small sum for a family of three, and two appearances constituted a very meager contract wherewith to give a good account of her accomplishments; yet, the proposition was accepted, the return passage to Italy deferred. Thus did Italy lose an opera singer and America acquire an artist citizen.

With some weeks to spare before entraining for the great white city of the Middle West, Galli-Curci engaged herself with polishing her rôles and setting her vocal apparatus in perfect order. Though she was to sing but twice, those two appearances must be the best she was capable of, and perhaps there might be more. Another turn of fortune's wheel, in the interim, brought her an engagement from C. G. Child, then president of the Victor Talking Machine Company, who invited her to make a test record on recommendation of a salesman who had heard her sing in Guatemala. Mr. Child was so impressed with the lady's first recording that he tendered her a contract under the same terms as Caruso's—a contract that developed many friendships and opportunities. Two other incidents of this interlude are important. After the Chicago contract had been signed, a Boston manager offered her a large sum to break it and tour the country under his direction. The other proved more resultant. Charles L. Wagner, a New York manager of artists, was asked to hear the singer whom Campanini had engaged for Chicago, but apparently made no move to secure the artist for his concert list; however, after the convulsion of November 18, he went to Chicago and concluded a triangular agreement. Thus began the new cycle that was to unfold a series of events, each more astonishing than the other, without apparent numerical limit.

Human beings are, in large measure, fatalists—prone to accept what they imagine destiny has assigned them, not realizing that, while fortune does open doors to opportunity, each individual is responsible for the particular one he elects to enter. It is true that Galli-Curci was born to sing. It is true that she chose her own vocational sphere, developed her own talent, and became the architect of her own career; nevertheless, in order to accomplish all this she did not rely on fortuitous currents to carry her to success, but sought to control all agencies to the purpose of her life.

She treated destiny as something to be governed, not to be governed by. To her the future depended on her own attitude toward existing facts and circumstances constituting the ensemble of life which, according to their acceptance or rejection, determine what that future is to be. Hence, here was a completely harmonious adjustment of a physical to an esthetic existence—an achievement requiring the perfect balance of all parts associated with or related to that existence. Few who have listened to this singer realize what it means to face, year after year, enormous assemblies of different racial characteristics, in varied countries, and hold them spellbound with matchless art. Perhaps they have never taken the pains even to wonder by what means she weaves this spell. Unless we understand so subtle a psychology, there is no inner significance to the Galli-Curci messages, though they may musically please and vocally thrill. The mysterious power, which was to reach its maximum at Chicago, remains a secret until we fathom the personality as well as the art.

Chicago

Galli-Curci had no thoughts for anything but preparation. Diligently she worked with scales and trills, with tones and breath, with phrases and melodic lines, with fortes, mezzofortes, and pianissimos, with vowels and consonants, with words, rhythms and tempi, with solos and ensembles, with attitudes and interpretations, with expressions and gestures. No detail was neglected, no point overlooked. If thoroughness meant anything and preparedness merited reward, it would be no fault of hers if the debut failed to register. The minds of the trio centered upon the outcome of the experiment. Would the big city—bigger than any other city she had ever sung in—accept her? Would her singing prove as likable there as in Cairo, Rome, Naples, Milan, Madrid, Buenos Aires, Palermo, Río, Havana, Petrograd? Were Chicagoans opera lovers—old style opera lovers? Would they bestow welcome upon an unknown after having heard the finest singers of the world? Was she nursing a foolish hope—to win success in spite of handicaps? Were her unvoiced musings merely idle dreams that she might, in this venture, find the harbor of her aspirations? So, without plan other than to make the most of opportunity, and trust in a benign providence to see her through, our singer toiled during those long days of waiting for the appointed time, singing the part in full voice the morning of the performance—a practice she had followed since 1909.

The most surprised person in Chicago over the engagement of Galli-Curci undoubtedly was Maestro Sturani, who had conducted the two Buenos Aires *Lucia* performances the previous year, in which our singer made her Colón debut with Caruso. He testified to her vocal gifts and reassured Campanini as to her capability. Two days before the Auditorium appearance, Sturani called her for a piano rehearsal, during which he became more and more astonished at the vocal splendor that caressed his ears. Duly impressed with her extraordinary vocalism, he communicated the discovery to his chief, advising him to engage her for twelve performances with a four-year option on her services, predicting a furore if she sang as well in public as in private.

Perhaps Campanini was a little perturbed, offering an unheard artist to an Auditorium audience in a favorite opera on a popular Saturday afternoon. Perhaps he felt some anxiety over the impend-

ing event, so, in order to satisfy himself on this point, the musical
director attended the orchestra rehearsal next morning. Whatever
perturbation or anxiety might have wrankled in his bosom and
caused a few lightly-penciled furrows to appear on that usually
serene brow was quickly dissipated, for with Gilda's first scene, the
maestro's forehead cleared. "Caro Nome" carried complete conviction. At the close of the number Campanini rose and, with an
alacrity that bespoke resolve, hastened to the Galli-Curci dressing
room. His face disarmed the singer, who met him with a direct in-
terrogation look. There is no record of the conversation that followed in voluble Italian, but the outcome was the extension of her
contract to cover the entire season at $1,000 a performance. The
agreement signed, Companini must have closed an eye in super-
satisfaction, for Lady Luck had handed him a star that would out-
rival any his confrere at the Metropolitan might offer; and he could
laugh in his sleeve at rival managers who, because of rash delinquen-
cy, permitted him to ensnare this golden treasure. The excuse, if
any, would be that an unknown, however promising, would be *de
trop* in a land already overstocked with famous stars and with scanty
opportunity for strangers to break through the operatic walls of the
opera houses sparsely scattered across the country.

Opera Rivalry

New York has ever been the hub of opera in America. From 1823
to 1850, when Jenny Lind made Barnum famous and turned Castle
Garden into a temple of song, residents of and visitors to Manhattan
Island enjoyed hearing the world's greatest artists, vocal and instrumental. With the Golden Era of the brilliant nineties and with the
twentieth century operatic stars, there was a continued development
of interest in this elevated form of musical stimuli.

In 1906 Oscar Hammerstein literally threw a hammer into the
smoothly running wheels of the "Met" by announcing his intention
of invading its special preserves—the City of New York. His declaration was the more startling in that it embodied the erection of a
new opera house wherein grand opera would be presented in a
manner quite novel to the residents of the borough, and as a suitable

name for the edifice chose "Manhattan," the same as that of his former house on West 34th Street, then located near Broadway.

The Hammerstein plan was unique in form. There were no directors, no trustees, no corporation—just Hammerstein—hence no impediments to artistic or business efficiency, and the strange thing is that the plan worked so well that, in three years, the clever manager had the "Met" worried. He produced, in that period, more works new to us than the older house had done in ten seasons under three directorates. Hammerstein stimulated interest anew and ended the "star" era. Oscar, the Brave, was experienced, able, far-seeing, fearless, sure. The new home of opera opened its doors on December 3, 1906, with *Puritani*, and announced an array of notable singers for the season, among whom were Melba, Nordica, Tetrazzini, Bonci, Sammarco, Gilibert, Dalmores, Renaud, with Cleofonte Campanini as conductor (the brother of Italo Campanini), while Garden, Nordica, Zenatello, Gerville-Reache, Sylva, Melis, McCormack, and Constantineau enabled him to produce more novelties.

The "Met" in 1908 brought over the Italian impresario Giulio Gatti-Casazza from Milan, accompanied by the brilliant young conductor Arturo Toscanini, and engaged a roster of prime songbirds. By 1910 the rivalry was in full swing, with each adding new names to its list of attractions in an endeavor to dazzle and capture the public. Gatti had Destinn, Alda, Amato, Clément, Gluck, Gilly, Matzenauer, and Witherspoon to assist his regulars—Caruso, Farrar, Homer, Gadski, Fremstad, Scotti, Case, Mason, Seleza, de Pasquale, Didur, Slezak, and Jörn.

The Manhattan series of *opera comique* added popularity to the new company, so the "Met" was pushed to the utmost to hold its clientele; indeed, it was forced to maintain a double company—one for home, one for the road; also practically two singing organizations—one for German, one for French and Italian repertory. The Metropolitan decided to launch a *coup de grâce*. Hammerstein must be stopped and the only way to its accomplishment was through the power of money. So, in 1910, for $2,000,000, it is said, the Manhattan owner agreed to take a ten-year holiday and for that period to refrain from giving opera in the skyscraper city.

The history of opera in Chicago is highly illuminative and furnishes an ominous corollary to the Manhattan débacle. Beginning December 10, 1889, with *Romeo et Juliette* and a cast headed by Patti, Ravelli and Del Puente, to the final performance of the same opera January 26, 1929, with Mason, Hackett and Defrere, constitutes a forty-year era (less one inactive season, 1914-15) of finely-motivated activity in the cause of musical art in America.

But it is the 1916-17 season which becomes epochal, for with it came the fireworks—a display that set eyes popping in wonderment and ears absorbing vocal joys such as they had not experienced in years of patient waiting. No sensation ever broke upon those Chicago opera votaries more unexpectedly than that of November 18, 1916. No bomb could have precipitated more excitement or created greater furore, yet occasioned by neither anarchist nor gunman but by a demure young woman celebrating her twenty-seventh birthday with a first American appearance. The kind of necromancy she employed was not black art or sleight-of-hand; it was the magic of her voice. The name—Amelita Galli-Curci—on the program was only a name to that Saturday afternoon throng assembled in the Auditorium to hear the Verdi masterpiece, for clever Campanini had not released the news of his "find" after the rehearsal. He preferred to give his supporters a genuine artistic shock which turned out to be more real than even he anticipated, and because of this, he reaped the glory of having discovered a great vocalist for Chicago.

There had been little advance publicity regarding the engagement. An advertisement called attention to the fact that "Amelita Galli-Curci, 'Successor to Tetrazzini'," had been "especially engaged by Cleofonte Campanini, Season 1916-17, Chicago Grand Opera Association, Auditorium Theatre, Chicago, Ill.," while a news item stated that the Chicago Opera debut of Mme. Galli-Curci was "an event awaited with great interest, for stories of Galli-Curci's summer triumphs in Buenos Aires (where she sang with Caruso) have preceded her to the city on Lake Michigan." Campanini was quoted as saying, "A fortunate engagement for my company is that of the celebrated coloratura soprano, Amelita Galli-

Curci. For her I shall revive Bellini's *Puritani*; *Lucia*, *Rigoletto*, and *Traviata* will likewise be used as mediums for her art."

Vocal Magic

During the first scene of her debut, the audience sat in quiet nonchalance, which state of mind continued for another quarter of an hour; then up went the skyrocket and up jumped the auditors after Gilda—slowly mounting the flight of steps to her room with lit candle, holding the final E for several measures—had concluded with the octave above, the tone hanging in the air like a point of light—a vocal rocket that always starts an avalanche of boisterous acclaim when perfectly executed.

The audience roared, shouted, yelled, screamed, stamped—all ordinary methods of applause engulfed in the din of the spontaneous wave of sound that welled up in increasing volume and vehemence. The singer who had aroused this vociferous demonstration must have been perplexed. She did not comprehend its meaning—it was all so sudden, so strange, so unexpected—this metamorphosis of a sophisticated assemblage into a frenzied mob demeaning itself by the most unseemly conduct, described by E. C. Moore thus: "This is the magic that happens occasionally in music. You cannot explain it. It just happens. Some of the best trained, best equipped, most intelligent musicians never find it; in fact, most of them never do. The technique of musicianship has little or nothing to do with it. Galli-Curci herself . . . was no niggling marvel of technical perfection . . . but she had that delicately lovely, that cream velvet, that entrancing quality of voice, and public and critics alike fell down and worshipped. From that afternoon on, the whole American public has apparently tried to shove the greater part of its opera and concert-going budget into the window of the box-office. Yes, there were others in the performance, but for all the credit they got in the public prints, they might as well have stayed home."

One late arrival, encountering the din and tumult when he entered the Auditorium lobby, enquired the reason thereof. "It's a new singer," someone replied, "name's Galli–Something-or-Other, and she's got them crazy." So momentous was the event in the eyes of Herman Devries that he hurried to a phone and stressed to his editor the value of holding the presses for a "scoop." This done, he wrote his review, then shot it to the *American* offices, where it was rushed through to appear in the late afternoon edition with the caption *Galli-Curci's Debut Makes Opera History*—all of which was against the *American's* rule to publish no reviews of Saturday musical events. But the rule was waived on this occasion.

So boomed the *Big Bertha* of a strenuous season, the new star repeating, three days later, the blast of vocal fireworks in *Lucia* to confirm the previous success. After the "Mad Scene," where Lucia flirts with the flute and vies with it in technical agility, the audience broke the bonds of decorous demeanor and, abandoning every aspect of formality, plunged into a tempestuous orgy of shouts and plaudits, necessitating twenty curtain calls and a repetition of the number. Her entrance was provocative of prolonged applause and stopped the performance temporarily. The "Sextet" caused another halt for bows, while the box-office was smilingly telling applicants for tickets the house had been sold out three days in advance and that few seats were available for forthcoming appearances. An interesting episode of the occasion was a reported short conversation between Campanini and Andreas Dippel during an *entr' acte*. Exclaimed Dippel: "What a find! What an asset! What a tone! What an art! Great coloraturas average one to a generation, and this is Galli-Curci's generation." He predicted accurately, for it proved to be just that. One auditor, years after, was heard to say that the Chicago Opera singer "had the most amazing skill in floating a tone which would die away to *pianissimo*, then seemingly partake of a bell-like purity and clarity and carry on indefinitely"—a feat that astonished and thrilled then as it has ever done when spun by a vocalist with perfect control of the head voice.

Traviata, the dainty prima donna's third opera, drew another record audience—the usual thing when she sang. Not only was she the sensation of the day but of the generation. Melba had sung the rôle of Violetta the year before, but the event was completely screened behind the blaze of the new star, whose presence in the cast wrought hardship upon her artist associates, as they were compelled to wait until the multitude had satisfied its enthusiastic vent. This performance, moreover, showed the dependability of our singer. Louise had been scheduled, but the sudden illness of her interpreter compelled a change of opera. *Traviata* was substituted, but something went wrong, for an hour before the curtain rising, there was no Violetta. A hurried call to Galli-Curci found the lady in bed with no knowledge of the change; but before the sixty minutes had expired, she was in her place ready for the cue.

Having already sung Juliette abroad, Galli-Curci was announced for a first performance of Gounod's work on December 15, and though an extra row of seats was placed in the pit, hundreds were turned away. With Muratore as Romeo the performance was of high artistic calibre, our soprano singing the rôle for the first time in French. It has been stated that for *Romeo et Juliette*, with prices raised, the $14,000 box-office was the largest paid attendance at opera the Windy City had ever known.

New Year's Day was celebrated with a first Rosina in *Barber of Seville*, which gave her a chance to prove her versatility. During the lesson scene, she sang the "Bell Song" from *Lakmé* and the "Last Rose of Summer" in English, to her own piano accompaniment. The audience, refusing to let her continue with her part, demanded another song, which she graciously rendered—Auber's "L'Eclat de Rire" with orchestra, Campanini conducting. The Chicago season closed with repetitions of her favorite rôles which, though but five in number, demonstrated her vocal powers and her linguistic ability.

Some in those vast audiences may have remembered the fourteen performances, in April, 1885, by the Chicago Festival Association at which Adelina Patti was the chief attraction but one thing is certain —they never heard finer or more finished proclamations of antiquated soprano parts than those by Galli-Curci in the same city a quarter of a century after.

The press was as loud in praise as the audiences were in acclaim:

"In thirty years, I, veteran opera-goer, have never heard such matchless, flawless beauty of tone, so satiny a timbre, such delicately lovely phrasing, such innate, God-given talent and feeling for the true *bel canto*. Art such as Galli-Curci's makes one welcome, instead of decry, the ancient form of opera."
—Herman Devries in Chicago American.

"Galli-Curci is one of the greatest artists who has ever stepped upon the stage of the Auditorium, or any other theatre."
—Karleton Hackett, *Chicago Post.*

"There have been singers with voices limpid and pure; Galli-Curci's is a little more limpid and a little more pure. There have been singers of outstanding dexterity and flexibility; Galli-Curci is a little more dexterous and a little more flexible. There have been singing artists who made a sincere effort to give a visual characterization of their rôle; Galli-Curci carried almost the entire burden of characterization. Few operatic singers have ever been able to do all these things at once; Galli-Curci did them all and more."—E. C. Moore, Chicago *Daily Journal.*

"She is the realized dream of the opera-ages."
—Frederick Donaghey, Chicago *Tribune.*

"So fluent, so brilliant an interpretation of Verdi's music has not been given in the town for many seasons. Galli-Curci has not much to learn about the art of song."—Chicago *Herald.*

The Galli-Curci "Caro Nome" became so popular that 10,000 phonograph records were sold in Chicago alone from the first pressing before the stock ran out. An interesting detail of the Juliette debut was the costume worn by our singer—of shimmering pink brocade without a seam, exquisitely silver-flowered motif, empire effect, studded with pearls in headdress and girdle, and silver embroidery, a gown specially created for the occasion. A replica was made for a doll that Galli-Curci contributed to the Christmas bazaar, with an exhibit of all gowns worn by the star on the stage.

A New Phase of Art

The triumph of Galli-Curci brought a new contract with Campanini with a $1,500 fee for future appearances. Having unexpectedly ensnared a nightingale, the astute director proceeded to hold her back even in face of increasingly clamorous throngs. Fifteen appearances in five operas constituted her contributions to a brilliant season that closed in January. The record reads: *Rigoletto*, 3; *Lucia*, 3; *Romeo et Juliette*, 4; *Traviata*, 2; *Barber of Seville*, 3.

The concert contract was triangular, whereby Galli-Curci was to sing opera in Chicago for ten weeks each season for three years, with option for road productions and a six weeks' spring tour, not to extend beyond March 1. The concerts, under Wagner's direction, therefore began in Indianapolis on February 7, 1917, but continued until June, a total of twenty-nine with fourteen in the fall. Among outstanding recitals were those in Chicago (Auditorium), Boston, Cleveland (Chicago Orchestra), Evanston (May Festival), Wash ington and Baltimore. The tour went as far west as Kansas, as far south as Texas, as far north as Toronto. Due to a heavy cold contracted en route, several concerts were cancelled. This experience taught our artist a valuable lesson, for it may be noted that, in all her later career, a postponement or cancellation was a rarity. This new phase of her art endeavors naturally added more work to her time schedule, for it necessitated selecting and preparing the concert programs as well as rehearsing them. For this, Galli-Curci went into retirement for the summer period at a quiet mountain resort in the Catskills, where she fashioned her programs and studied the rôle of "Dinorah" for the coming opera season.

Two of the spring concerts were substitutions for other singers unable to appear—Destinn and Schumann-Heink—both in Detroit. Everywhere Galli-Curci was received with enthusiasm, winning a notable triumph at Buffalo and in Boston to three overflowing houses. These recitals gave our youthful artist a new hold on American music lovers that became more tense as appearances increased. By the end of the season, she had firmly established herself as the reigning vocalist of the continent. Though essentially an opera singer, her art was so flexibly versatile as to enable her to grace the concert platform in the same inimicable way as she did the opera stage. She dominated both because of her wholesome personality, captivating charm and natural manner, without any of the usual prima donna idiosyncrasies. She never attempted an up-stage demeanor; indeed, that form of egotism was wholly absent from her physical make-up. *Bel Canto* and *bel anima* form a combination of conquering power and intensity, and Galli-Curci had both.

The astonishing thing about this phenomenal response to a new singer is that it was a spontaneous outburst to the appeal of an old form of opera at a time when the world was plunged in a life-and-death struggle. Nothing in a decade had so aroused a nerve-tensed population, nothing in half a century so stimulated interest in coloratura singing. The Galli-Curci advent was the inspiration for reawakening a love for a decadent style of music. None save a genius could have evoked enthusiasm with such antiquated relics. Hers was a type of composite art not portrayed by opera singers in America since the previous century, i.e., a blended performance of brilliant singing, unstilted action, technical facility, artistic instinct, high intelligence and dependability, to which was added a graciousness of person wholly captivating. And to accentuate the type, our artist dressed for the concert platform as she dressed for the opera stage, costumed to suit the locale.

The operas of the Italian florid period, which were primarily her vocal vehicles, were being ousted from favor by the modern dramatic school, so that their renaissance, through the dispensations of a single voice, was little short of miraculous. Yet, when the matter is analyzed, one finds a logical reason therefor, as did Geraldine Farrar, who said: "There is something in her voice like the heart of a pansy. There are no tricks in her singing. We have no voice like it. She has a special gift . . . to me, she seems as nearly perfect as possible. What she presents to the hearer is unequaled, and Galli-Curci can put her heart in her voice." Those who listened to her and marveled at her art no doubt wondered how she attained such proficiency. There were many things contributory to it, one of the most valuable being her study of the phonograph records, which she analyzed with minute care, hunting for imperfections in rendition and then working for their eradication. Acknowledging that there was room for vocal improvement when she began her career in America, Galli-Curci started at once upon locating faults and defects, then eliminating them.

Tours and Tests

The first opportunity New Yorkers had to listen to the new songstress was in March, 1917, when she gave a recital in Albany. Those who tripped to the capital to hear the Chicago star in concert found a musician, a personality, a singer who had command of every vocal resource, who held her audience thrilled and satisfied.

Galli-Curci, at this time, was making frequent trips to Camden, New Jersey, for recordings. Of fifty-nine made for the Victor Company, all but seven were double numbers, a total of 111 separate items. These consisted of songs, arias and ensembles with other noted artists, including Caruso and De Luca, covering a tremendous range of vocal music.

During the fall tour of the Chicago opera forces there was a highly significant numerical tabulation whenever Galli-Curci appeared. At Kansas City the record sales at Convention Hall were given as follows: 1905, *Parsifal* by Metropolitan Opera Company, $12,500; 1912, Lyne concert, $11,000; 1913, Melba-Kubelik concert, $12,500; 1917, *Lucia*, with Galli-Curci, $13,500.

The first week in June Galli-Curci demonstrated her friendly spirit to the country that had received her so cordially by subscribing for $25,000 of Liberty Bonds, and in September there was a dinner tendered to her by the Victor Company at a dealers' convention in Atlantic City, New Jersey. The table was graced by many notables of Victor fame.

Artists of a feather flock together, which accounts for a musical event of unusual interest although entirely informal. Kreisler was visiting John McCormack at the latter's home in Connecticut on a mid-July day. Galli-Curci motored over from the Catskills to call. After exhibitions in tennis and diving by the McCormack family, and a tour of inspection through the beautiful grounds, the party adjourned to the music-room where the evening was devoted to an impromptu musicale, with Kreisler at the piano and the two singers, on left and right, reading opera scores.

The middle part of Galli-Curci's voice was of a velvety smooth quality, but coloratura music lies almost entirely in the upper regis-

ter, which is the best for vocal display, hence a singer with lower
quality must occasionally resort to lyric rôles. Experts noted this
exceptional tone characteristic without break or diversity, thereby
insuring a flowing legato such as few singers had. As the distinguish-
ing element of fine violin playing is tone quality, so in singing, which
is lovely or unlovely according to the fineness of the tones emitted.
Galli-Curci proved her right to sing lyric rôles with her Juliette, then
cast about for other suitable media. Those available for this expansion of her art were numerous, including, perhaps, Eva and Elsa.
Human nature, however, is a conglomeration of absurdities, no
more vividly displayed than in musical taste. People determine
policies, set standards, establish vogues. Twentieth century opera
devotees were content to hear her Gilda, Rosina, Violetta and
Lucia, in the presentation of which she had no rival. But our diva
was determined to carry the experiment further, so we find her
choosing Lakmé, Manon, Mimi, Butterfly for future presentation,
with Dinorah, Linda, Juliette, Norina, Coq d'Or Queen and
Annetta in mind to meet the public preference for the lyric sort.

Galli-Curci did not inherit the cloak of Patti, of Melba, or of any
other great singer, whether contemporary or predecessor. She wove
her own and wore it. "I am what I am," she declared, "with special
musical characteristics, virtues and defects of this time and this day.
No great artists are alike, no two voices are alike. Nobody can be
taught to do a great thing."

That is a specimen of the common-senseness of her attitude toward art. Continuing, she said, "If I were carried off to a desert
island where there were none to hear me and left there to my own
resources, I would sing while there was life within my body. I am
like a bird which, perching upon the branch of a tree, warbles from
the sheer delight of living, warbles because it is a part of its nature
to give vent to the music within its heart. I sing with the same spirit
in summer weather when I run up the mountainside or clamor by
the brook in laughter and lift my voice to my sisters—the birds in
the trees. I sing with my whole heart to the last and the first member of my audience."

The consequence of fame is publicity. For an idol of the public, privacy is an impossibility, particularly so against sieges of the press. As soon as Galli-Curci had convulsed Chicago with her song, she became the tempting target for a horde of editors seeking articles, interviews and intimate photographs. The Chicago *Examiner*, first in line, secured a contract for a series entitled *How to Become an Opera Singer*. The initial article appeared November 26, 1916, captioned "Breathing." The others covered "How to Study," "What to Study," "Singing the Scale," "Studying an Operatic Rôle," "Acting a Rôle."

One of the publicity benefits gratuitously received by celebrities is having their names linked to certain things or personages. Next to being sponsor for a new baby, a perfume, a soap or a cigar, perhaps the sincerest compliment is that of imitation. As an instance of this mode of flattery, a certain juvenile soloist of the Paulist Choristers was styled the "Boy Galli-Curci."

The astute manager of the Chicago Opera destinies was, at the beginning of the 1917-18 season, fully convinced of the mighty drawing power of his new prima donna and saw an opportunity to utilize this tremendous popularity as an offset to the usual threatening deficit; so he flew his golden falcon as often as permissible, anticipating that her song would lure more quarries to the Auditorium. After the opening of *Lucia*, Campanini presented Galli-Curci in a first *Dinorah*, which rôle she had prepared during the summer. It was just the kind of bait to draw another record audience, but there was still more luck in the director's bag. Not content with giving him a meteoric star to boost his show and stuff his coffers, fate arranged a most sensational publicity for this Galli-Curci debut.

Having sung her opening "slumber song," concluding with those incomparable phrases in imitation of the birds, and beautified her vocal contest with the bagpiper, our singer left the stage to Correntin and Hoël, but their duet was suddenly interrupted by the orchestra breaking into the "Star Spangled Banner," at the first strains of which Galli-Curci ran from the wings to lead the singing of the anthem in ravishing tones, although she did not know the words. The audience stood in awed suspense, then added their voices, not understanding the cause for such irregularity, which

proved to be only a scare. It seems that while the duet was in progress, a foul odor filled the hall, followed by a hissing sound like that
of a lit fuse. There were excited cries and muffled whisperings, then
the *dénouement*—a dud bomb that some joker or maniac had
placed under a center-aisle seat. The package was quickly removed
by the fire chief, who rushed in, wrapped the smoking missile in
his coat, dashed out into the street, and dropped the whole into the
gutter, where the awesome article sputtered and expired. The audience displayed marvelous coolness and nerve control until a fireman
appeared on the stage to assure them of the danger passed; then the
show resumed its glimmering way with Galli-Curci's "Shadow
Song" as full compensation for those who remained. The shock,
however, was deleterious to Campanini's heart, and as a consequence
he missed several performances during the following weeks. His
vitality, too, from that time on, seemed to ebb perceptibly, but he
was a man of iron, meeting crises superbly, even in spite of shattered
health.

This season saw another feature offering—*Lakmé* with Galli-
Curci and Muratore; yet with all the glory, came the proverbial rub
—the rub that ruffled Campanini's financial brow. The great soprano, who had been a life-saver for the Association, showed signs
of overwork. A continuous stream of concerts that engaged her from
September until the middle of October, then sixteen appearances
in seven operas, two of them new and requiring constant rehearsing,
brought her to the end of December mentally and physically fagged.
So the songbird flapped her golden wings and peeped "Enough!"
She knew that New York, which had been kept waiting more than
a year, looked eagerly toward her arrival in January, and she must be
fit, hence the ultimatum: *no rest, no sing.* She got the rest—two
weeks' layoff—which she turned to account by entraining for the
town of Father Knickerbocker, there to face the test supreme. The
Chicago season completed, all moved to the assault upon New
York's fortress of art.

"Après Moi le Deluge"

January, 1918, contributes a notable chapter to operatic history in the making when the Chicago company opened in the Lexington Avenue Opera House. The first week was devoted to the regular repertory with the regular personnel, Campanini holding back his singing ace until the second week, thereby raising the curiosity of the opera public to frenzied pitch. Finally came the evening that has become memorable to Gothamites—January 28, 1918. Galli-Curci in *Dinorah* drew a massive audience. Pandemonium reigned in auditorium and back-stage as the city capitulated to the witchery of opera's newest glory. Masses hurtled to do homage to this miracle worker. There were sixty-one curtain calls. Tickets sold for $25 on the curb. Those who could not pay the price might elect to go home or invent a ruse to get inside. The press was agreed upon the merits of our artist. James G. Huneker wrote, "She sang with a lark-like freedom that floated the sensitive listener on the wings of song, and every now and then, she let go and we tumbled earthward."

For ingenuity and determination that of several student girls deserved success. Ascertaining that supers would be needed to swell the number of villagers in the final act, they applied for the jobs and were accepted. At seven o'clock they reported at the stage door, were assigned to dressing rooms to be fittingly costumed and made up. These silent supers had orders to stay behind scenes, which did not suit their mood—they were there to hear the diva sing. Each time they resorted to disobedience by slinking into the wings, they were sternly ordered away by a merciless stage-manager; but not for long. Lining up outside Galli-Curci's room for a peep at the celebrated singer, they were rewarded with a pleasant nod, which set them all aglow to hear that voice, though made to suffer for such imprudence. With Act II and the "Shadow Song," each girl disappeared amidst a maze of scenery to find a likely lurking-place where, unobserved, she might see and hear. It was 11:30 before they were called, but what mattered time or four hours and a half of hectic waiting? They had seen and heard—that was recompense enough.

Some amusing incidents marked the aftermath. Melba, scheduled to appear as Marguerite the following week, when asked for an opinion, is quoted thus: "Galli-Curci I suppose is wonderful. I have heard her only once and on the road. I know that I have the most beautiful voice in the world, and as long as I know that, I shall keep on singing." Melba at fifty-nine seemingly was unwilling to concede the palm to a successor. How different the attitude of Geraldine Farrar, who applauded vociferously from an orchestra chair and, when twitted about how it feels to see another take the crown, replied: "Simply great! Isn't she glorious?" It was quite in order that Galli-Curci should have a memento of that evening which was provided unexpectedly during an *entr'acte*—a gold wreath inscribed "To Galli-Curci, incomparable artist of the Chicago Opera Association, admirers offer a token of great admiration for her exquisite art."

The New York season reaped a harvest reported to have been over $168,000. Then came *Lucia*, another *Dinorah*, *Rigoletto*, *Barber of Seville*, and finally on February 15, *Traviata*, which proved a spectacular climax that will be discussed as long as there are those who follow operatic happenings. No such demonstration of wanton wildness ever gripped the Gotham public. Even the farewell of Jean de Reszke at the Metropolitan on April 7, 1901—an orgy of enthusiasm which incidentally capped a season that permitted a 150 per cent dividend—faded by comparison; nor did the tribute accorded Caruso, Tetrazzini, Renaud and Homer in *Rigoletto* on February 5, 1912, at the Metropolitan, approach this occasion, although characterized by a human tidal wave that blocked all avenues in the vicinity of the Broadway house with an estimated 3,000 turned away. But the immovable crush on Lexington Avenue was epochal. A special cordon of police endeavored to hold in check a swaying mob of ten thousand irreconcilables that stormed the entrances. Streets were choked with autos, sidewalks jammed. Those nearest the doors, constituting the main line of standees, had held their positions since early morning, some with lunch boxes, others with chairs, stoically waiting and ironically consoling later arrivals whose chances of getting to the box-office were negligible.

A captain of police, supported by twenty-one men and a score of firemen, strove valiantly to keep the lobby clear for ticket-holders, but the shouting mob pressed firmly on toward every possible inlet, delaying entrances to the auditorium already filled with 2,569 seated and 800 standing. The performance was on a par with previous Galli-Curci dispensations of choicest vocal art, climaxed, at the close, by an almost concerted movement of that vast audience to the footlights. Their clamorous recalls were not to be denied so, at five minutes to midnight, a piano was shoved across the stage and the curtain raised. Then from the wings out tripped the modest diva, graciously acknowledging the overwhelming tribute, set herself before the instrument, and sang "Home, Sweet Home," which turned three thousand humans into cheering madmen, while others stood on seats and waved whatever they had in hand.

The winning of New York was perhaps the greatest triumph ever achieved by a newcomer, outstripping that of Caruso and Farrar some twenty years before, when these mighty exponents of song burst upon the musical metropolis as an unrivaled combination. After so glamorous a welcome, Galli-Curci decided to make New York her home because, she said, "New Yorkers were so splendid to sing to, so appreciative and so understanding of the good things in music." Tit for tat. She took an apartment, and there received the onrush of press representatives, interviewers and photographers. While posing for a portrait by her husband, the Marchésa di Simeri was free to discourse on many topics, both trivial and timely—clothes, for instance. But she astonished her hearers by declaring her slight interest in such mundane things; in fact, she vowed that the Marquis had actually to drive her to the dressmaker. We can imagine the chorus of poo-poohs! to that incredulous pronouncement.

"New York is magnificent, glorious, the one great city that is mine!" is expressive of her enthusiasm, for after the *Dinorah* performance she said, "Now our wanderings cease! That audience surcharged with electric energy, no doubt aroused by curiosity and expectation, that twenty minutes of tumult after the 'Shadow Song' and those five minutes after the repetition of the final part—that was a tribute not to be forgotten, and those sixty curtain calls—ah! fatiguing but . . ." Nor must it be forgotten that she fulfilled hopes, surpassed expectations, satisfied curiosity, dispensed doubts, surprised critics—in a flash, joined the lyric·queens on Musical Olympus, showed herself a great singer with a winsome personality; but above any personal achievement, she won the honor of restoring the art of coloratura singing to its pedestal from which it had fallen through lack of an interpreter. The mellifluous shadow aria was, in the language of one reviewer, "Bottled Moonshine"; another said, "Hers is a pure flute voice."

Galli-Curci, who had appeared at the Hippodrome opera concert on February 3 (with receipts of $13,000), wound up her New York visit at a second Hippodrome concert which was unique in that the final orchestral number was played during a tumultuous uproar. Moving on to Boston, she sang *Lucia, Rigoletto, Dinorah, Barber,* and *Traviata,* the box-office income reaching an amount that required a payment of nearly $12,000 war tax. These appearances were noteworthy in that the advance bills had to announce "Seats for this performance all sold out."

Back to New York for the Rubinstein Club concert at Carnegie Hall at which Mrs. Whitman, wife of the then Governor, was the guest of honor. In the audience were some notables and musicians of prominence, including Mme. Sembrich. Our singer was supported by her faithful partners—Samuels, pianist, and Berenguer, flutist. For the occasion, Galli-Curci wore a special gown, an 1860 model with underskirt of mauve faille and silver brocade, over which was a tunic of point d'esprit trimmed with tiny colored bouquets, a quaintly-fitting bodice of mauve velvet hanging below the shoulders. Evidently her garments were modern models of that exquisite taste which dominated her life both on and off the stage.

The season continued until June, a few of the highlights being another Hippodrome recital with 600 seats on the stage, a double appearance with Cincinnati Orchestra under Eugene Ysaye, a record-breaking recital at Wichita, Kansas, a Minneapolis Orchestra debut, a Chicago Auditorium recital before the usual admiring multitude, compelling a second on her return from the West, when 500 extra seats had to be placed on the stage; a Portland, Oregon, sell-out with 400 additional seats; a San Francisco avalanche with a sale of 22,000 seats in two recitals within two weeks, the Red Cross profiting thereby $15,000 due to the benefit granted by our artist.

The wind-up was at Evanston with Minneapolis Orchestra, constituting a season embracing twenty-eight opera and approximately seventy concert appearances.

Literary Exercise

Early in 1917 magazines and papers began to seek articles and interviews, all in an endeavor to tell their readers about this new song sensation, to give a mental picture of her person and a qualitative idea of her voice—a task of course impossible, but it served a goodly purpose by awakening interest in fine singing, and that is something that never goes amiss.

The next article from her pen was a translation from the Italian, published in the *Chronicle* in January, 1918. It had, of course, to do with opera. "The operatic future of America depends not so much on native artists, impresarios and other dispensers of art, as upon the public itself. The talent is here and needs only development and encouragement. What Europe has in plenty, and America lacks almost entirely, are lesser opera companies in which promising young singers may gain their experience, prove their worth, and graduate to organizations of the first order. This early experience is most important in the development of the artist and is only to be had in the less important companies.

"The Italian artist has the advantage of a home and a circle of friends and relatives to furnish assistance. The first engagement is not so hard to obtain. Then Italy does not have the mental attitude toward beginners that America has. Italy gives her children a fair hearing and encouragement. My own career has been too smooth for romantic recounting. I had the good fortune of an audition in Rome, where I was engaged. Since then my experience was one of steady advancement in other opera houses. It has been a career of hard work, but with no serious hardships or difficulties. There should be an opera company for each of the ten largest cities in this country and each city of less importance should have its annual season of grand opera.

"The star system is responsible largely for the lack of interest in opera in the smaller cities, where the music patron takes the ridic-

ulous stand that *he will hear the best or none at all.* The resident of
such a place in Italy accepts the artists obtainable with approval,
enjoyment and satisfaction, consequently he acquires a familiarity
with the operas that enables him to enjoy more fully the work of
greater artists when he hears them later in the same rôles. America
has become so accustomed to the *system of great names* that this
habit of mind interferes with her artistic progress . . . but there is
still that outstanding fact that there should be quantity as well as
quality."

At this time Galli-Curci was slender, graceful and petite. In repose, the oval face was pensive, but lit, when speaking, with an inner
glow. The raven hair, parted and worn unusually low on both sides
of the face, almost covered the ears. Eyes, deep-welled and dark, yet
sweet and kindly in expressive moments, gave indication of quiet
strength behind a manner reposeful and serene. Poise, one might
say, was the most observable of her qualities, for not even when
conversing did she resort to other than the briefest gestures and
then only by way of quiet emphasis. She moved with ease and
rapidity and without effort. Her speaking voice was delicately clear
and of that same ingratiating *timbre* which she employed when
singing. The lips, as if always ready for a smile, were rarely closed,
exposing a set of well-matched teeth.

The Curcis spent the summer of 1918 in the Catskills, to which
enchanting region our singer had lost her heart, but the vacation was
to be fraught with trouble and annoyance of a distressing kind to
her who sought recreation as well as quiet solitude for study. Her
activities were devoted to driving—for she had a passionate love for
horses—walking, climbing, spying out song-birds, haying, motoring,
feeding chicks, playing with her dogs, rehearsing rôles two hours a
day, and initiating her pet cat "Dinorah" into the secrets of song
life. During this rest period, Galli-Curci prepared Linda in *Linda
di Chamounix* and Annetta in *Crispino e la Comare,* also four new
concert programs.

Suits and Counter-Suits

As early as July a rumor began to circulate that Galli-Curci was to join the "Met," which rumor was denied by Manager Gatti-Casazza. September furnished front-page copy with the suit brought by Luigi Curci against Wagner and Samuels for $250,000, charging alienation of affections and combined conspiracy to turn his wife against him for their own purposes. To this, prompt action was brought by the singer, who filed a suit of replevin to secure possession of her automobile and of her belongings in the New York apartment occupied by Curci and his brother Gennaro. She stated that, from the time of their marriage, her husband had earned practically nothing, but had lived entirely on her earnings; that he squandered her money, and by his conduct interfered with her career; that he refused to become an American citizen and had tried to prevent her from doing so; that he had depleted her bank account, thereby compelling her to change banks and revoke his authority to sign checks. The singer charged that she had given her husband 250,000 francs wherewith to purchase bonds, which he did, but in his own name, refusing to turn them over to her. She proposed therefore to support him no longer. This provoked a surcease for marital relations. So the lady left her husband and went her way alone.

During the separation period, Galli-Curci kept her own counsel. Finally, however, she was compelled to throw off the matrimonial yoke by instituting divorce proceedings which Curci, at first, sought to defend but allowed the case to go by default, realizing that he had no defense. The divorce (granted in the Superior Court of Chicago, January 6, 1920) provided that Curci should have no interest in her property and should pay the costs of suit. Four hours after receiving her freedom, Galli-Curci applied for citizenship, and received her first papers on January 8. Curci on July 2 married Wanda, daughter of Professor A. P. Tirendelli of the Cincinnati Conservatory of Music. They returned to Rome, where Curci died in 1924. His only contribution while in this country was a series of articles, published in the Chicago American in 1921, in which he aimed to make out a good case for himself with a recital of his married life with Galli-Curci, but as many of his statements were grossly exaggerated as to fact and detail, the effort proved ineffective.

Our diva, always appreciative of acts of kindness and courtesy, endeavored to express somewhat of that appreciation by subscribing $10,000 more for Victory bonds. The American people had given their money to hear her sing, she would return the compliment by re-investing some of it in the country's time of need.

Came Labor Day, with Galli-Curci singing at the Ocean Grove Auditorium, the third big event of the Jersey resort, following concerts by Caruso and McCormack. In a varied program, the audience expressed itself mostly in favor of the coloratura arias, which aroused them to outbursts of uncontrolled enthusiasm, extending even to the stage door, where her exist was made difficult due to the throngs outside and the large floral offerings she tried to hold in her arms. Then she returned to the Catskills to await the fall activities. One other notable incident of the early summer was her serving as god-mother, with Caruso as god-father, for the son of Giulio Crimi, former tenor of the Chicago Opera.

1918-1919

The fall season opened at Binghamton, New York, and wound up at Detroit and Cleveland, the former place turning out the largest paid audience the Arena had ever held, the latter turning away many from admission to the Armory. In October she appeared with the opera company in St. Paul, Minnesota, returning to Chicago to open the season on November 18 in *Traviata*. The war had ended, and there was appropriate recognition of the Armistice. During the intermission after Act I, a procession of conductors marched upon the stage in front of the massed chorus. A different conductor led each of the national hymns, concluding with the American national anthem under the direction of Campanini, sung by Galli-Curci, who was escorted by the ballet, with the standing audience enthusiastically assisting. The diva completed the evening's joy with a finely-colored Violetta. *Lucia* followed and received another tempestuous demonstration. After the "Mad Scene" a group of soldiers and sailors gave our popular prima donna the famous "rocket" cheer, calling her out innumerable times.

The 1918-19 season comprised a very healthy one for Galli-Curci, with ninety-seven appearances—seventy concerts and twenty-seven operas—covering a wide territory, with New York getting as many as seven recitals, in addition to operas. As a climax came *Crispino e la Comare*—a most delectable entertainment by Galli-Curci in the rôle of Annetta. Other high spots were a previous Mimi in *La Bohéme* and a *Linda di Chamounix*. So successful were these new appearances that she won a new title, "The Comet." Muratore, claiming a nervous breakdown, left the company, thereby depriving our artist of her best Romeo. Rumor had it that the French tenor was headed for the "Met," where Galli-Curci also was to appear. Denials followed rumors, with no authentic statement from either side.

Not to be outdone, the "Met" revived *Crispino* on January 17, 1919, with Hempel and Scotti in the leads. Galli-Curci, however, was winning the West in a series of new triumphs. At St. Paul, where she had appeared with the Minneapolis Orchestra and the Chicago Opera on previous visits, her recital drew a tremendous crowd which she literally swept off its feet. Returning East for the New York opera season, she sang six rôles to the usual throngs, also appeared at two Hippodrome concerts, each before approximately 6,000 people, with hundreds of chairs on the stage. She sang also at a Biltmore Hotel musicale; then to Boston for two recitals at Symphony Hall in two different programs on two successive days. Back to New York for a final Hippodrome recital, then *en tour*, again including an Atlanta recital appearance in April—a noteworthy occasion, inasmuch as it followed the opera week by the Metropolitan company. The Atlanta *Constitution*, commenting on this concert, said in part: "To describe the beauty of Galli-Curci's singing would be an impossible thing. As well try to describe the light or the air or a summer breeze through the trees . . . as to tell its effect upon an audience of more than 6,000 people who had just completed seven performances of grand opera in a week's time and yet sat enthralled by one singer."

1919-1920

Marinuzzi succeeded Polacco as conductor, but all activities palled by the death of Campanini on December 19. Funeral services were held at Holy Name Cathedral with a solemn high Requiem Mass together with other musical numbers by opera members, one of which was the Bach-Gounod "Ave Maria" sung by Galli-Curci, accompanied by organ. The wavering tones of her voice, which almost broke at times with excessive emotion, were nevertheless sufficiently controlled to enable her to invest the number with such incorporeal power as to cause the congregation to weep in reverential silence. Among those present were Samuel Insull, Harold McCormick, Charles Dawes with Mary Garden, Rosa Raisa, Tito Schipa, and the full company constituting the choral ensemble. A second service was held on the Auditorium stage, with the public, during a three-hour period, filing past the bier. The body was returned to the maestro's former home in Parma, Italy.

The passing of Hammerstein and Campanini in the same year quashed a promise of each pertaining to operatic interests. The former, three months before his death, reaffirmed his intention of opening the Manhattan in January, 1920, when his Metropolitan agreement would expire. Campanini had announced *Semiramide* for Galli-Curci, but it never materialized.

The end of the Chicago season saw a first *Sonnambula*, a first *Barber of Seville* with Schipa and Galli-Curci, and a first Norina in *Don Pasquale*. The New York visit, with our artist in her two new rôles, provided great attractions, making her record for the season sixteen opera appearances and approximately seventy concerts.

CYCLE OF EXPANSION

1920-24

"We cannot give anything without having something. There must be a message in every note a true artist sings."

—GALLI-CURCI

New Management

The fame of the young artist, by this time, had extended to all parts, and the Savannah (Ga.) Music Club made application to Evans and Salter, Atlanta managers, for a sponsored recital. The request for a date was wired to her manager, who was incredulous as to the club's ability to pay the large fee, so declined the offer. These hustling futurists, however, were not to be so thwarted—they were awake to opportunities, hence disinclined to let this one pass unchallenged. Evans took train for New York and returned to Atlanta with a contract which was duly executed by the Savannah Club and the Galli-Curci event definitely fixed for January 19, 1920.

Galli-Curci was now entering upon that part of her career which necessitated a major managerial change. For some time, her associations with Wagner had not been congenial, so, following the enormous success of her first Atlanta appearance, and with an ever-ready eye for efficiency, naturally the two young men who had initiated the series and carried it through so brilliantly were not forgotten. So she sent for them, and when closeted in a hotel suite, announced her intention of changing managers. Impressed by the capable handling of the two affairs with which they had been associated, which proved the biggest musical attractions ever given, with the largest receipts, she invited them to come to New York, where she would establish them as her managers for both opera and concert appearances. Acknowledging with appreciation the confidence thus imposed, they promised to give the matter careful consideration. The decision was favorable, and within two months the firm

Galli-Curci gives vocal lesson to Jack Dempsey, Universal City, Calif.,
early 1920's

As Manon, Act 3, 1920

Wedding picture, 1921, Galli-Curci and Homer Samuels

As Mme. Butterfly, Chicago, 1922

New York, 1922

In recital, Edinburgh, Scotland, 1924

In recital, Albert Hall, London, 1924

Visiting "His Master's Voice" factory, Hayes, England, 1924

name of Evans & Salter graced the door of an office suite in the then Harriman Bank Building on Fifth Avenue.

Lawrence Evans is a native of Georgia, Jack Salter of South Carolina. They met in Atlanta, where both were identified with the city's musical life, the latter acting as sales manager, the former as salesman for the Cable Piano Company. Later the company took on the local agency for Victor products and Victor artists. Evans withdrew to give full time to concert work, and shortly after was joined by Salter, the two forming the Evans & Salter Musical Bureau.

After several years of well-directed activity, in 1919 they were asked to manage the Metropolitan opera season in Atlanta. This they accomplished with such success as to induce them to inaugurate the Star Concert Course. It required vigorous persuasion on their part to win approval from the foremost music patrons of the city, who had come to think of Atlanta as an opera, not as a concert, city. With the necessary backing secured, the first course for 1919-20 offered several stars—Galli-Curci, McCormack, Amato, Mary Garden, Destinn, Hofmann and Heifetz.

Events now moved rapidly. On June 26, 1920, Galli-Curci prepared to sail for a visit to her mother, in Paris, whom she had not seen in seven years, but on the pier was served with a summons in a suit brought by Wagner for breach of contract. Since the agreement, dated November 30, 1918, had been cancelled by her in April, she claimed that she was under no obligation to fill engagements for the 1920-21 season. The suit was settled out of court and, upon her return from Paris, the singer rested during the summer, appearing for her first engagement under the new management on August 19, in the Ocean Grove (N.J.) Auditorium.

Mission of Art

The mission of artists is to keep art alive. This is accomplished through preserving the bond which unites successive cycles so as to form a consciously-perceived progression. Whereas each cycle is per se definite, in that it represents a complete expression of thought, it is necessary to keep changing that expression so as to produce new cycles, yet without destroying the continuity of the whole. The awakening of artistic consciousness in individuals to this evolutionary process constitutes esthetic vision. History ought to be a selective record of the high spots of civilization's progress, not a running account of events irrespective of their importance. So with art. Only the best can possibly constitute a true record, for art is not inclusive, but particular; in accordance with Kant's definition, "Beautiful art is the art of genius." Art that is not born of genius is not beautiful, hence to label all artistic effort as art is obviously preposterous.

The record of art should be a composite of the most beautiful examples from the several chain cycles which may be taken as the history of that particular art branch. Any era that loses contact with the one just emerging therefore fails of its purpose and so reduces its effort to nihility. Only those contributions live that are inseparable from the march of time through living contact. The precise thing that most singers overlook is this: the business of art is to give people something they cannot themselves create; to provide a new world in which they can expand though unable to add anything thereto; to establish an esthetic inheritance which can be passed on to succeeding generations. Those who sing without this higher motive dominating their endeavors are not messengers of art, but mere automatons.

The important thing in a singer's life is to impart musical vision, not musical knowledge, and thereby direct thought toward that vision. Adherence to stereotype programmatic schemes or traditions of interpretation does not create musical vision—it can impart only musical knowledge. Vision is an inherent faculty. One has it, or one has not. So the duty of those who have it is to hold it up for others to gaze at steadfastly until they catch at least a portion of its real significance.

In addressing masses of people, whether vocally, dramatically, or oratorically, we have to consider their natural capacities. A minimum will suffice for some unable to digest more, while others will require a maximum, and these, if not given sufficient nourishment, are apt to starve. What and how much to serve constitutes a considerable problem for anyone who faces cosmopolitan assemblages with intent to feed them art, science, politics, or religion. It is a delight undefinable when a singer finds herself amid those who show a capacity to absorb and a desire to acquire cultural improvement.

Art must conceal art. This Galli-Curci did perfectly. One did not think of art when she sang, but of beauty and of sweetness. Her success was the natural sequence to a preponderant talent. People are not stones; they respond to stimuli; they recognize genius. The public knows what it likes, so when someone gives it that, there is no question of success. Galli-Curci's ease and naturalness—evidences of her absolute command of her tools—was the quintessence of art concealing art. This rarity was the subject for numerous articles, the New York Times *Magazine* of February 10, 1918, having devoted a first-page story to it, entitled *Galli-Curci's Voice*.

"If I had not been a singer, I would have been a painter," said our artist one day while discussing art tendencies. "I have never held a brush, but I am always painting in my mind. I love the mystery, the subdued colorings as in the Turner landscapes. When the lark ascends into the blue sky, it sings and sings. The higher it goes, the greater is its song. But I! When I go into the air I am mute before we have gone up a mile—mute with fright. I don't like flying. Nor do I swim. I haven't the temperament to get fat. The fat prima donnas of the past were quite unnecessary. I think those very plump singers must lose some voice power through their huge proportions. I drink a lot of milk, eat a lot of fruit and vegetables, fish, chicken and perhaps, lamb—but no beef or steak." The *Prima Donna Cocktail* invented by Galli-Curci likewise serves her when fatigued or disturbed, guaranteed as a great bracer for singers. "Fill a large glass with cool, or iced, milk. Add a teaspoonful of powdered sugar and a tablespoon of strong black coffee. Stir vigorously and sip slowly."

How so much volume could be possessed by so small a container was somewhat baffling to the listener, but less baffling when one knows the woman behind the singer. The more she sang, the more able was she to make her voice do what she required of it. When not practicing, she hummed. She never stopped singing because she loved it and could not desist even if she would. Let none imagine that she did not have to work to win her crown. No singer worked harder or longer or more diligently than she, and here's the climax of it all: "True, there has been the thrill of a forty-five minute reception after a concert, of a crowd at the stage door, but there have been other forty-five minutes in my life that have held only heartache and wretchedness. *It is those hours that have molded me—not the glorious, triumphant ones!*"

Until 1920, Galli-Curci was partial to old-fashioned modes for the concert stage, but fashion proved too strong a counter charm and so she yielded to time's progress. Accustomed to her *outré* wardrobe, she startled a Boston audience by appearing, not as a living picture of some painting, but in an ultra-modern frock of brilliant apple-green, the skirt of taffeta trimmed with ostrich feathers, barely covering her knees, accentuating the black lace stockings and high-heeled slippers, smartly buckled. A black sash, tied front and back, and a diamond-pearl necklace with pendant about the neck, heightened the piquant effect. Ear sparklets and hat of black maline, bedecked with feathers, set off the unusual ensemble.

Does Galli-Curci like jewels? She is a woman; hence, like Fricka, may be pardoned her acquisitiveness. "Yes," she says, "when I was a little girl, I wanted to have a big diamond. Perhaps I got the idea from some picture book or story, but I wanted a large brilliant to hang about my throat and promised myself some day to earn enough to buy one. Well, it was many years before my wish was realized." After four seasons in America, she finally repaid herself for her diligence—a fifteen-carat stone suspended from a platinum chain. Was there a hidden charm in this talisman? Who knows what influence those pure white rays had upon the imprisoned vocal chords? Yet that one item satisfied her desire for gems "I got what I wanted. What more could one ask for? The trouble with us is that *we don't want hard enough to work hard enough to get it*"—the wisdom of a Solomon for a modern world.

"When I came to America how my head swam with the talk of millions and billions and trillions! Even when they talk of poverty they do not know what it is. They would say a man is poor because he has no butter to put on his bread, yet he has the loaf packed away under his arm. That is not the poverty I saw in my younger days in Italy."

Engaged by the "Met"

In 1920 there was an expected, but unvoiced, move in operatic circles that was to place Galli-Curci on the top-most pinnacle of fame and position. With Hempel and Barrientos out of the Metropolitan for the coming season, Gatti-Casazza needed a coloratura, and there was but one of Metropolitan calibre—Galli-Curci. So quietly and without ado, overtures were extended to the diva's managers, with the result that the lady's services were secured for the Broadway opera house, at a $2,500 fee—equal to that drawn by Caruso. Thus did Galli-Curci become a member of the two leading American opera companies—a unique position in the annals of operatic art. This engagement was to cover New York and Atlanta appearances only, leaving her free to sing elsewhere with the Chicago company.

With this new development in her futuristic schedule, an extension of repertory was essential and the preparation of new rôles taken under immediate advisement. According to her formula, study begins with a reading of the libretto to get the story and its psychology. Next comes examination of the vocal score for a visualization of the relationship of words and music. Then follows the setting-apart process, which involves elimination of all scenes in which she does not appear, enabling her to concentrate upon those parts which concern her individually, i.e., solos and ensembles. Memorizing is the least arduous task, for it is accomplished during relaxation periods, therefore without physical exertion or nervous strain. Either she takes the score to bed or lies on a sofa where, in peace and quiet, she can let the composer's thought and the significance of the music percolate, as it were, through her being and in that way give a clear idea of its significance and purpose.

Now comes the working out at the piano in detail: words and music together, phrasing, tempi, interpretation. For a big rôle, she takes ample time to prepare, since to properly learn voice parts, ensembles, acting, characterization, orchestration, is not a matter of speed but of thoroughness. No completely satisfactory enactment of an operatic rôle is achieved at a first performance; only after numerous appearances does it get into the groove and become automatically yours. Even then the polishing is never finished—that happens when one lays it down for good.

Languages are important adjuncts to a singer's art, and must be mastered in order to secure facility of vocal delivery and pronunciation accuracy. Other details have to be considered, particularly breathing, which is perhaps the greatest factor in securing proper melodic valuation. This demands endless study if the tone is to be floated on the breath so that a *pianissimo* may carry to the top gallery. Such was the Galli-Curci formula.

It has never been a trait of our artist to disparage other people's prominence or gain the spot-light to the exclusion of another equally entitled to it, yet there are occasions when she finds it impossible to avoid the honor. As an instance of this, the congestion due to the simultaneous appearance of Galli-Curci, Franklin D. Roosevelt, and "Babe" Ruth at Binghamton, New York, in October, 1920, may be cited. The first-named was there for a concert, the second for a campaign speech, the third for an exhibition ballgame. The Arlington Hotel was thronged with a motley mob surcharged with curiosity to see the noted singer, who was in a vortex of pressing welcome when the candidate for the vice-presidency arrived. Mistaking the plaudits of the crowd as a tribute to himself, he turned to one of his party with the remark that it was certainly fine to see so much enthusiasm for the Democratic ticket, and was much amused to learn that the demonstration was not political, but artistic. So, with a characteristic smile, the candidate accepted the situation most gallantly and consented to pose with the singer for a photograph which was nicely balanced by the inclusion of the home-run king. "Two kings and a queen," remarked F. D. R. facetiously. "Ruth is the king of swat, Galli-Curci is the queen of song, and I am becoming the king of talk since I have been making so many political speeches." There is no numerical record of those attending the ball game or the political meeting, but 2,200 persons

went to the State Armory to hear the little lady sing. She was intensely interested in the election, and deemed it unpatriotic not to
be considerate of candidates and issues instead of parties; also
pleased over the part women play in the affair and commented on
their intelligence in voting. She would have liked to vote, but was
not yet naturalized.

Making records had become a Galli-Curci habit, so we are not
surprised that, on November 7, she broke the Hippodrome attendance record with a $12,000 box-office. Then on to Chicago for the
opera opening, her first appearance for the season commanding
more panegyrics from the press. And it was she who forced a suspension of the 'encores not permitted' rule.

The year 1920 brought her a first *Manon* appearance, boosting the
total new rôles to eight and one re-sung in French, in addition to
keeping up her regular repertory and learning many songs for concert programs. Certainly, four years packed full of industry and
accomplishment.

L'Amour

The forces of evolution have an inexplicable way of bringing together persons qualified for companionship. Some call it *fate*, some
predestination, but sages call it *love's affinity*. Toward the close of
the year Galli-Curci announced her engagement to Homer Samuels,
her accompanist. "It's a case of real love," she explained. "I am very
happy. I want all my friends to know it." In those words our prima
donna communicated to the world another side of her character—
the sentimental side. Galli-Curci is nothing if not individualistic.
Who ever heard of a prominent singer falling in love with her accompanist? The usual procedure would have been to *fall out*.

After her first hapless matrimonial adventure, the lady expressed
herself emphatically as through with wedlock, but—the love-bug
brooks no interference. There is no antidote for such inoculation.
This was a case of congeniality born of pure affection and brought
to flower through the constant contact of two esthetic natures attuned to similar harmonies.

Accustomed as she was to scoring "hits," this *coup de main* provoked almost as much comment as one of her flamboyant operatic demonstrations, and to give spice to the event, the bridal day was set for the coming January 15, when she would receive her final naturalization papers. Her marriage to an American, however, automatically granted her that citizenship, so the ceremony was performed a day earlier at "Edgebrook," Minneapolis, the home of Mr. and Mrs. J. C. Samuels, parents of the groom.

The ceremony was graced by utmost simplicity, neither principal having an attendant. At the stroke of noon the pair advanced to an improvised altar of roses over which the country's flag, a gift to the singer by a Texas regiment, formed a canopy. Lawrence Evans and her personal flutist, Berenguer, were the only witnesses other than relatives. The wedding gown, likewise devoid of ostentation, was of soft pastel gray silk, draped with silvery lace, its one distinctive touch furnished by kolinsky fur trimmings and silver slippers with French heels. The bride wore a rope of pearls about her neck, jade and diamond ear pendants, and carried a bouquet of orchids. Among the many gifts and congratulatory telegrams was a message from Mary Garden, newly-appointed director of the Chicago Opera. To satisfy the gatherers of news, the event was recorded in a film picture and the customary press courtesies extended.

Again Galli-Curci did the unusual. She kept her professional name and made the wedding merely an interlude of the concert tour, which served also as a honeymoon trip. The party left the same evening for continuance of the schedule. Not to be wholly unromantic, the bride indulged in several feminities pertaining to inquisitorial overtures. If one ask a hundred brides why they marry, he would get ninety-nine answers all alike—*for love!* But this bride's is perhaps the most unique, for she cannot be commonplace. Her answer was, "If at first you don't succeed, well, your next venture may bring happiness—if not, try, try again!" Another salient bit of psychology injected into a healthy philosophy is her attitude toward any bygone *contretemps.* "I am living in the present and am marvelously happy, as happy as a bride should be. Our romance was wonderful. Homer became my accompanist in 1917. We grew to be great pals, good friends, neither thinking of love—oh, no! for I was not then divorced, though separated from my husband. The awakening came only in 1920 when I was free and went to Paris for a visit to my mother. When I got there I discovered that I was lonesome, more lonesome than ever before. I was what you might call miserably happy. Then I knew it—it was love for Homer. So back to New York I came. He met me at the dock and his first words were not 'Did you have a pleasant trip?' but 'I was so lonesome here without you.' I said I was, too. He said, 'I love you!' I replied, 'I'm in love, too.' "

As a corollary to this Cupid and Psyche episode, the words of the latter's votary are pertinent. "No girl should marry before thirty. Before that age, she cannot know how to distinguish between love and emotion, but if she does marry and finds unhappiness, well then —try again, for happiness depends on one thing, and only one—*both must be in love with each other.*"

Homer Samuels is his wife's senior by ten months, having been born January 15, 1889, at Eau Clair, Wisconsin. Overmodest, he claims that there is nothing interesting about him—his life has been devoted to, submerged in, music. Both he and his twin brother, Harvey, were musical. Father Samuels was an organist, and at the debut of the twin organists, then seven years of age, played the foot pedals with his hands while the boys played the console keys. Eventually, Homer switched to the piano and Harvey to the cello, later taking up dentistry as a profession. In 1909 Homer went to Berlin to study with Josef Lhevinne, returning in 1913 as accompanist with Carl Flesh for the Hungarian violinist's first American tour. Re-engaged for a second season—which was cancelled because of the war—he was engaged to assist the Italiant violinist, Arrigo Serato, likewise on a first tour of the country, but Italy, entering the conflict, kept Serato at home. Luck did not entirely forsake the young pianist, for he secured an engagement to accompany Emmy Destinn who, however, was unable to leave Bohemia, and again he lost his job; yet, in spite of three contractual annulments, they brought him a bigger and better opportunity. Galli-Curci was secured to fill some Destinn bookings and needed an accompanist. Samuels wired the singer, received a favorable reply, left hurriedly for the West, arrived at his destination with just time to rehearse the program and appear at the concert in the evening, the satisfactory conclusion of which established him as her permanent pianist; indeed, so well pleased was she, that she offered him a life contract, but Homer's modesty of course forbade. Being a woman, she eventually had her way even if extremes were needed to effect it. She credits the odd circumstance to one of fortune's wiles, for it was written in the stars that she would make two marriages and so recorded in the tell-tale cross upon the palm of her hand.

Samuels has played in every prominent city of the world, participated in over a thousand concerts with his wife, without a miss, and proved himself both a capable and a sympathetic associate in proclamations of the masterpieces of vocal art. He is an erudite musician, and a composer with an operetta and many songs to his credit, not a few of which appeared upon the programs jointly rendered for the delectation of enlightened throngs. From the first concert date in which the two worked together to that which closes this record constituted a period of rare cooperation, without friction or disagreement either as to *what* to sing or *how* to sing, *where* to go or *when* to work, an harmonious blending of two wills and two souls into a unity of strength and purpose so manifestly evident in all their artistic ministrations.

In February, 1921, during her last New York appearances with the Chicago company at the then Manhattan Opera House, the news of Galli-Curci's Metropolitan engagement broke with many varied versions. Some papers carried absurd statements, one of the most absurd being that she had been rejected by Gatti-Casazza in 1916.

In an article in the *Musical Observer* for May, 1919, *My Career as a Prima Donna*, she said: "I did not attempt to get an audience with Gatti and, when getting it, receive from him a curt refusal to engage me. I never sang for Gatti."

"Sul Monte"

As an American citizen and an American wife, Galli-Curci wished to stabilize that two-fold circumstance, so began planning a permanent home, and in her usual individualistic manner, did so in a way quite contrary to expectation. The Catskills had ever proved hospitably pleasant for jaded bodies and tensioned nerves, so thither she cast about for a likely spot whereon to set up her *Dolce far niente*. Highmount was the final choice, and with the purchase of 188 acres of picturesquely fashioned land, a site for the mansion was selected upon an elevation from which a natural terrace descended to the highway below. That summer Mr. and Mrs. Samuels occupied a cottage within easy access to the rising edifice that was to cost $200,000.

"Sul Monte" came into being for genuine living. "I wanted something far away from my usual life," she declared. The skytop rendezvous was the answer to that wish. To get away from the world so as to commune with nature was the motive that vitalized the idea. Everywhere books—highbrow books in five languages—among which was a set of Swedenborg, which the mistress considers healthy reading. "Why be concerned wholly with things of present life?" she asks. "We ought to think about the future also. A musician must feed his mind on other things than music. When the voice goes, when the fingers grow stiff—then the mind that has been stored with good things will have something to feed upon." Spiritual people, she holds, are more deserving of appreciation than intellectual people, for "when you know people and understand life, there's not much room for vanity."

Simplicity in all things is the code by which this most normal of women always lived. She never dressed for fashion's sake nor followed vogue's irregular maneuverings. The importance of sleep she stressed volubly as most essential to singing—ten hours, if possible, and advocated the early-to-bed formula. She is a milk and water advocate—a gallon of the former and two quarts of the latter daily, also plenty of fruit. Lots of air and no heat at night is another *obiter dictum*, but here is a remarkable manifesto: "A little worry now and then is good for us. It stirs the blood. Apathy is worse than worry." Almost stoical in purport, nevertheless rationally right, as is her belief that it is a blessing not to be born rich. "*We get most out of life when we have to struggle for a living and get the taste for work."*

Even those who did not know her felt that Galli-Curci loved to live, loved the pleasure of existence, looked for no special dispensations of Providence, disliked over-attention, and when singing was done, wanted to play and laugh and enjoy her friends. In summertime one saw a different person—the artist become a woman, an energetic life-conscious being, animated by the vital principle of creation, radiating health, energized by nature's tonic and open-minded to the beauty of mundane things. When she climbed the hills and roamed the mountains, when she galloped astride a favorite mount, drove over bumpy roads, cavorted in her private pool, picknicked on the lakeshore sward, played at baseball, football or golf and danced in the old-fashioned barn, with now and then a visit to the village one-night show—then, and only then, was the candid naiveté of this whole-hearted humanist disclosed in its inherent state.

Evenings were devoted to music, art, books and conversation on topics appertaining to some suggested mental trend which, no matter whither it led, the hostess of "Sul Monte" could meet and carry on with erudite assurance, for she was a reader and a thinker, a scholar and a sage. Nothing gave her more delight than to scramble with a flock of gladsome children, "over hill, over dale, through bush, through brier . . . go seek some dew-drops here, and hang a pearl in every cowslip's ear." Another time, they would inspect the cows and chicks and wind up in the dairy to sip sweet cream from earthen jugs, then lick their coated fingers clean 'mid laughter and enraptured merriment. If perchance they came upon a babbling brook, she would always throw herself upon the mossy bank and drink the cooling water, then upward turn a dripping, smiling face for the glowing sun to dry.

When she spied some tree or flower, some bird or animal with which she was unfamiliar, she would give an enthusiastic shout. Sometimes, when motoring, she would take the wheel, and no sooner started than she would begin a song in which the other occupants were enticed to join. No stray dog or cat or bird applied in vain at her open door for succor, nor did any ever feel the sting of slight, for in her code there is no substitute for hospitality. It has been said that Caruso was first a man, then an artist. So with Galli-Curci, who was first a woman, then a singer. It was this supersensitiveness to life and living, to beauty and truth, to goodness and sympathy, to understanding and human relationships, that formed about her person an aura of congeniality.

And Then the Metropolitan

In August, 1921, the news of Caruso's death, flashed from Naples, shocked the world and deprived the "Met" of its leading artist. The management, however, was not left stranded, for it had Galli-Curci under contract; but the question was, would she be available for the opening, heretofore a Caruso gala night. Negotiations were immediately opened for four additional appearances, including the opening performance, and were successfully concluded at $3,500 each.

When the opera season opened on November 14 with Galli-Curci, it was the first time in eighteen seasons that the "Met" began its schedule without Caruso, and the first time since his debut in 1903 that *Traviata* had served as the opening opera.

Gatti-Casazza knew that, under the circumstances, his new prima donna would provide rich glamour and add needed brilliancy for the opening night so, as Violetta, Galli-Curci began her engagement as a member of the Metropolitan Company. There have been many instances of an artist of one company appearing as "guest" with another company, but rarely, if ever, in America had one been a member of the two premier companies at the same time. Galli-Curci's double membership thus constituted a record unique in operatic circles, particularly so as the record was achieved within the space of five contingent years.

While every subscription night at the "Met" presents a brilliant scene, a first night is different—it has a distinctive glamour. There seems to be a little more atmosphere, a little more brilliancy of toilettes, a little more éclat, perhaps a bigger audience and a greater demand for seats; yet on this particular night there was present a little more supersensitiveness in the atmosphere. Surrounded by a balanced cast, including Gigli as Alfredo, De Luca as Germont and with Moranzoni conducting, the performance moved with smoothness and finesse. At least a thousand opera "fans" had stood in line from noon to 7:30 in the rain, with sandwiches, umbrellas, and raincoats, reflecting the Galli-Curci debut at the Lexington three years before. Not all of these gained admission, the unfortunates joining another thousand who had been turned away. Three hundred limousines dropped their occupants at side doors, while hundreds of taxis landed passengers at the main entrance. It was stated that speculators went a-haying, even in the rain, darting hither and thither among the pressing lines of ticket holders scrambling to project themselves into an already crowded lobby, and used their tongues so glibly as to dispose of their stock of tickets in great excess of box-office prices, one pair of seats fetching $150 cash.

From the first strains of "Ah, fors è lui" and "Sempre libera," that evoked a storm of applause, to the last agitated "Oh, gioja!", the spell of the singer's art was supremely manifest in its humanizing appeal, in its gentle charm, in its caressing tones. The memory of Caruso was revered that night through the tribute bestowed upon his successor, and a great sigh of relief must have been silently wafted upward by many in that great throng when it became apparent of the certainty that the cloak of their departed favorite had fallen upon the shoulders of one worthy to wear it.

That debut is history, hence extended comment is superfluous. The natural beauty of Galli-Curci's voice, the host of admirers who packed the auditorium, the audience of pre-war brilliancy, the radiant performance by the new soprano, the glamour of her vocal interpretation, the enthusiasm of the listeners, the truthful impersonation—ingratiating vivaciousness in the first act, gentle pathos in the second, tragic insouciance in the third—all blended to make the event both memorable and cherished. Critics seemed to be agreed that Galli-Curci had scored another triumph.

Lucia, three days later, was but a repetition of the opening night. On this reminiscent occasion, how the Caruso presence must have been felt by the new prima donna, who recalled the time when she and he had sung together in this opera at the Teatro Colón in Buenos Aires—perhaps, had he lived, they would have been singing Lucia and Edgardo again that night; yet, without that assistance, she gained entrance to the enchanted garden of fame which some reach early, some late, and others not at all. After the brilliant debut, Galli-Curci was flooded with telegrams and floral gifts. "Here's to the greatest triumph of your life. I wish I were there to cheer (John McCormack)." "All our thoughts and good wishes to you tonight (Mary Garden)." "With my sincere wishes for your triumphal success this evening (Rosa Ponselle)." "At the moment of departing for Chicago, I wish you an unfailing and brilliant success (Tito Schipa)." "A heart full of happiness and good wishes for you (Florence Macbeth)."

With respect to Shakespeare's triplex classification, it is obvious that Galli-Curci was not born great, unless that consists in having a God-given voice and a God-given power to make use of it. Nor had she greatness thrust upon her, unless that consists in having universal honor, prestige and popularity without its seeking. She did, however, achieve greatness by a judicious use of talent and thereby placed a higher valuation on accomplishment through industry efficiently applied. It was claimed, at the time, that next to the President of the United States and the Prince of Wales, she was the most photographed and the most publicly discussed person in the world, and with the exception of Caruso, had the greatest earning capacity of any artist, past or present.

"I wonder how many people who listen know what it means to go through an opera, what a singer has to encounter!" exclaimed our artist after that first strenuous week. "The actress has only to act, the violinist only to play, but a singer must make her tones and sing and act. She must feel the part. She must have control of her throat, her breath, her placement, her lines, her enunciation, keep an eye on the conductor and her attention on the *tout ensemble*. Of course, some of these things become more or less automatic with experience and practice, but one must always supervise. How does it feel to make a Metropolitan debut? I was not nervous, I was not frightened, I was not sceptical. One thing perturbed my usual calmness of mind—could I do the rôle satisfactorily to myself? The result pleased me, for I realized that I had done a faithful job. Seen from the stage when one takes curtain calls, it is a sight the magnificence of which none can realize from the auditorium. Then a complete change for eye and mind—the dressing-room, change of costume, thoughts upon the music and the action of the coming scene, then the call and once more upon the stage. But the final thrill comes after the opera is over and one meets a throng outside the stage door to catch a glimpse of the singer and, sometimes, shower her with kindly words and cheers."

New Horizons

As early as December, 1921, Galli-Curci admitted that she was not content with her position as foremost coloratura singer of the world. She had a desire to be something more—in a word, a consummate actress. Her success in lyric parts—those that were important dramatically as well as musically—aroused her ambition for characterization which the coloratura rôles did not adequately provide. "I had lots to learn in Butterfly—the little Japanese movements, the fluttering gestures, the quick, light manner of walking. I love to interpret the joy and sorrow of the maiden through my acting as well as through my voice." This was the new Galli-Curci speaking. The music allotted to Verdi-Donizetti-Bellini-Rossini manikins is intended to be sung with everything focused upon vocal technic, little focused upon characterization. When, however, one has advanced from the vocalizing to the singing stage of art, then it becomes evident that there is a higher type of ministration than that by which she became known and beloved. Did or did not Galli-Curci belong to lyric opera? If critiques be taken as a criterion of opinion, then we say she did. If lyric rôles suited her style admirably, as all admit, and if the lovely middle quality of voice found in such music be a more perfect medium for her winsome personality, again we say she did. This was noted by the Chicago Journal: "The voice itself is of heavenly sweetness and remarkably resonant, even greater in *cantabile* than in *coloratura* singing. Of all great sopranos, she is the only one whose art is quiet and subdued. It is the finest singing and it is a natural means of expression."

Does art become static with fame? When an artist's life can no longer be affected by circumstances or be shaken by failure; when there is nothing more to win, no greater goal to gain, must he or she become the machine of art to do and live according to the dictates of the world? After the top is reached, with no new horizons to seek and yearn for, the downward path begins; for anything short of one's best immediately starts the march of jealous lilliputians with their cords of critical disapproval and malicious whisperings to bind this Gulliver and render him a helpless prisoner. Therefore, the peak must be maintained.

"Who made you a success?" asked a curious admirer.

"Everybody after November 18, 1916. That was my artistic birth, the one that counts most. So many claim to have had a hand in it. One recalls how he told me to produce the tones, another how to sing the rôle, others how they coached and taught and advised and warned—so many that I must have had more instructors than acquaintances."

Galli-Curci responded generously to the numerous calls for articles. These covered her advance to stardom, early life, views on singing, opera and life—furnishing excellent material for study and pleasant reading, for they are couched in simple style with no attempt to garnish or to preach. In addition to *How to Become an Opera Singer* previously mentioned, she wrote several articles on her opera successes, on her vocal method, and on her manner of study.

Many quotations might be taken from these records, with respect to her art—all important, all interesting, but they would shed no further light upon the narrative or upon the cyclic evolution. Let one suffice:

> "Singing is the most natural means of expression and has a human appeal that cannot be obtained by other means, and it

is a much greater triumph to succeed with an unsophisticated
audience which has a definite idea of what kind of enjoyment
they are to have."

Hyper-critics had their fling at Galli-Curci, but it was the lay men
and women that set the criterion of valuation. They judged by
effects produced. Did she arouse emotions? Did she awaken nobler
impulses? Did she inspire love, ambition? Did she fill the soul with
rapture? Did she give the impression that life is not all callous and
unsympathetic but full of poetry and beauty? Did she create a
dream world, transfigure commonplaceness, radiate warmth? Did
she glow? We can answer in the affirmative if we accept her motto:
"Look upon your work as a joy. Let nothing discourage you. The
only way to succeed is to put every ounce of energy you possess into
your every task."

Voice analysts have sought to ascertain how great singers produce
certain tones, how they color them, how they float them, but there
is no scientific means by which such analysis can be secured—that is
the singer's secret. Anyone having a voice, intelligence and urge to
work, claims Galli-Curci, can acquire this art, but that is only the
initial step. "To know how to sing is one thing, to know how to use
it for the interpretation of a song or the impersonation of an opera
rôle, is quite another. Quantity of vocal mastery is no guarantee;
quality is the yardstick and proficiency the gauge. Only years of
constant study will give the needed fluency and finish for acceptable
performance. Tone production and breathing are the two essentials
of good singing and they depend upon right functioning by many
organs of the body which, in the process of singing, must be relaxed
and pliable. Some of these organs are the diaphragm, throat, larynx,
lungs, nose, lips, tongue, palate, head cavities—of which perhaps the
larynx is the most important, and when properly managed, the rest
is easy . . . It is not enough to emit beautiful tones—one must know
how it is accomplished so as to be able to do it always whenever
desirable, even when indisposed or under adverse conditions." Galli-
Curci learned the secret early in life by application, by listening, by
study. To feel tone sensations in throat and head and to know there-

by whether or not they are correctly placed is the first acquirement. It is this tone sensation that decides for the singer. "Il tono fa la musica." (The tone makes the music.)

The Human Element

While her journalistic efforts always brought a liberal remuneration, she was over-generous in donating her artistic services to worthy causes, such contributions amounting in value to many thousands of dollars. On the afternoon of November 27, 1921, she appeared at the Metropolitan Opera House in a benefit concert from which $12,000 was raised for the Verdi Home for Aged Musicians in Italy. The stage was draped in black, presenting a scene of cathedral solemnity, with an heroic bust of Caruso resting on a pedestal in the center and presented during the ceremonies by the widow with her daughter, Gloria, attending. Participating artists, all in black, were Galli-Curci, who sang the Bach Gounod "Ave Maria" with orchestra; Sundelius, Farrar, Alda, Gigli, Martinelli, De Luca, and others, also six conductors, the opera chorus and orchestra. A similar event took place on the same stage February 19, 1922—a concert for the benefit of the Caruso Memorial Foundation Scholarship for Talented American Musicians—the receipts of which amounted to some $20,000. Artists on the program were limited to those who had been associated and had sung with Caruso: Alda, Farrar, Ponselle, Matzenauer, Rothier, Martinelli, De Luca, Gigli, and Galli-Curci. At the same place on February 12, Galli-Curci gave a benefit recital for the New York Osteopathic Hospital fund. The sale of tickets was so enormous that for the first time in the history of the opera house the stage was utilized, to the surprise of the management, for seating the overflow. The receipts were $10,500. On January 15, 1922, she sang a group of songs on a gala charity concert benefit for Illinois Children's Home and Aid Society.

Radio, at this time, was in its infancy with respect to broadcasting musical events, but the Chicago operas were put on the air from Station KYW, the first on January 1, 1922, with *Rigoletto*. In later years these broadcasts from the Auditorium stage afforded delight to many listeners although the reception was not good, at least in the East. Three men in a small room at Ft. McPherson, Georgia, reported that they had heard Galli-Curci sing from Pittsburgh, 1,000 miles away, on February 16, by means of a new radio set.

Galli-Curci sang her first Chicago *Butterfly* on January 7. This proved to be an advance in her art, notable in its sincerity of por-, trayal and command of stage technic. Dramatically and vocally convincing, she disclosed artistic growth surprising to many, much of which was due to her painstaking devotion to details. In the preparation of the rôle, she not only went over the book with the author, John Luther Long, but coached the part with its dramatic producer, David Belasco.

"Queen of Song"

It looked, in 1922, as if there might be a Galli-Curci craze, with many racking brains for some new idea where-with to glorify the Queen of Song. Pupils of Omaha were invited by the Omaha *News* to enter a poster contest, the subject to be Galli-Curci. There were fifteen prizes, the winner to receive two tickets for the concert, $25, and a personal introduction to the artist. Other awards covered tickets only. The first prize was won by a university boy, the second by a high school girl. Another inordinate event was staged in January, at the Congress Hotel, Chicago, during the progress of the Friends of Opera ball. Galli-Curci was hailed from her seat by the master of ceremonies who, with cordial familiarity, grasped the tiny hand, drew it through his arm, and led the laughing lady to the center of the room, where she pirouetted to the song of her extemporaneous singer escort, all of which put her *en rapport* with the delighted audience, who applauded so rapturously that it was with great difficulty the rioters were induced to resume dancing.

At the Atlanta opera debut in *Traviata* on April 25, 1922, with the Metropolitan Company, Galli-Curci received the greatest ovation since that memorable debut in Chicago six years before. The audience gave itself up to wild enthusiasm and extended the singer an electrifying welcome. The immense auditorium was packed with 6,000 devotees, and many were turned away. The receipts, approximating $24,000, were the largest in the history of the opera association, seats selling on the curb for $50 a pair. But it's an old, old story. Next day, the newspapers skyrocketed their superlatives until their vocabularies became exhausted. The visit was climaxed at the next performance when Galli-Curci occupied a box, with other artists of the company, where she received the tributes of the audience with bows and smiles.

Before she arrived in town, reporters and camera men got lost trying to locate the singer. Misleading reports sent out led them a merry chase from one station to another, but Galli-Curci did not arrive at any—she entered the city by motor.

Entering the hotel, the prima donna inquired if her rooms were ready. "Not only a suite," replied the gallant manager, "but the whole establishment." He was rewarded with a rose from a bouquet she carried. Her arrival was heralded by the press on white, green and lavender newsprint. After this single appearance she resumed her concert tour.

Interesting things are ever happening to those who attain an exalted place in their distinctive spheres; several are associated with Galli-Curci's journeys as she zigzagged over the United States. For her Cleveland recital, that year, the manager of the theatre turned the diva's dressing-room into a bower of flowers and provided a wedding-cake, which at the post-concert reception was cut by the bride, and even the stage-hands were invited to share the feast. Another tribute came from a news gatherer who was as much impressed with her personality as with her art—surprised that she would welcome him as a guest, that there was nothing stilted or up-stage about the attitude of this celebrity, that she proved vivacious, quick, witty, brilliant at repartee, and a gifted conversationalist in any language offered, with a ready and facile command of American slang, which she dispensed with piquant relish, darting from theme to theme with astonishing ease.

Experiences en Route

Honored by the Camp Fire Girls on November 1, in the auditorium of Scottish Rite Cathedral, Minneapolis, Galli-Curci was given the name of "Cante Waste" or "Singing-Heart." What title could be more fitting? The singer was robed in a scout dress, received the symbol—the bluebird of happiness—and wore the beaded headband of the order. The initiation consisted of the Fire-Light ceremony. That a singer must be impervious to heat and cold, as well as to fatigue and nervousness, is obvious, as shown by a contrasting pair of examples in the career of this winged warbler. At Victoria, Vancouver, where the theatre proved too small to house the expected audience, an ice-rink was engaged. The weather suddenly turned cold and transformed the skating palace into a refrigerator. The emptied ice pipes were filled with steam, but failed to serve other than to give forth sizzling sounds. Galli-Curci met the difficulty by bringing her fur coat on the platform and gladly donned it when the audience called "Put it on!" Then she sang to the shivering assemblage, likewise wrapped in furs, coats and rugs. In San Antonio, Texas, with the thermometer at 101 in the shade, the only available auditorium was the theatre playing a show matinee and night, between which the concert had to be fitted. So at 5 P.M., before a crowded, sweltering house and on a stage with temperature increasing, Galli-Curci gave her program as unconcernedly as you please, although her accompanist had to change his collar three times. The glow of singing, she explained, enabled her to forget the heat and devote herself to getting across music's message.

In the audience at the Los Angeles concert was a deaf mute who "heard" the singing through the sense of seeing and the perceptive impulses set up by the vibratory oscillations of the air. It is a scientific fact that musical sounds are felt externally and that tone sensation may be experienced without ear perception. This young man missed the silken beauty of the voice, but his digital dexterity flashed before his companion's eyes in a manner that declared high enjoyment of vocal climaxes and he commented on the singer's ability to woo with song. He read her emotional states of mind in her face, her tonal gradations in the full sweep of the throat like a bird's. He noted that the intricate runs on the flute were timed to the fraction of a second in the cadenzas; indeed, he heard far better than some with quickened ears but not in tune with nature's harmonies.

A Psychic Votary

Galli-Curci first sensed the psychic world at the age of sixteen.

"Every intelligent person must recognize the nearness of such a world," said she when asked her views on this occult science. "Study Swedenborg. Read his interpretation of the Bible and you will find quite a new Bible, one that never contradicts itself or becomes ridiculous. The Bible is allegorical. If you once grasp its symbolism you will understand why men writing at such widely-separated periods of history wrote things which so perfectly convey the same meaning. Through symbolism, Masonry was preserved and passed down its message through the ages. Why not the Bible? Swedenborg will give you the key. Then you have only to listen to the inner voice and you never go wrong. Truly, talent and genius are handed down from above. Something inside told me to sing." With respect to spiritualism, she is interested only to the extent that she feels, as many others do, that there is something in the heart that must go on—that cannot stop with death. She has read Lodge and Doyle, but is no convert to their theories, though recognizing spiritual influences. She is interested in the psychic field as pure enlightenment which cannot be had through contact with the physical world alone. To further her power of apprehension she studied languages, art, politics, literature, human nature. She sought the depths of art and of religion.

Emanuel Swedenborg, whose philosophical works captured her attention, became her spiritual mentor and she began a serious study of his principles. This study led her to become a votary of psychic belief, following the Swedish scientist-theologian's excursions into the arcana of the unseen. His tracing of the soul in its relation to the body and his studies in physiology she found deeply affecting, as also his theory of the relation between the finite and the infinite, between body and soul, his aim to discover the nature of the soul and spirit by means of astronomical investigation.

The faculty of divination is highly sensitized in certain individuals —some having an uncanny power of occult perceptivity, others subject to powerful spiritual influences. Galli-Curci is one, not due to her studies and predilections in this sphere of knowledge, but due to personal experiences with such manifestations, the most striking of which was that associated with the death of her mother in Milan on April 14, 1923. The daughter, while on tour, had been kept posted about the sick one's condition, but did not become uneasy until one night at Houston, Texas, where she had given a concert, following which she was handed a cablegram reporting the illness as pleural pneumonia. In the middle of the night Samuels awoke to find his wife staring out of the window into the darkness. Inquiring the reason for such an unusual act, he was informed that she felt certain that something dire had happened. Samuels tried to reassure her, but Galli-Curci held to her premonition. Next morning the party moved on to Alexandria, Louisiana, for a recital at the university the following evening. During the day another cable arrived announcing Mme. Galli's death. Samuels and Salter agreed to withhold the news until after the concert and to prepare the artist by framing an Italian-worded message stating that her mother had grown alarmingly worse. This was presented upon their return to the hotel, but their good intentions were futile; for as soon as Galli-Curci read the spurious communication, she said, "This is not the truth. Why do you try to fool me? I know all—my mother is dead." There was naught to do but hand her the original and excuse themselves on the ground of consideration for her. When the question of discontinuing the tour was mentioned, she promptly dismissed it, declaring that her mother would wish her to go on and that she proposed to do so, expecting to receive spiritual strength from the other world. This determination was all the more difficult in view of the fact that Mme. Galli had been expecting to come to New York to live with her daughter as soon as she had recovered sufficiently to make the journey.

The Onward March

With ninety-one appearances in fourteen capitals and twenty-six new places, with nineteen in New York and thirteen in Chicago, yet with the demand still unsatisfied, Galli-Curci completed her seventh season, in which she earned five times the salary of the President of the United States. From October, 1922, to June, 1923, was an uninterrupted period of triumphs without a cancellation or postponement. "Too bad it's all over!" she exclaimed. "I feel so good!"—an almost incredible condition after three strenuous seasons of continuous concerts and operas. Naturally there were some unusual features worthy of record. In January she stood godmother for the second time, with Ruffo as godfather, to the infant daughter of Tito Schipa, her operatic associate of long standing. In April she drove through the National Park at Vicksburg, Mississippi, and visited the Naval Observatory. Mounting to its top, she sang to the souls of the dead—a decided contrast to the shrieking guns of sixty years before. She also stopped at the Illinois monument to sing to the memory of the dead heroes listed thereon. In Dixon, Illinois, she gave a recital in a big barn-like building known as the State Arsenal. Many birds had built nests among its rafters and set up a concerted twittering chorus, whereupon Samuels whispered to his wife, "Are we giving a concert in a henroost?" After a time, the birds ceased and Galli-Curci felt flattered, for she had outsung them.

The private life of every prominent person is subject to intrusion by certain individuals who hold no respect for the sanctity thereof, evidenced in no more annoying manner than through communications, many of the begging kind. Galli-Curci continually received epistolary requests for financial aid, and while unable to grant all such calls, she did respond to those deemed most deserving. Not a few of these SOS solicitations bordered upon the ludicrous. One in 1923 from a woman in Idaho read: "Will you let my daughter sing for you? They say she has the makings of a great singer. She is a soprano and contralto (sic). The organist of our church said he thought she was going to be the highest soprano we have ever had. She is only fifteen now, well-built and healthy. I cannot afford to give her the musical education she needs and I thought if you would only hear her sing and you found her voice was worthy of it, you would give her a free scholarship." Another plea from Toronto: "I want to be a singer. I have been studying about a year and have made good progress, but on my way to my teacher's residence to pay for my last term, I lost my purse containing the sum of twenty dollars and have not been able to make it up again. I am praying night and day for help that I may start again. You are kind to others, won't you be kind to me? Do please help me, just this once. I do so want to study again and I thought that you, being so great a singer, would sympathize with an ambitious girl."

Sympathy Galli-Curci had in abundance for such unfortunates—most of them obsessed with an unwarranted urge fostered by unenlightened parents and preyed upon by unscrupulous pseudo-instructors. Galli-Curci is strong in her denunciation against the influx of fake music teachers who promise short-cuts to fame and fortune. "*Beware of the Singing Teacher!*" is no idle pronouncement. To many letters asking advice she sounds a warning against that brand of dishonesty which advertises special methods for quick results. "No one," she asserts, "can manufacture a voice. A canary in an opera-house can be heard as clearly as an opera singer because it sings naturally." To the first admonition should be added a second: *Beware of the Career Promoter.* The disappointments, heart-breaks, financial ruins, pathetic dramas and fatalities resulting from negligence in avoiding these two pitfalls constitute the Tragedy of Music.

Chicago Dénouement

The passing of the 1921-22 season marked the last of the Chicago Opera Association, the annual deficit amounting to so high a sum as to forbid a continuation under the same conditions. So with 1922-23 came into being the Chicago Civic Opera Company, with Samuel Insull as the president and Polacco as musical director.

The dream of the Insull directorate was to make opera permanent, place it in a new and worthy home, and establish a sinking fund sufficient to carry on *ad infinitum.* The dream came true but ended in a nightmare.

For two seasons Galli-Curci had appeared as a member of both opera companies under the mutual agreement, but now there arose a dispute over the opening opera for the Chicago 1923-24 season. Should it be *Dinorah* (her choice) or *Lakmé* (Polacco's choice)? On November 1 Lawrence Evans advised General Manager H. M. Johnson that Galli-Curci desired to open her season on December 3 in *Dinorah* and was not agreeable to other suggestions, inasmuch as the matter had been fully discussed by them and supposedly settled.

To this Johnson replied "We must insist upon *Lakmé* as Mme. Galli-Curci's opening performance. We must consider other artists and general program for the season."

This elicited an ultimatum from the artist direct in which she expressed surprise at the attitude of the management and insisted upon her rights to be consulted with respect to what she should sing, as had been done in the past. She called attention to this right of choice made to him two months before while in New York and that changes had been made in previous seasons, even after her arrival in Chicago. The ultimatum concluded, "Should this interfere with your general program please feel relieved of any contractual obligations toward me." Samuel Insull wired her on November 5 that he had just returned from Europe and regretted her action and requested her consent to *Lakmé*. "Shall esteem it a personal favor," he added. Galli-Curci's reply was explicit and explanatory. She protested against the "curt, high-handed manner" in which her desires were over-ridden. "All that I am asking is that, on a month's notice, the order of the first two performances be reve sed." To this Insull answered: "The request you make is that I interfere with the carefully arranged repertoire of the company to suit your individual desires. This I cannot do . . . the management of the opera company must be supreme in the matter of arranging the repertoire."

Galli-Curci concluded the controversy November 12 with the following directed to Insull: "I am obliged to accept your decision inasmuch as I am bound to the company for this season. I deem it but fair, however, to inform you at this time that . . . I shall not be with the company next season." While there was no written contract covering the last two years, the artist recognized a verbal agreement as binding, therefore bowed to managerial dictate until the expiration thereof.

Explaining the break, Galli-Curci stated that it was instigated, no doubt, through back-stage jealousies of which the public knew nothing and which made her work unbearable. When Mary Garden was director she said of her chief singer: "Galli-Curci can have anything she wants. Just let her ask. She can sing anything at any time. I am going to give the public what it wants." The news of our artist's resignation raised a storm of protest among Chicago music-lovers, even greater than that occasioned by the Muratore-Garden combat which caused the exit of the polished French tenor. Public opinion was with Galli-Curci, whose wishes should have been acceded to under any circumstances. Those on the inside declared that the root of the trouble lay, not in the choice of opera, but in a dictatorial policy which permitted certain artists to pick their operas and even select their rôles, which privilege was denied Galli-Curci. "If they can choose," she asked, "why can't I?" A just question entitled to a just answer. She further declared that she was embarrassed by the public statement of the conductor inferring that the company would be better off without the stars.

Commenting on the affair, the Chicago *Journal*, in an editorial captioned "Chicago's Favorite," said in part:

> "The big operatic question of the moment is this: shall Chicago's first-class artists be driven out of the organization by the intrigues of a jealous conductor and other operatic politicians? Shall this city lose a voice, for which New York bid in vain for years, to satisfy a conductor whom no other musical center seems particularly eager to secure? Public sympathy in this difficulty is wholly on the side of Galli-Curci. Opera-goers of this city can never forget that this diva became a world-famous star from her singing of the role of Gilda in *Rigoletto* on the Auditorium stage . . . and from that hour to this, Galli-Curci has been the city's favorite soprano. Her gracious manner has endeared her to all patrons of the opera."

Other editors commented *pro* and *con*, and for days the flame of controversy burned the pages of newspapers until it went out of its own accord. On December 3, per schedule, Galli-Curci sang *Lakmé*, with Panizza conducting, as if burdened by neither cares nor disappointments. The performance was stopped while the audience took time to welcome its favorite, many rising from their seats to do her homage. After the "Bell Song," a second demonstration retarded the opera's progress, but applause and ovation failed to alter the decision of the opera's star concerning next season, which in the meantime had been completely booked with concert engagements and Metropolitan performances.

Dinorah on the 17th evoked another tempestuous scene of appreciation for Galli-Curci in which Insull, as reported, did not join, but sat silent in his loge, even omitting his customary visit back-stage to congratulate her. Perhaps he felt the sting of retribution over a hasty act which lost the company its best attraction and the greatest singer of the day. In spite of all, Galli-Curci never indicated, by act or word, her feelings over the outcome. She was content to let unpleasant happenings dissolve into oblivion. Her philosophy of life does not permit of discontent, hence her recipe for contentment, "Give up worry!" Formerly, she was given to worrying over trifles and the prescription is simplicity itself, though sometimes hard to follow. "Do not think of things that threaten to worry." In due course, she found that she was in love with the whole world, and from time to time she discovered additional improvement in her singing because of this sane attitude. Psychology, science, self-hypnotism, foolishness—call it what you will, it worked with her; and more—she felt that her happiness was communicated in her voice to her audiences. Her aim was not to measure Art in terms of money but in terms of popularity. She wanted to please, wanted everyone to enjoy her singing and in order to accomplish this, she had to sing with beguiling tones. If but one thing is preserved of her song career, it will be that her voice *caressed the ears*. When she faced crowded auditoriums she found happiness—perhaps the happiness of gratitude—then she expressed that gratitude in sweetest tones. It is not extravagant to claim possession of an art that woos affection, subtly charms the inner senses, and in so doing, soothes the troubled spirit and gives the heart a fresher kind of joy.

Farewells

The Chicago final performance on January 4, 1924, was the opera *Romeo et Juliette* which Galli-Curci had not sung there for three years, yet was scheduled without her knowledge or approval. But the musical vehicle which was to serve for this unhappy exit mattered not to the masses that besieged the Auditorium—further witness to the fact that our singer had sung to more "Sold Out" houses than any other member of the company. Those gifted with keen observation might have seen tears in our singer's eyes, but all could not detect the farewell color in the tones she uttered in her good-bye rôle. The audience came that night to hear a singer, not an opera, and tendered her a touching and devoted "Godspeed," thereby testifying to their deep affection and loyalty. There was one distinguished auditor at that last performance who occupied Campanini's erstwhile box—Eleanore Duse, who broke her rigid rule of attending public functions while on tour.

The apartment of the Italian actress was directly over that of the Italian vocalist in the Congress Hotel. It was prophetic that these two notable representatives of high art, each greatest in her sphere, should meet, particularly at this time, in a romantically dramatic rather than in a socially formal manner, during the Chicago farewells of both. After the matinee performance of *Ghosts*, Galli-Curci called at Duse's stage-room to tender her respects, but the maid, following instructions, informed the caller that the signora was ill and could see no one. Galli-Curci thereupon left her card and departed. While resting next day for the evening's opera, there came a timid knock upon her apartment door which, when opened, disclosed the figure of a black-robed little woman whom Galli-Curci recognized immediately as the great tragedienne, and sprang to give her welcome. With affectionate kisses a friendship was cemented, then and there, to be severed only by the elder woman's death later in the year. Expressing pleasure at the honor, Galli-Curci asked the particular reason for the call. Duse explained that it was in the nature of an apology for the stupidity of her maid the day before. So these two of divers character—divers because of the difference in their life viewpoints—came together for a time. Duse said, "Open my heart and you will see graven inside of it, Italy." Galli-Curci would have phrased it: "Open my heart and you will see graven inside of it, Love."

Galli-Curci's farewell was characterized by two contrasting features—the one a warm, the other a frigid, send-off. At a good-bye luncheon on January 5, tendered by the Italian Chamber of Commerce in the Congress Hotel, each of the 150 guests wished to speak. Those who received recognition by the chairman eloquently voiced, in the smooth Romance language of their race, a unanimous opinion couched in flaming words, which read: "May Galli-Curci always be right, but we're for her, right or wrong." The guest of honor responded in her native tongue and gave out a final statement which said, in part, "I feel that I cannot leave Chicago without expressing my heartfelt gratitude for the loyalty and affection which has been shown me by the public, so strongly contrasted with my treatment from the opera management. To you, my beloved public, my best wishes and thanks for many of the happiest and most treasured moments of my life." As a conclusion, fitting because so true and so characteristic, was the final epitome: "She is of our country and we appreciate the wonder of her art as none others can."

Referring to the statement that not one of the opera people responsible for the break called on, or even spoke to their biggest box-office attraction during her last days in the city, one paper commented thus: "Galli-Curci did not leave Chicago. She was driven away in defiance of the wishes of nine-tenths of the opera-going public."

CYCLE OF
FULFILLMENT

1924-1930

"Individualism must be asser-
tive but should never run wild."

—GALLI-CURCI

Last New Role

A MEMBER now of but one opera company, Galli-Curci opened the Metropolitan season in *Barber of Seville*. Records show that it occurred on the night of a great storm that tore the dirigible "Shenandoah" from her moorings in a seventy-mile gale. The house nevertheless was full, with three hundred standing. For *Traviata*, the house was again overstocked with humanity, while *Lucia* drew a double line of standees from Broadway to Seventh Avenue, most of whom got to the door only to behold the familiar "Sold Out House" sign.

As a money-maker, Galli-Curci was *facile princeps*. She was not only a famous singer, but was receiving several thousand dollars every time she sang and enjoying a steady income from the sale of phonograph records. Her earnings as always, were shared with others, so we find her singing at the opera house in February for the benefit of the Metropolitan Opera Emergency Fund, electing the "Mad Scene" from *Lucia* as her contribution to the occasion.

The new rôle of the season was that of the Queen in *Coq d'Or* on January 21, commenting upon which, our artist said: "The singing part of the Queen is only half an hour long but there is no better half hour. In that brief period the singer meets all vocal difficulties, including many the old composers never thought of. The roulade in the 'Hymn to the Sun' has intervals that are simply fiendish and all but impossible." Of her performance, one critical comment will suffice: "The voice of Galli-Curci gave a lyric loveliness to the Queen which had an animated counterpart in the dancing of Rosina

145

Galli. Her clear, flute-like notes, now mocking, now gay, reflected the bewitching caprice of the airy dancer."

Literary Work

Galli-Curci's literary work was now assuming considerable proportions, her articles appearing in some of the leading magazines. A *Ladies Home Journal* series begun in 1923, *Beginnings*, covered a discussion of chance and choice, disclaiming the power of superstition. "I carry no amulet or charms nor do I pick up nails. I have no fear of ladders or black cats, no faith in fortune-tellers. None of these fetishes ever touched my life or thought. But I do believe that the whims of chance or fate—some call it opportunity—have made me Galli-Curci. Yet I cannot say that I was a wholly inactive pawn in the hands of fate." In the second installment, "Singing Secrets," she discussed the matter with intelligent unrestraint. The life of a prima donna, by virtue of its very nature, is subject to inopportune incursions, perhaps the most frequent and conspicuous of which is the demand for voice secrets during extensive journeyings.

How, How, How? wells up the yearning chorus from every land. *What, What, What?* reverberates from thousands of zealous throats. The deluge of questions is almost engulfing with no escape other than to withhold replies on the ground that the secrets of every art are immune from publication. Secretiveness has value as a time-saver, and to some may serve as a curiosity provoker, but according to Galli-Curci, there are in reality no vocal secrets which, if known, would lead to musical accomplishment unless it be that of genius, which is itself unfathomable. That, however, does not satisfy; so now and then our artist must resort to print as evidence of her willingness to tell her "secrets" to an impatient world. In this article she advocates *charting the voice*, each according to its individual character. Other recommendations are: "Begin early and sing lightly. Learn to hear a tone in your head before attempting to produce it. Get the sense of pitch, the feel of rhythm, volume, timbre and color. Use imagination, master easy breathing, learn to float the voice on a stream of air, control the breath, open the throat, study vocal anatomy. Learn the difference between open, closed, dark, nasal, head, forward and back tones. Care must be taken in the selection of vocal exercises. Do not coddle the voice, yet avoid straining it. Try to mix vowels—the best teachers for this are the birds, particularly the nightingales and larks. Shun consonants in practice. Never sing translations. Imitate the feathered singers of the Hartz Mountains if you would learn to trill. Eschew carelessness. Never be satisfied until you have mastered every problem. Set a watchdog on yourself and think. Adopt healthful modes of living, with special attention to eating and moderation in all things—which is the greatest secret of all."

This article concludes with a description of how a great career is built, and also is a timely dissertation on accent and stress; but rules necessarily are applicable only if one has the talent, the industry and the ability to apply them. In "Singing Roads," Galli-Curci says she finds herself regarded as "a complete guide to musical secrets, an animated folder on the scenery along the road to greater music, a human blue-book along the way to opera." Young singers hunted her out, questioned her eagerly about the musical way over which she has travelled. The hundred-and-one questions pertaining to this topic are enumerated and analyzed under various sub-heads. In the last article, "The Greatest Thing in My Life," she tells of experiences and acknowledges her debt to America.

Success! What does it mean? Here is Galli-Curci's recipe: "Real artistic success cannot be reached without matrimony. They go hand in hand. It is not a case of one dominating the other, for together they make a complete career. One cannot separate one's work from one's life." Asked if a great career interfered with woman's work in woman's sphere, she replied, "No, because our need for a home is all the greater. I must have its relief, its repose, somewhere to be myself. The American woman is most wonderful in her home —when she stays in it." Success depends, too, on beauty and charm, which according to our vocal psychologist may be had without actually possessing them, i.e., through illusion. "This may be made by unique hairdress, by unusual costumes, or by *feeling* beautiful. Beauty means a clear, velvety skin, an alert mind, bright eyes, a fresh sane outlook on life, and an enthusiastic manner. These attri-

With Tito Schipa on a "singing lark," at Victor Recording Laboratories, Camden, N.J., 1924

Portrait, around 1925-1926

Sold-out house in Melbourne, Australia, 1927

*With Homer Samuels, in the quiet surroundings of their summer home,
"Sul Monte," Highmount, N.Y., 1927*

butes, if not natural, must be acquired. One should scintillate and laugh with joy, also be gay and colorful. The secret of acquisition is rest and relaxation. But—the greatest asset to beauty is to be feminine. If we women lose that we lose our power and we gain nothing, because we shall never be so successful as men in men's sphere. None can succeed in a sphere not their own."

During this year she wrote a series for *The Etude*, the first captioned "Are Singers Born, Not Made?" Here the author handles the subject with fine grasp and understanding. One paragraph in particular is worthy of quotation: "America, like Italy, is a land that has produced many lovely voices; but the American singer, on the threshold of her art, must learn to speak with an open throat. Americans do not realize it, but the observer coming here from a foreign land notices first of all that many of the people seem to talk with mouths almost closed. The jaws are stiff and there is no thought other than that of expressing oneself forcibly and positively. The educated Italian tries to show his culture by talking beautifully. Such habits have come down to him for centuries. He has very little to overcome. The American, the German, the Englishman, on the contrary, has to upset his vocal ancestry before he begins his voice work."

Continuing in another issue with "Thresholds of Vocal Art," the writer says: "The material that one sings is not nearly so important as how one sings," she herself using only the simplest materials as illustrated in the exercises by Manuel Garcia—those he gave Jenny Lind wherewith to restore her voice. Looking at them in print one might mistake them for the initial sessions of a violin beginner, so simple are they. "The singing student should make it a practice to assimilate, as much as possible, the vocal wisdom of the great singers and teachers of the past." Americans, she claims, "spend entirely too much time at lessons studying mere songs, often very poor songs. One hour of *Sonnambula*, *Norma*, or *Lucia* is worth five hours of ordinary songs."

A Little Nonsense

As an uncritical expression, this of a concert in Medford, Oregon, is delightfully refreshing:

"While a lot of her singin' went over our heads, yet Mary an' me, we liked it fine. Nice little lady, an' got a good voice too. I caught Mary wipin' a tear out o' the corner of one of her eyes just about the time the lady got thru singin' Silver Threads among the Gold. Gosh, but she sure can sing—it was wonderful! The man at the pianer was mighty good at his job. The feller with the nickel-plated broom-handle which he tooted on, was pretty good too—but he done purty well at that, only Galli-Curci's voice is so much clearer than what he was a-tootin' on that it made the tooter sound kinder poor. But, takin' it by and large, it was a mighty good show."

—*Medford Herald*, June 5, 1924.

On another occasion, when she came out to sing, her attention was drawn to a man in an aisle seat, the picture of despair. It was obvious that he had been brought to the concert against his will. "Aha!" said our singer, "there is my doubtful customer." She began to sing to him, watching the effect. At first, the only observable response was irritation. He would not even look at her, but glared at the program, shifting in his chair, clearing his throat, and growing more and more fidgety. By and by, he cast sly, reluctant glances in her direction, then his scowl faded, and one could almost hear him say to himself, "Well, it's not so bad as I imagined." With each song, he showed keener interest, finally giving his whole attention to listening. By the time Galli-Curci had finished the program the man was leaning forward, with face beaming in blissful rapture. "You didn't want to come, did you?" was the greeting he received backstage from our smiling singer. The convert grinned sheepishly as he asked, "You saw me?" Assuring him that she had, she expressed delight in having been able to sell him her music. She conquered because she believed in her art.

In May, 1924, while en route from California to Phoenix, Arizona, for a concert, the party was halted at Yuma, a quarantine station. While being subjected to the disinfection and inspection process imposed on all passengers, Galli-Curci hummed a gay tune and complimented the authorities upon their diligence against the spread of foot-and-mouth disease, then prevalent in that section. The *dénouement* came, however, when the artists' trunks were held and she had to proceed without them, necessitating appearing at the concert in a borrowed gown loaned by a local dress establishment.

Did she exhibit temper or dissatisfaction? Not unless a smile and a nonchalant mien be indicative of that ill-humored discomposure, and her words mean other than they say: "Temperament is necessary to art, but unless it is controlled, the artist is a walking potato. Temperament is another word for selfishness nine times out of ten. Temperament merely means that one is inconsiderate of those around one. Those artists who are really on top are those who are least temperamental. It is the same with business or anything else. One receives the best treatment, the most consideration, from the persons who have arrived, and the worst treatment, the least consideration, from those who are merely bluffing their way along. Just because one is famous and talented is no reason why one can't be a real human being."

It takes more than the ordinary forces of nature to stop a Galli-Curci concert. Many times she had to leap seemingly impossible barriers, but she always succeeded—unless we make exception of the few missed through illness. An example—in March she and her associates made part of the journey from Montgomery, Alabama, to Meridien, Mississippi, on a flat-car of a freight train. Starting the trip in an automobile, they came to grief in a mud slough ten miles from Demopolis, which distance they covered aboard the freighter to spend the night in that place.

Hollywood and London

Now loomed upon the great horizon the flare of interest afar. Foreign countries had not remained unenlightened as to the epoch-making progress of the young soprano America had discovered, so a tour abroad was inevitable—the first, perhaps, in history where a prima donna earned a reputation in the New World before seeking acclaim in the Old, a direct reverse of the usual procedure. In January came the startling announcement that the first Galli-Curci London concert, scheduled for the fall, had been sold out exactly eight months in advance and that for the second performance, the larger portion of the house had been booked—the first instance since the era of Jenny Lind that an artist's fame had been so pronounced. A month later it was reported that over 20,000 tickets had been purchased for the two events.

June 5, 1924—a keystone date because capping a structural career in a country used to superlatives and accustomed to high achievement, yet roused to astonishment by the compelling influence of a single woman able to attract, through the power of song, a mighty multitude estimated at 27,000 persons who paid $25,935 to hear her sing at the Hollywood Bowl, on the outskirts of Los Angeles, California, in conjunction with the Symphony Orchestra directed by Alfred Hertz, former conductor of the Metropolitan Opera, New York, and later of San Francisco Symphony. She was met at the station by a corps of United States Marines assigned as a special guard of honor to escort her to the Bowl on the eventful night, marking her first open-air appearance and her hundredth performance in America. The intake of $25,935 not only topped the Paderewski recital record at San Francisco of $24,590, but was one of the largest sums ever accredited to a single artist. Moreover, it was the fifth appearance within a period of three months, the other four being two recitals in Los Angeles and one each in Pasadena and Pomona.

Several other factors entered into this concert to make it an outstanding event in musical history. In addition to singing to the largest audience ever assembled to hear a singer at popular prices and breaking all monetary intake records, it occasioned the greatest throng ever witnessed in those parts. By 5:30 P.M. several hundred persons stood in line before the box-office. Many brought suppers and seats. By eight o'clock the police were face to face with a terrific traffic problem, so much so that it was with difficulty that the artist, escorted by two motorcycle policemen and two automobiles of marines, was able to make her way to the stage. Of course, the supply of seats was exhausted early, compelling the overflow to take refuge on the slopes of the surrounding hillsides.

One of the nigh-impossible technical feats accomplished that evening was the picture, the taking of which necessitated the co-operation of six cameramen using the largest instruments made. More than 4,500 feet of double feeder wire were used to secure the flashlight photograph, which required five and a half pounds of powder from thirty-six pans, simultaneously exploded and producing a report like a gun, at an expense of $450. Another interesting

feature was the presentation of a large American flag to Galli-Curci
by a body of United States Marines while the orchestra played "The
Star-Spangled Banner."

During this California visit Galli-Curci met Jack Dempsey at
Universal City, where the fistic champion was making a film picture.

Said the singer: "Oh, Mr. Dempsey! you must each me to box."

Said the boxer: "Fine! I'll do it right now if you teach me to sing."

Whereupon Galli-Curci showed Dempsey how to take "high E,"
but the latter, after one effort, decided to stick to gloves in preference to notes.

England

Now for the next rung on the upward flight to vocal sovereignty,
Galli-Curci did not view her British tour as that of an invading
conqueror but as a messenger of song. "I do not feel that I am great,
for when I compare myself with my ideal, I find I am much back
of what I desire to be. All artists are idealists; it is religion for them.
As religion strives for perfection of spirit, so an artist is ever reaching
after the elusive—ah, but it is elusive!" On October 1, 1924, our
singer, accompanied by Evans, Samuels and flutist Berenguer, sailed
for England.

Reputation is like a flag: one cannot escape it, so on the crossing
our dainty prima donna was the center of attraction, climaxed by
her appearance in a benefit recital aboard ship in a program made
up of several songs together with the "Shadow Song" and the "Mad
Scene" with flute obbligato.

A portion of a wireless message to the ship from the London
Music Club read: "We hope your visit to our island will bring you
great happiness. To forewarn and prepare you for the welcome that
awaits you is the pleasant purpose of this letter." Galli-Curci replied,
concluding: "I only hope that I may give as much happiness as
shall be mine in the giving."

Arriving at Plymouth the party was met by a deputation headed
by His Worship, Mayor Solomon Stephens, and his daughter, who
presented a bouquet to Galli-Curci. Lionel Powell, the London

manager of her tour, was also on hand to assist her down the gang-way to the tender after a luncheon on board. How reminiscent of three quarters of a century ago, when Barnum escorted the Swedish Jenny from the steamer to Manhattan Island crowded with curious welcomers! Arriving in London, our artist was domiciled in the rose suite of the Ritz Hotel, frequently occupied by the ex-Queen of Spain, which she found a floral bower. This was not her first visit to the British capital, for she had spent several days there in 1920 on her way to Paris to see her mother.

The continuous flow of glowing accounts from America of our singer's achievements, of her miraculous drawing-power, of her huge fees, of her irresistible charm, of her magical singing, of her amazing technic, together with an enormous number of articles in magazines under her name, anecdotes, experiences and *bon-mots*, supple-mented by advertising of divers kinds and in vast quantities, consti-tuted a stupendous propaganda that stimulated the usually calm Britishers to the point of curious excitement. The common impulse therefore was to see and hear this vocal phenomenon, hence the tumultuous surge toward Royal Albert Hall on the afternoon of October 12, thousands holding tickets which they had purchased months before, others hoping to get within the auditorium, if only to stand. Here's a touching communication scribbled on a bit of paper torn from an address book and sent to Galli-Curci: "We have been waiting at the gallery entrance since 8:30 A.M. and have failed to get to hear you sing. We are bitterly disappointed. Can anything be done for six forlorn souls?" They were taken care of. Such devo-tion deserved its own reward.

Lack of space prevents more than a brief mention of the columns of reviews, some of which can be compared only to a novelist's idea of the amazing scenes enacted. The singer's triumph was described by various flashing headlines:

MAGIC SPELL OF GALLI-CURCI
10,000 Thrilled by "Home Sweet Home"
Voice of Silver—Flowers and Kisses for Admirers
—London *Express*.

GALLI-CURCI TRIUMPH
Brilliant London Debut
Singer Stormed by Crowd
Flowers Flung to Audience
—Westminster *Gazette.*

MME. GALLI-CURCI'S TRIUMPH
Brilliant Singing at her First Recital
—*Star.*

10,000 GRIPPED BY SINGER'S SPELL
Mme. Galli-Curci's Great Albert Hall Triumph
Kisses Thrown to Audience from Flower-strewn Stage
—Daily *Mirror.*

GALLI-CURCI CONQUERS LONDON
Cheering Crowd of 10,000 at Albert Hall
Songs in 5 Languages
—Daily *Chronicle.*

MME. GALLI-CURCI
First Concert at Albert Hall
London, or as much of it as could be packed into the Albert
Hall, heard Mme. Galli-Curci sing for the first time yesterday
afternoon.—The *Times.*

MME. GALLI-CURCI
Enthusiastic Reception in London
"She came, she sang, and she conquered"
—The Morning *Post.*

GALLI-CURCI SINGS TO 10,000 PEOPLE
Wonderful Reception at Albert Hall
—*Lloyd's Weekly News.*

GALLI-CURCI'S TRIUMPH
Platform Stormed at Albert Hall
Audience Refuse to Go
—Daily *News.*

A few unprecedented facts: the house was sold out nine months
in advance; three other London concerts sold out six, four, and one
in advance, respectively. Concerts in the twenty-three provincial
cities sold out long before appearance dates, several before local
advertising began. Tickets for London concerts sold at one guinea
(normally $5) each, whereas tickets for other major concerts sold

for twelve shillings (normally $2.90), establishing a new box-office record for England.

Galli-Curci's attitude toward criticism is very liberal—so much so that she pays no attention to it. She harbors no animosity against reviewers of her work, recognizing that they are a necessity to journalism, but thinks that they might show more leniency toward the aspiring musician, especially the singer. She says: "It is unwise for an artist to read, much less heed, either praise or censure. If a singer reads criticisms after a recital, her next will not be a success, for she will be so aware of her shortcomings that it will upset her nerves and she will lose control of her art. The singer under a strain is never a good singer or a great artist. Fortunately, all of us know our faults in our humbler moments and learn to conceal them, but the vocal organs are so delicate that they are not always at their best—then defects cannot be hidden. It is then that the critics begin to ply their pencils with relish. In my operatic beginnings, I was ignorant enough to read all that was written of me. Now, I never do."

The concensus of reviews throughout the tour may be summed up in this statement of the *Daily Mirror*: "It was certainly a triumph which has never been excelled and seldom equalled either at the Albert Hall or elsewhere." The *Tatler* said: "No great singer, not even the divine Patti, has ever had such an ovation as that which was accorded Galli-Curci on the occasion of each of her big concerts. London succumbed a willing victim to the power and charm of Galil-Curci's marvelous voice."

After the first recital she received a green-room call from Joseph Hislop, whom she greeted with "My Romeo! my Romeo!" Bystanders were startled, but the artist's husband showed no uneasiness, for the English tenor had sung Romeo to her Juliette in Chicago several years before.

Fewer things shed more light upon an artist's character and upon the several environments through which she has to pass in the making of a career than the intimate episodes associated therewith. After the adulation and the crowds of the initial recital, it is little wonder that our singer exclaimed, "Heaven save me from my friends!" Not to be unresponsive to such acclaim and to leave an ineffaceable memento of her appreciation, she cut the letters G-C in the bark of a tree in Green Park, which faced her hotel.

Aftermath

On one occasion, while Galli-Curci was dining in the Savoy restaurant, two Italian waiters who had been members of the chorus at her Rome debut sixteen years before, presented her with a duplicate of a jewel similar to the one she lost on that evening and for which they had searched through Italy, holding it for her London coming. Among other queer happenings in the course of her English journeyings was a letter postmarked Manchester and addressed *Madam Galli-Curci, Queen of Song, London.* The letter was delivered.

During October, Galli-Curci visited the Gramophone Company factory at Hayes, where "His Master's Voice" records are made. She was photographed, filmed, recorded. She signed the Golden Book of Celebrities, but did not sing a note, to the disappointment of the 3,000 workmen who greeted her during the dinner hour. Over there they called it "Galli-Curci Fever." London took it first, then passed it along to other cities until it became quite an epidemic. Here is an advertisement from the London *Times* in September: "Galli-Curci. Royal Albert Hall. October 12th and 19th. Loggia, Box, eight seats; £40 each day." There were others of similar kind, offering seats and stalls at unheard-of prices.

A limited time necessitated a limited number of appearances, hence many places in the kingdom had to be omitted. Many of these found fault because so discriminated against, considering it a slight upon their intelligence. A Reading firm took the matter more philosophically by issuing the following announcement: "Galli-Curci Will Not Visit This Town but Records of Her Wonderful Singing May Be Had at the Advertiser's Premises." Another dealer circulated a letter which stated that, whereas all tickets for the Galli-Curci concert had been sold and many music-lovers disappointed thereby, he had arranged to hold a series of thirteen Galli-Curci concerts in his new gramophone recital room. Invitation by ticket only. Enterprising Englishmen, those!

The Liverpool *Post* sized up the situation in succinct fashion with an article captioned GALLI-CURCI RAMP: "When is it going to end? For months past we have been flooded out with some of the most masterly propaganda that has ever heralded the approach of a new star in the singing firmament. Before ever she set foot in the country—which is waiting impatiently to cast itself at her feet—the prima donna has already written extensively in our journals . . . stories have been assiduously put about concerning her. Her picture has been on the boardings for months. Already she is a legend. None in this country has ever heard her sing, but nevertheless everyone knows that she is the greatest musical event of the year. Certainly a tribute to the power of the gramophone and of the press." Not to be outdone, an ingenious London manager inserted this notice in the papers: "The Galli-Curci tea will be held at the Royal Palace Hotel, Kensington, W., on Sunday, October 12, when the lady guests will be given a special Galli-Curci Souvenir."

It may be stated in passing that the tour had been booked by Powell & Holt on the International Celebrity Subscription Concerts. The firm received over 180,000 applications for Galli-Curci tickets covering twenty centers. For the thirty-five appearances scheduled, a guarantee of $135,000 had been given, and notwithstanding the enormous amount pledged, the tour receipts doubled that of any other artist in Britain, while her concerts in the series, everywhere, were almost an individual matter, as the filled houses were due to single ticket purchasers—not to series subscribers—as a result of the gramophone, which made her a popular idol long before she reached the country. "Fame in Celluloid" was one English way of expressing this popularity, which was claimed to cover a gramophone audience of half a million.

The most popular favorite in England, in those years, was Dame Clara Butt, who became almost a national factor there as well as in the colonies, where she received fees larger than any other artist. Fritz Kreisler, too, was a big "draw," also Tetrazzini, who never got less than five hundred guineas an appearance. Galli-Curci broke all records, however, from box-office standards.

Our artist's last appearance, on December 14, was the climax of a tour that set minds a-thinking and tongues a-wagging. It also gave

Galli-Curci a broad conception of national character. Of the places visited she considered the audience at Manchester the most musical, while London furnished the most politeness of all. "Tell the people that I love them very much," she flung from the train window as she pulled out of Waterloo station for Southampton.

And here's a pretty aftermath. From Bray in Ireland came a letter from one who lived in blissful anticipation of her Dublin concert, telling how he had been thrilled by her records and giving this account of a little incident associated therewith: "On a bleak November evening last year, as I was playing one of your records—a kind of bird song with flute accompaniment—five little blackbirds perched on a shrub outside the window listened attentively with little yellow ears, and flew off when the music finished, only to return when it was replayed. I put on several records, but this one of yours was the only one that they repeatedly paid homage to. By comparison, your largest and most enthusiastic American audience grows insignificant before this little array of five tiny music-loving blackbirds."

The party sailed for home December 18, arriving December 24, Mr. and Mrs. Samuels entraining immediately for Minneapolis to visit the Samuels home for the holidays.

Australia

1925—a year that brought more territorial coverage and more ocean travel, necessitating ten months of continuous activity. Beginning January 12 in *Barber of Seville*, Galli-Curci concluded her Metropolitan appearances February 22 in *Dinorah*, then hied to the Catskills for a short respite prior to sailing for Australia; but before leaving the city, she purchased an apartment suite on Fifth Avenue, finding it essential to have a town home during opera season and at other times when she might be in New York. So she indulged in a period of relaxation until the time for leaving late in the month. With Salter, Samuels, and Berenguer, our singer, accompanied by the usual paraphernalia of a prima donna, set off for San Francisco, from whence the party sailed March 3 on the "Ventura."

When Galli-Curci reached San Francisco for the outward journey, she had no thought of singing in Hawaii; but her sailing, as reported in the Honolulu press, at once begot so vigorous an acclaim to have her sing as to cause a cable to be sent: "The whole island wants to hear the queen of song," resulting in an agreement that, if the steamer arrived in time for a mid-day concert, the lady would sing. The vessel's captain brought them into the harbor at the scheduled hour, thereby making possible one of the quickest and most unique overseas bookings on record.

As the steamer approached the island, two delegations sailed out to meet the diva—one from the Chamber of Commerce, the other composed of newspaper men. On the pier, black with people, a band gave musical welcome. Immediately following the landing, on a brilliant South Sea morning, Galli-Curci, dressed in one of her love-liest gowns, was driven through the streets to the Hawaiian Theatre, crowded to the last small space with the native populace augmented by visitors from outlying islands.

Artists of the introvert type probably would not have been inter-ested in racial diversity—but Galli-Curci was an analyst. She wanted to know. It was important for her to familiarize herself with what kind of an audience she would meet at the noonday recital to be given in the Hawaiian Theatre. The people assembled there to hear her in no wise resembled those to whom she had sung in Europe, the Americas, and Britain. These slightly variable divisions of Asiatics were of an entirely different racial character, but any initial fears she might have entertained were immediately dispelled when she saw the crowd of 1,700 that had come to hear the concert.

What! Japs, Filipinos, Hawaiians, buy tickets to listen to an un-known singer from America during a few hours' stopover *en passant?* That is just where an intimate understanding of these peoples and of their lives, their pursuits, their opportunities, proves an aid to one contacting them upon an esthetic plane. A goodly representation from the American colony, including the Governor-General and his staff, perhaps a few English, gave a touch of home to the occasion, in contrast to that strangely unfamiliar sea of faces that wore no masks, to swarthy countenances expressly intelligent, to eyes that glowed with comprehensive pleasure. Again we might evince surprise over the type of music sung—operatic arias and classic songs—hardly calculated to thrill a community way off in the Pacific and out of contact with the world of art. This audience appeared familiar with Galli-Curci's art, with opera and with the masterworks of song. It showed an appreciative grasp on a par with that of continental centers. During the intermission two girls, in Chinese costumes, went upon the stage to decorate the singer and her accompanist, each with a golden flower lei of gorgeous blossoms.

The recital began promptly at noon 'mid sunlight and soft breezes filtering through open windows, only the stage in shadow cast by electric lights. After the event our singer was treated to a motor trip, while the captain held the steamer an hour to afford his distinguished passenger this extra pleasure. As she sailed away, hundreds of voices sang to her the Hawaiian national song, "Aloha Oe," to which Galli-Curci replied with a promise to repeat the recital on the return journey.

En Route

Two events of interest on the way—the ceremonies prescribed for crossing the Equator and the stop at Pago Pago. Galli-Curci, who had contacted that imaginary dividing belt half a dozen times before on the Atlantic, could stand by and enjoy the initiations meted out to Salter, Samuels, and other oceanic neophytes, for until one becomes a member of Neptune's Order he is not rated a full-fledged seaman.

American Samoa, composed of five small islands and a coral atoll, has an area of only 76 square miles. Pago Pago, on the Island of Tutuila, is the capital with a meagre population at the time of 611, yet so great was the interest in the famous singer that a dispatch was sent to the ship requesting a recital under a $1,500 guarantee, which, however, had to be declined.

Now comes the strangest part of the voyage. It was midnight of March 17 when the "Ventura" came up to the "Sonoma" in mid-ocean, going in the opposite direction. When about a hundred yards apart, the boats stopped. Voices called back and forth. For a few moments there was a great buzz of comment as the searchlight of the "Sonoma" swung toward the forward deck of the "Ventura," where, outlined in the brilliant glare, stood two famous travellers—Galli-Curci and Pauline Frederick, one in white, one in black.

Suddenly silence, then a voice floated out upon the muted air. It soared on the tones of "Home, Sweet Home," while a thousand people were transported out of their solemn thoughts to the higher plane of memories. But that was not the object of the stop. While this impromptu song held all in a sweet, calm stillness, a boat put off from the "Sonoma" containing three men in chains and held to silence and obedience at the point of guns by officers. Through cargo doors they were transferred to the "Ventura," unseen, unknown by all on board save the officials—all the rest were too much engrossed in listening to even note the passing of a boat between the steamers. When the transfer had been effected, the vessels resumed their respective courses while the delighted double audience applauded and cried for more. *Au revoir!* echoed through the night as quietly the distance widened till finally only blank darkness stood between them.

As early as January, 1925, Australian papers began the publicity of Galli-Curci's approaching tour, stressing the "importance of her visit as a lesson in good singing." When the box-office at Sydney opened in March, there was a human queue four deep, curling down the street; it had been forming since early morn, headed by messengers who had been in line all night. This interest was continued and grew steadily up to the actual moment of arrival. In other cities where our artist was to visit, the same exceptional excitement prevailed, all following the news of the vessel's progress from day to day. As the "Ventura" steamed up the harbor, a plane circled overhead and dropped a bouquet of roses on the deck addressed to the famous passenger. Flag-bedecked launches swarmed about and a throng of closely-herded living units jammed the wharf over whose heads hung an enormous banner bearing the kindly inscription: WELCOME, GALLI-CURCI.

The official welcome assumed the form of a reception given by Lady Fuller, Mayoress, in the Hotel Australia. On a table was a "Ladder of Fame" surrounded by laurel leaves on a base of pink cactus dahlias. Our artist wore a smart Paris dress of black satin and lace, set off by a black hat. Souvenir programs of the musical numbers rendered in her honor, with her picture, were presented to the guests. The Lady Mayoress' address concluded: "It is delightful to welcome to our continent such a happy interpreter of the sweetness of music, and our dear wish is that her stay with us will be the happiest stage of her life." Galli-Curci replied: "It makes me very joyful and I hope to give you, too, a little joy,"—always grateful and ever eager to repay happiness with happiness.

The Sydney Sunday *Times* carried a three-line caption across an entire page with picture and a special story of the artist's life. The *Sun* gave a first-page spread with photo of Town Hall during the first recital. The *Times* captioned its review "The Greatest of Living Coloratura Singers," and headed its critique "Hark, Hark, the Lark!" describing Galli-Curci as looking like a "proud, white peacock." Little use quoting from the columns of praise bestowed, which in themselves fill a large volume. Over there they called it "Galli-Curci-itis." As in England, Australia was prepared. All had read of our artist and of her triumphant march from place to place. Sydney capitulated, as did Melbourne, Adelaide, Perth, Brisbane, and Wellington. The record of consecutive concerts is astonishingly impressive: Sydney, 9; Melbourne, 9; Adelaide, 4; Perth, 3; Brisbane, 3; Wellington, 6—a total of 34, the more remarkable as no city heard the same program twice and every audience was of capacity size, the last "request" appearance in Sydney, April 14, 1925, following the eight already made. A remarkable feature of these nine Sydney concerts was the $5 scale, averaging $10,000 each. American newspapers commented on the unusual features of the tour and printed items of the homeward trip.

This overwhelming success was not without distressing moments. Immediately upon arrival, a prominent critic called at the hotel to announce that a large gathering had been invited to meet our singer at a certain hall, which function she was expected to attend. Manager Salter objected on the ground that Galli-Curci was tired, that to attend a reception before the recital would be inadvisable and contrary to their established policy, whereat the man took offense, remarked that she would have to suffer the consequences because these sensitive people would show their displeasure by absenting themselves from the concerts. Salter, however, stood firm, the result proving the absurdity of the gentleman's imagined boomerang. This capture of a new and strange territory further demonstrated Galli-Curci's power of allurement, the more particularly as she had invaded the special preserves of Australia's most illustrious Daughter, Dame Nellie Melba.

The farewell concert was described as "unique in the history of Melbourne." The people shouted, stamped, and waved hats, handkerchiefs and programs. Many broke in at odd times with the song "For She's a Jolly Good Fellow," and when a raucous masculine voice called for cheers, there was a deafening response. Time after time Galli-Curci returned, but the crowd was disinclined to leave, even after the singer had given them a speech. Hundreds surrounded her on the stage, but only a few succeeded in shaking her hand. She was bombarded with programs for autographs, some floating down from the gallery. Other hundreds pressed forward to the green-room to bid her goodbye, while another regiment took up positions outside. The universal press comment was that the reception given proved "the greatest accorded any artist," and bookings were of a magnitude hitherto unknown there. Said one reporter: "Galli-Curci has so long been to us a voice out of the darkness that one can quite imagine her as a bird or a spirit." There we have the gist of "Galli-Curci-itis." It was strange for them to find her a living woman—as if a celebrated portrait had come to life.

Particularly in Australia are musical activities strong. An isolated land, yet unlike Hawaii, its inhabitants, aside from the aborigines, are of Anglo-Saxon stock, which consanguineous strain makes for expansive, extensive, expressive world-inclusive contacts. Because of her complete acceptance of English-American ideals and ideas and her adoption of the United States as her permanent home and country, Galli-Curci formed a closer tie with this aspiring race, and with such affiliation seemingly was able to strengthen that tie through the medium of her song.

The Nationality of Soul

Egyptians and Hindoos believe in the transmigration of souls.

Metempsychosis is a tenet of Buddhistic, Egyptian, and Brahminic religions. Where the soul originates, whence it comes and whither it goes, is not given man to know, yet he cannot refrain from speculating thereon or framing a philosophy to cover his imagined findings. Though peering into depths beyond our province or ability to fathom, we wish to emphasize this essential point: one may be born upon a particular geographical spot, surrounded by a particular environment, yet feel that he belongs to another section of the world and kin to a different racial element. He may even feel that his earthly parentage is contra to his own tendencies and character. He may be educated along lines which promise business success, yet switch to another avocation. He may marry one of his own kith and kin and find in other kith and kin a more harmonious relationship. He may be reared to beliefs that, in time, become irreconcilable with his inner intuitions, necessitating revision or rejection.

Galli-Curci was born an Italian, but the Italian was a mixture of Spanish and Milanese. Her schooling, associatons, and early entrance into an activity that required travel and commingling with many races and peoples made for a broadening of mind and an expansion of soul, both intimately associated with her art. No mere idiosyncrasy, no crass hallucination, suggested the idea that she was more Anglo-Saxon than Italian, nor have her repeated and always kind receptions in English territories produced in her any form of Anglomania; on the contrary, it was a most natural consequence, for any life devoted to a universal art and to a universal good must, of necessity, outgrow all limitations of nationality and emerge a composite, most adequately represented by the term Anglo-Saxon.

If a soul could choose where to be born, no doubt it would seek a physical endowment in accordance with its spiritual aspirations. If for vocal or pictorial art, if for science or invention, if for poetry or drama, if for opera or orchestra, if for politics or government, if for travel or discovery, if for any of the innumerable avenues accessible to human urge and industry, it would elect a body indigenous to that territory wherein the specific activity finds fullest expression. Did the soul of Galli-Curci choose such progenitors as could secure a wholesome body in which to dwell and push it forward to a preconceived and predetermined goal? Did the soul of Galli-Curci have an Anglo-Saxon essence with which to transfuse its earthly habitation? Who knows? Should you ask her about her nationality, she would reply, "I was born in Italy because I love to sing—but my soul ancestry is Anglo-Saxon."

Here is a proclamation of Socratic profundity as difficult of comprehension as Christ's pronouncement to Nicodemus that, in order to enter the Kingdom of God, *a man must be born again*. By metaphysics or ontology it might be possible to show that the mind can conceive a proposition so utterly abstruse. By psychology it might be possible to show that the soul is capable of spiritual rebirth. Occultism offers many fields for experiment and investigation, not the least of which is the relationship of art and spirit, of music and soul.

Regarding her Anglo-Saxon leaning Galli-Curci said, "Opera is pompous and stiff. It is not in the Anglo-Saxon's blood and therefore artificial to them."

An article in the *Occult Digest* for September, 1932, "Famous Hands Analyzed," showed a correspondence between Galli-Curci's hand lines, her mental and artistic characteristics, and her life. "The line of fate, the line of life, and the mounts all play their parts, as do the fingers and the spacings. Nothing was added to what we already knew, but the concurrence of the palm disclosures with that knowledge helps us in presenting a full, well-rounded fixity of mind, soul, body, and character nicely co-ordinated to function at the maximum. Moreover, her record shows the greatest and most numerous successes achieved among English-speaking peoples—in Great Britain, Australia, South Africa, New Zealand, Tasmania, Hawaii, Philippines, Canada, and the United States. This preponderance of racial acclaim indicates, on the part of these blood-related folk, something other than love of singing or cultural attainment—an affinity begotten of mutual attraction such as emanates from the association of kindred souls."

Chirography, too, divulged characteristics. In "An Analysis of Handwriting" by May Stanley in 1931, we find: "In the writing of Galli-Curci, the fine, tenuous lines show a degree of refinement almost spiritual, a fact which is again emphasized in the long loop of the capital G . . . displays tenderness and an excessively sympathetic nature in the extreme slope of the writing. Everything she does she finishes perfectly, and the carefully closed a's indicate a spirit of reticence and modesty."

Home

Sailing from Aukland, July 9, en route to Honolulu, the steamer touched at Suva, Fiji Islands, in British Oceanica. With but a six-hour stay during the evening, there was time only for dinner in the environs and a short period of sight-seeing, although the hours might have been utilized for an impromptu concert at the hotel under the auspices of a local club which offered $1,500 for the privilege of hearing the celebrated songstress. So at midnight the steamer cast off and headed for Hawaii, where it arrived on the 18th. Here a halt was made for several days, during which Galli-Curci learned to swim at Waikiki Beach, coached by a native instructor. During this second visit another concert was given, as promised, to the delight of a large assemblage. Continuing the homeward journey. the ocean voyage was completed on August 4, the arrival at San Francisco embellished by a crowd of admirers assembled to welcome home their favored singer.

Back to New York after a five months' absence, having completed a journey of some 30,000 miles. "Sul Monte" was waiting for its mistress, so to the Catskills went Mr. and Mrs. Samuels for a relaxful vacation, to reminisce upon the happenings, now merged with others that, in combination, make the cycle of historic art; to relive the joys experienced, not the least of which our singer crystalizes thus: "Everywhere smiles greet me. Everywhere people are kind. It is a tremendous thing to know that you belong to the whole big world and that it has called you friend."

The 1925-26 season began in October with a tour of the eastern states, a Metropolitan concert at the month's end, followed by another tour through the West and Canada until the opening of the opera season. On November 15, in Orchestra Hall, Chicago, two years after that memorable farewell in Romeo et Juliette at the

Auditorium, Galli-Curci faced another great assemblage and cast her usual spell over those who listened to . . .

"A dazzling agility and accuracy, perfect mastery, delicate ease, ravishing beauty and magnificence of tone, a human and intimate quality—an artist of singular power and distinction— singing that satisfies the deepest desire of the musical sense."
—Chicago *Daily Journal*.

"The people still love to hear her sing and there is no more to be said."—Chicago *Post*.

"A voice one can never forget, peerless, unsurpassed."
—Chicago *American*.

"Returned to gladden the hearts of the many who bewailed her departure . . . revealed again the Galli-Curci who sang her way into Chicago hearts in one brief day eight years ago."
—Chicago *Tribune*.

Publicity plays queer tricks. Here is a "Today's Birthday" item in a Connecticut paper in November, 1925: "Amelita Galli-Curci born in New Orleans, 70 years ago today." Another from Kalamazoo, Michigan: "Miss Galli-Curci, Kalamazoo's native daughter. Former schoolmates will attend in a body. Owing to the fact that Galli is singing in her home town, it is hoped that she will sing 'School days,' 'That Ol' Gang of Mine,' and 'Down by the Ol' Swimmin' Pool,' which are great favorites with Kalamazoo people."

Back to Earth

The forepart of 1926 was devoted to concerts and opera in the United States and Canada, a record season culminating in June with a *Rigoletto* performance in Cleveland—her sixteenth appearance in that city—concerning which Archie Bell wrote in the *News*:

"The empress still sits upon her throne. The queens and princesses cast longing eyes upon it. There are heirs apparent, heirs presumptive, yes, even pretenders. But Amelita Galli-Curci has no equal in the realms of song. At least, not in the opinion of Cleveland.
"There was $30,200 in the house. This meant something over

one hundred admissions over capacity—owing to additional
seats, the audience numbering over 8,000 persons."

After a summer's recreation period our artist resumed her activities through Canada to the Pacific Coast and south to Texas,
then the Middle-West until Christmas; then a holiday interim, pre-
paratory to the Metropolitan Opera in January.

Several interesting happenings furnished a little extra glow for
the now habitual conquests which were reaching into the realm of
commonplaceness, saved only from that fate through our artist's
genius for attracting upon herself the spot-light beams of publicity.
Galli-Curci held the public eye and commanded front-page attention because she was "news" and that means the opposite of "commonplace." One event that aroused considerable interest happened
in El Paso, Texas, where her coming turned even thieves into musicians. While the owner of a valuable violin was attending the
concert, some freebooters acquired possession of the instrument,
together with bow and case, from a parked automobile. Perhaps the
guardians of the law were likewise basking in the shade of the Galli-
Curci lotus tree.

"Adventures 'Round the World" appeared in the Ottawa *Journal*
in December, 1926, in which our singer-author recited the main
events of her life to date, much of the matter being incidental with
that previously used in other articles. But her oral proclamations
proved of greater value to the public, hence were freely quoted by
the press and often commented upon because of their extreme bold-
ness and novelty. While week-ending at Atlantic City, New Jersey,
back in August, Galli-Curci attended a musical comedy, and up-
setting the expected commentary on that form of entertainment,
remarked: "I would rather go to a good musical comedy than to a
grand opera." Enigmatical words from a grand-opera singer, but
they were founded upon logic. "Americans are not opera-loving.
They like musical comedies and I don't blame them. Opera is not
the highest form of art. It is billboard with a lot of colors—just a
show with a little more aristocracy about it. Why bother the poor

people with so much opera? Grand opera is all right for the masses when the masses are ready for it. Right now they need—and I need, too—something to make them forget those little trivial worries which seem so great to all. Musical comedy does this. I like the gaiety of the light shows. I enjoy the fun in them."

That declaration induced an avalanche of questioning surprise. *Knocking her job!* Perhaps, but there was a logical reason for so doing. As a medium of self-expression, opera afforded her no real satisfaction.

Another observation, quite as bold and quite as characteristic, followed. Galli-Curci refused to lend her voice to the air because what she had heard gave so little art satisfaction as to decide her against it as a medium for vocal transmission. She owned a radio set, but its function was to provide amusement for her employees. "The radio," she said, "is undeveloped, is in the experimental stage. Art is half merit and half atmosphere. I do not want my voice affected by static. I refuse to be sandwiched between a bedtime story and a jazz orchestra. I do nothing in which I am not wholeheartedly interested and of which I do not enthusiastically approve. When I make a Victrola record, I do it over and over until it is perfect. I make a new record for the sake of one wrong note. Radio does not give this opportunity; besides, it is perilous to our profession. The people will not be permanently satisfied merely with hearing. I do not believe in rushing into anything. When the radio is improved as to instrument and when programs are arranged differently, I may change my mind. If radio is controlled, I may sing at some later date." She did, in January, 1928; February, 1930; and June, 1934. The first two were on Victor programs, the last on a commercial program.

Her first radio experience was not a happy one. She calls it Big Bad Wolf. Smile, laugh, gesticulate—one can't do that on the radio. Her personality counts for as much as voice. She wants to face her audience. "To broadcast," she said, "is like making love to a wall—one misses the personal touch. I like to see faces, to feel contact with my audience. Broadcasting is blind work. Crooning is a disease, a distortion, a caricature of singing, and it ruins the voice. Crooners will never be able to sing again properly."

Some Side-lights

Music hath charms to upset as well as to soothe. Galli-Curci had been practicing one morning at "Sul Monte." Outside some work-men were repairing the road. After a time, the foreman appeared and inquired, "Is you the lady wot's beein singin' all mornin'?"

"Yes," replied the singer, "have you enjoyed it?"

"Well, mum, it ain't exactly that. I was goin' to ask you if you'd mind not 'anging on to that top note so long next time—my men 'arve knocked off for dinner three times already."

In October, 1926, the editor of a Spokane, Washington, paper—so the story runs—sent a cub reporter to interview Galli-Curci. That was an assignment on a par with attempting to force a way through the Pearly Gates on a busy day. The cub called at the hotel and lodged his request, only to receive the crushing reply: "Madam never sees anyone on the day she sings." "I don't care if she won't see anyone," bellowed the infuriated editor to the quivering youth. "Get the story or don't come back." The cub reflected. "No inter-view, no job—no job, no food—must get interview." He returned to the hotel, tipped a bellhop to show him to the diva's sanctum. He heard her practicing. The "must-get-the-interview" idea had crystal-lized, so he knocked. The lady herself opened the door.

"I am a reporter," he began.

"Oh!" she smiled. "You newspaper men . . . but I will not be interviewed. I am always interviewed. I will change that . . . I will interview you. Come in."

She chatted and talked for two minutes. The essence of what she said, supplemented by facts garnered from her companions, fur-nished the needed material, the gist of which is: "Galli-Curci is an artist. Galli-Curci sings because she must. So great is the artist in her that she must have expression for the greatness of her emotions. That is why she is such a great artist. There is in her this great urge for expression and whatever she produces is art. Her public is something very near to her. She sings to the hearts of people, not to their intellects."

In 1927 rumors were heard of fabulous sums offered for her services—one stating that she had refused $200,000 for a ten weeks' tour of movie houses; another that she might agree to sing at the Roxy Theatre, New York, for a $25,000 weekly fee. Bubbles! A real compliment, however, was bestowed upon her art in January when two English girls, working in a government office, arrived in New York. Three years previous they had attended the London concerts, after which they decided to save and follow to America to hear Galli-Curci in opera. When our artist heard of their sacrificial mission, she presented the girls with orchestra seats for her performances during their three weeks' visit.

Operas, concerts, and travel until July, when Galli-Curci once more was to play a unique rôle. She received an assignment from the Universal Service to cover the Dempsey-Sharkey fight at the Stadium, New York, on July 21, and as a special favor for a Chicago paper. Art and sport? "Yes," says our singer-reporter. "To the artist a prize fight is beautiful! . . . as an exhibition of skill, as a magnificent conquest of sheer physical manhood, as a thing of beauty, as a triumph of the will to do." She valued the sight as an educational thing. The ring faces of the contestants especially interested her, Dempsey's "showing how a man, who can be a gentleman in private life, would look in the prize ring and what a human face can express," as contrasted with the "cocksureness" of Sharkey's eyes. There was more than fighting—there was craftsmanship, skill, strength, rhythm of movement, coordination of muscles, quickness of brain. "What I saw was the technic, so cunningly covered, yet so cleverly displayed. I saw the steady advance of Dempsey, slowly but surely advancing to the goal to which he had set himself—a showing to the world what he could do after the world had thought he couldn't. One could see that purpose gleam in his eyes and that's what won the fight." She also studied the crowd, which seemed to have a national significance just as at the bull-fight in Spain and at the opera in Italy. But the thing that impressed her strongly was the sight of 80,000 orderly, good-natured people. Her final comment in this remarkable sports report was "America seems to stand for law and order."

Still another honor awaited her in September, when she chose a rare, deep, fiery, crimson dahlia to be named after her at the Dahlia Show on the Steel Pier, Atlantic City, where she sang for the first time and where a special arbor was erected for the display.

1927 was brought to a close with another Canadian tour and concerts throughout the East and West, with a Chicago recital, and a Minneapolis concert that drew 9,000 auditors. Who claims that a singer is not without honor in her husband's town?

Another incident, peculiar because of its nervy novelty, but ingenious nevertheless, was that of a small radio station announcing to its audience that "Galli-Curci chooses as her concluding number . . ." which of course was a transcription played from a phonograph record, but presented in such a manner as to lead auditors to think that the artist was actually in the studio.

Opening her opera season at the "Met" in January, 1928, our artist went steadily along until the middle of February, when she was stricken with laryngitis at Charleston, West Virginia, hence forced to cancel several engagements in order to visit her Chicago physician. This is the only time in eight years that she had been unable to fill a date due to illness, for that is something singers must conscientiously avoid. "No artist," said she, "dares risk a chance. When I am billed to sing, I must sing and I must give my audience that which they came to hear—the very best in me. No matter how far I have travelled, I must never be fagged or nervous. I must never get hoarse or headachy or suffer from indigestion. I must always be fresh and radiating vitality. Sore throats and tonsils are things unknown to me and no doctor has ever looked down my throat." But the time comes to everyone when the best intentions prove of no avail and one has to submit to the inevitable demands of nature.

First Radio Concert

January, 1928, marked Galli-Curci's first radio appearance, as guest with the Victor orchestra. This debut was significant in-

asmuch as her managers had persistently held out against all overtures for broadcast appearances and consented to this only as a
special concession to the Victor Company. It is not generally known,
but one of the offers declined was that of a prominent radio manager
who promised to furnish any orchestra desired with any conductor
and pay any sum for a broadcast contract. The radio, however, did
not as yet possess sufficient power of allurement to induce Galli-
Curci's own managers, Evans and Salter, to run any risk with their
artist in a problematic field.

When asked about the possibility of a future radio concert Galli-
Curci said: "I will do it with pleasure for the people who cannot
come to my recitals. It is very difficult to restrain one's voice in a
studio after singing in a large auditorium, but my great idea is always to reach everybody. That is all I can say—maybe once in two or
three years, or perhaps only once. I was really won over for a radio
appearance by hearing how nicely a certain well-known operatic
singer's voice came from the loudspeaker to which I was listening.
Thus I made my decision to sing before the microphone, having
been convinced that it was actually possible to send and receive a
singer's voice over the radio and preserve its qualities."

On January 15 there was a seventh wedding anniversary in the
New York apartment, attended by Mr. and Mrs. J. C. Samuels—
celebrating their own forty-third—and Homer's twin borther, the
sons adding an additional festive touch to the occasion because of
their thirty-ninth birthday. There was a farewell to the season in
March at Carnegie Hall, followed by an appearance at Atlanta in
the Barber.

Still contributing to magazines, Galli-Curci wrote an article for
McCall's on "Choosing a Husband," the sum total of which was:
"A union of interests is, to my mind, absolutely indispensable to a
happy married life." She also gave her views on the proper feminine
figure. She said: "The Venus figure with curves of womanhood must
return. American girls must cease being lengths of animated
spaghetti and regain those curves that are woman's natural birth-
right. I am so tired of no figures on women. I want curves to come

back. I want to see waistlines and hips and bosoms again." This from decorous Galli-Curci elicited wide interest, but her prediction that "women will give up smoking soon" proved erroneous.

One thing we are assured of—Galli-Curci never ran out of topics or was in want of a catch caption. In a rather striking discussion of her activities during the summer at "Sul Monte," under a heading "A Prima Donna Farmer" (in the *Country Gentleman*), she declared "Farming is my pastime." In this interesting article she describes her work associated with house, barns, gardens, dairy, stock, poultry, and grain fields, but admits that she cannot get wholly away from her art. The cows bore the names of Favorita, Tosca, Butterfly, Zaza, Mimi, Louise. Her boss cock was Don Basilio, her sheepdog Fagin, her cat Dinorah. Rhododendron is her favorite flower, and when not engaged without, she likes to knit rugs of clipped wool, but she never cooks. She reads philosophy but no fiction, and advocates young singers "to learn to play an instrument, for it might come in handy if the voice fails."

Oriental Vistas

And now the beckoning finger of the Orient stretched over the Pacific with an overwhelming appeal. A pronounced peculiarity of this polyscopic career is the universal, constant, and extraordinary interest Galli-Curci as a name evoked and the popularity accorded its bearer even when unheard. One might suppose that the drawing power of an artist, appearing for the first time in distant lands and known only by photographs and phonographs, might be hypothetical, the popularity equivocal. But there has never been any such doubt concerning this artist. Years before the Far East trip was planned Galli-Curci's managers had been receiving requests and contractual overtures from distant promoters of cultural entertainment for a Galli-Curci visit, but heavy demands elsewhere made any consideration of an overlong journey impossible because of the time required to accomplish it. Only when solicitations became burdensome was the demand finally acceded to and then only for the following year.

This announcement roused a considerable fuss in newspaperdom.

Withdrawing America's most cherished singer for five months when so many places at home were begging for dates seemed unkind, if not unjust. Baffling is such admiration unless we construe it as a sort of heroine worship, not a blind reverence for some legendary being or artificial adoration of some current idol. The Galli-Curci quality of reverence consisted of something quite apart from the usual brand bestowed upon famous personages. Her hold upon the fancy of individuals, her grip upon the imagination, her power of rousing them to enthusiastic outbursts arose, not from any mass impulse of adulation nor from any irrational desire to do as others do—hers had a far subtler, deeper source, one that springs from spiritual wells and excites the pleasure centers within ourselves without relation to any other person, thing, or circumstance.

There was a magic in her name that defies analysis, a charm in her personality that cannot be defined, a captivating timbre in her voice that cannot be described, and an allurement in the melodic flow of her song that is inexpressible. Galli-Curci was one of those rare creatures whose superb endowments were used to put a little more joy into a world harrassed by care—to give a little more pleasure to those who came to hear her sing.

Announcements of her coming produced in every town and country an effect almost of national significance. Before she uttered a note, officials were ready to hand her the keys of the city, and after she had sung, to award her the town. No returning hero could expect more, yet this honor was not for one of their own but for a stranger, a foreigner. There is only one interpretation of so odd a situation. Galli-Curci was monumentally unique in every phase of her existence—the most unique factor of which was her radiant self, from the glamour of which there was no escape.

One of the potent contributory forces to the growth of Galli-Curci's art was her wanderlust and her skill in applying such acquired benefits to cultural improvement. Constant mingling with peoples of dissimilar dispositions, customs, environments, habits, beliefs, and training in their native habitats, many journeys over wide expanses by land and water, contrasting personalities of divers types, facing innumerable strangers, sensing reactions to the vocal message—all this intimate intermingling with a world-wide population could not have wrought in one so completely attuned in mind and spirit to immutable relationships a state of mind other than ethereal. One thing is inescapable: Galli-Curci knew and understood people and countries perhaps better than they did themselves. Most truly is this so with respect to the United States. From Vancouver to Quebec, from Maine to Florida, from Oregon to Texas, from Southern California to Cuba, she travelled many times, touching at countless inland points wherever railroads ran and people sought diversion along esthetic lines. She knew the land, the customs, the characteristics everywhere and numbered among the citizens more friends than she can ever tell.

"Tire of travel? Not a bit!" she declared. "There is always something new to see, always improvements to note, always old friends to meet, always progress to contact. Bad weather never bothered me. When it rained, I was in finest voice, but always wanted to go out and shake the hands of those who stood in line, perhaps for hours, and thank them for the trouble they had gone through to hear me."

One American invention she appreciated—the railway lunch-counter—which proved a needful friend on many an occasion after leaving a concert-hall and in a hurry to catch a train; the high stool and clean counter were ever a joy whereat to eat her cornflakes and milk. Much of her reading was done on trains and steamers, also considerable sewing and embroidery.

By the fall of 1928 the Orient bookings had been completed so that when Galli-Curci, Samuels, Evans, and Alberghini, flutist, left New York on February 3, 1929, the itinerary embraced twenty-three concerts in Japan, China, the Philippines, and Hawaii. The party embarked February 9 at Seattle, Washington, on the "President Taft," and after a twenty-day smooth and pleasant voyage, arrived at Yokohama. The initial appearances, however, were to be given in reverse order, i.e., beginning in Manila, to antedate the hot season there and escape the yet cold Japan. After touching at Kobe, Shanghai, Hongkong en route, the vessel reached the Philippine capital where four concerts were given in eight days, a fifth having to be cancelled so as to catch the north-bound steamer for Hong-kong.

With a then population of twelve and a half million—all Filipinos except approximately 70,000 made up of Chinese, Americans, Japanese, Spanish, and a few Germans, French, and Swiss—one might suppose it an impossible task to secure sizable audiences for a series of four song-recitals within so short a space of time; but that number was insufficient to satisfy the insatiableness of these people for singing, with audiences sixty to sixty-five percent native.

The press had warned the public to buy tickets in advance because, it said, "there may not be any on the last day," so full houses were assured. A reception in the garden of the Mayor at Santa Mesa was one of the first honorary tributes given for our artist, at which students of the conservatory rendered some Filipino music. There was also a reception by Senate President and Mrs. Quezón at Pasay, at which were acting Governor and Mrs. Gilmore.

The first concert attracted the largest audience in the history of the auditorium—one of international representation, three-fifths of which perhaps did not understand English or Italian; yet the program scheme was not designed with special care, for Galli-Curci never catered to nationality in music, feeling assured that pure music, as a universal language, is intelligible to all peoples when properly presented.

"One doesn't need to know music," said she, "to appreciate it. If you take a picture to pieces, you cannot see its full beauty. If you dissect the petals of a rose, you destroy it. That is why the naturalist cannot appreciate a flower—he is so intent upon the minute points that he misses its fragrant loveliness. An audience should not want to detect or understand technicalities—they are there to be thrilled by the art, and it is our job to thrill them. We cannot be perfect, but we can have absolute sincerity. The whole mind, heart and soul must be given up to expressing the spirit of the song." Her programs therefore always pleased because they were designed to please, first herself, then the public. She puts herself first because, if the numbers pleased her, she felt that they would please the public.

The enormous success of these concerts was noted by the press. Papers carried front-page stories about the audiences, which contained many distinguished persons scattered about the capacity houses. The final concert, on March 15, furnished a brilliant and impassioned climax with a packed auditorium tendering a continuous ovation during the recital, at the end of which Galli-Curci left in a whirl of admiration.

China

Farewells were said amid much cheering and waving, with the concert party aboard the steamer returning the salutes in kind. Hongkong was the next concert stop.

As the "President McKinley" passed into the harbor at night, a thrilling sight was presented to the passengers, enhanced when viewed from a steamer's deck. In the background, mountains with electric-lit encircling drives; above, the ebony sky star-tinselled, cold and distant; below, frail ghostly sampans lolling on the surface swells, their decks strewn with bronzed and scant-clad bodies of the dwellers, who vied and chattered among themselves as they poked upward long poles with baskets affixed for alms to be therein dropped. A floating city without song or joy or uplift. Within these tiny barks recur the cycles of births, marriages, lives and deaths— existence of one dimension occupied with fostering it and nothing else. These miserable folk, forgotten and forsaken, never heard of Galli-Curci, perhaps never heard of God or Love, and never may. They came not to welcome or to honor a famous artist, nor had she come to their demesne to bring them happiness through song, because between the two extended an infinite gulf which neither could bridge nor lessen.

As a race, Chinese are not interested in occidental music; indeed, not even in their own as far as outward appearances showed. No street musicians were to be seen, no native instruments heard. Any attempt to introduce modern jazz in a hotel was little else than a passing gesture; no surprise, then, that natives did not attend the Galli-Curci concerts. Yet it is somewhat puzzling when one considers that these people possess artistic instincts of high order expressed in other arts; evidently they have no adaptability to transfer those instincts beyond their own narrow sphere and in whom the inquiring mind is truly apathetic. Even their curiosity to see an artist of world renown was not aroused, due, no doubt, to certain racial characteristics which for centuries have been developed introspectively, focused more upon the glories of the past than upon progress and culture. Whatever music natives hear or make is but an expression of their submission to Fate's decree—its chaotic cacophany registering an impulsive protest against a destiny they cannot alter or avert, hence for them there is no music message, no ministry of song. A like condition exists on land where the daily grind for mere existence is the sum total of human effort. It would be odd indeed if audiences there were other than non-Chinese. Hence the gathering that greeted Galli-Curci on March 25 was a mere 25% native and that almost all of the younger set. Americans and British were in the great majority, which proportion prevailed in other Chinese cities. Four concerts in Manila and wanting a fifth, against one in Hongkong—nearly four times bigger, numerically. A paradox? No, for the Filipinos and the Chinese are opposites with respect to sensorium susceptibility.

In selecting Shanghai as the third point of contact, the management of the Galli-Curci appearances took into consideration those factors indigent to the territory.

A reception was given in honor of Galli-Curci by the China National Committee of the YWCA and Shanghai Women's Club which afforded our singer a first opportunity to meet native women. The three concerts were given in the Town Hall on March 30, April 3 and 6, but the greatest thrill came with dancing in the world's finest ballroom, with a floor that accommodated 600 couples, built on springs, with two orchestras—one for classic, one for jazz music.

The next stop was at Tientsin. While waiting for a train to convey them to the former capital, a six-year-old beggar offered to sing a song for ten cents. The offer was accepted, which filled the gamin with delight, with the improvised recital caught on a portable movie camera. Galli-Curci was entertained on arrival by naval officers, and the recital, held in the Grand Hotel ballroom, was attended by an audience mostly of foreigners—the native portion of the audience being relatively small. Seats sold for $8, and the event, which took on a social and diplomatic character, began at 10 P.M. The occasion was marked by an unusual circumstance: four hundred tourists from the steamer "Franconia," bound on a world tour, attended in a body, some of whom our artist had met in the States, others who had heard her sing before.

There was much to interest our party in this Forbidden City, with its old Imperial Palace and the summer palace of the Dowager Empress as memorials of an art typical of the old spirit of beauty and a dynasty typical of a spirit that flared up intermittently but never took root.

A three-day voyage across the Yellow Sea brought the travellers back to Japan, arriving at Shimonosiki, where they boarded a train for Tokyo. Five concerts were scheduled for the Nippon capital (April 26–May 19). Advance notices of her arrival, during the preliminary stop and upon her approach for the scheduled appearances, preceded the actual arrival, which assumed the nature of an international welcome. Our singer was greeted by oriental artists of the Imperial Theatre, where the concerts were to be given and where she received one of the most flattering receptions ever tendered a visiting singer. Galli-Curci was presented with huge bouquets and a decoration bestowed only upon notables in the field of art.

Nippon

In 1929, Japan was alert, modern; China somnolent, olden. Japan stood for the present, China for the past, a condition observable in opposite attitudes toward art. The reaction to fine art in Japan was big, expressed in the same big way as in Europe and America. The Japanese apparently possessed an intimate knowledge and understanding of what they heard. No idle curiosity led them to the Galli-Curci concerts, but a desire to listen to a renowned artist with whom they made themselves acquainted. That fact accounts for the amazing interest displayed, which required five full programs to satisfy audiences averaging 2,200 each in a theatre that seats but 1,600. No such up-to-date auditorium is to be found in all China as this Imperial Theatre of Tokyo, well-equipped to serve theatrical performances by the resident company.

For these concerts the programs were carefully planned, preference being given to familiar songs and arias, with the thought in mind that the Japanese audience is oriental by birth, if occidental by education. Hence the appeal was directed less to the emotional, more to the esthetic. Thus we can appreciate the difficulties facing an artist undertaking such a tour for the first time. With Galli-Curci's departure for the final concerts southward, one Tokyo paper said: "Galli-Curci has been the greatest drawing card in musical circles in this country."

> "Galli-Curci's popularity in Japan is so great, indeed, so unprecedented, that she enjoyed a capacity audience and received a splendid ovation. She was in beautiful voice and charmed the whole house with her incomparable singing. She proved herself to be a singer of the highest magnitude."—*Miyako-shimbun.*

> "She is not a mere technician of irresistible sensuous appeal, but an artist of a noble calibre and lofty intellect."
> —*Asahi-shimbun.*

> "Ten years have passed since we devoured the canned Galli-Curci—the Victor records—with such marvellous appetite. How we longed and sighed and pined for Galli-Curci during those ten long years! At last, kind fortune brought us our eternal Love."—*Yomiuri-shimbun.*

> "The fact that the first-class tickets were sold at a premium testifies to what degree the pitch of the public enthusiasm had been raised."—*Jiji-shimbun.*

Kobe, Kyoto and Osaka form a trio of cities where five concerts were given—two each in Kobe and Osaka, one in Kyoto—during the latter part of May. Alas! Such lovers of art, such esthetic instincts have been crushed by war perhaps never the be revived.

Departure from Yokohama was made with a satisfactory remembrance of the pronounced success of the undertaking and with the prospect of another delightful visit to Honolulu, where they arrived aboard the "President McKinley" on June 5, in time for the scheduled concert on the sixth. The tour completed, our little quartet put in several days of rest before embarking for home on the "City of Honolulu," which conveyed them safely to San Pedro—port of Los Angeles—on June 21. With no further ado, they left immediately for the East, where the little family dispersed, the singer and pianist going to the Catskills after a five months' absence.

A New Phase of Art Psychology

From 1929 the Galli-Curci programs showed an attempt to break away from the types standardized over many years of singing. We find numbers of the quieter, classic kind, less of the coloratura display sort, but there was method behind this seeming imprudence. Galli-Curci was laying the foundation for a larger mission of song. There is a significance in this phase of art psychology—a phase that few understood at the time.

The *Evening Telegram* of Toronto caught the trend of her musical thought, expressed in a comprehensive article captioned "Galli-Curci Shows Change," which closed with these lines:

> "Her brilliant warbling in coloratura numbers will always endure, but it is in gentle lyrics of similar sympathy that Galli-Curci's singing will live in the hearts of music lovers the world over . . . The runs and trills were shadowed by something more profound . . . The Galli-Curci of coloratura fame used to set all listening ears tingling with delight. The Galli-Curci of last evening *set all hearts throbbing with sympathy and understanding of a more enduring kind.*"

Here is a digest that contains the gist of Galli-Curci's change in method of approach—an approach to the heart instead of to the ear. *Bel canto* superseding warblings, the impersonal becoming personal, the glow of warmth melting technical coldness, heart-throbs taking the place of wonderment, the woman illuminating the artist, music transforming the medium—in short, Galli-Curci *emerging from a vocalist into a singer.*

Artistic Hornets' Nests

Stirring up hornets' nests is an exciting pastime, provided one avoids the sting. The year 1929 proved to be one for considerable activity along this line by Galli-Curci in her particular domain. She was born to opera, educated to opera, apprenticed to opera. She began in opera, rose through opera. She became one of its most illustrious exponents, one of the greatest of prima donnas; yet she knew intuitively that there was a higher sphere of musical art, a nobler vehicle of esthetic expression, a finer channel of emotional communication. Having thought the matter through, she began to prepare the public for the inevitable shock, the first inkling of which came in a reply to the reported utterances of Mascagni contending that jazz and the modern demand for something new in music were sounding the death-knell of opera. This reply was in the form of an article entitled "Is Opera Doomed?," printed in a prominent newspaper, October, 1929. "We are living, so far as opera goes, on the fruits of yesterday. Today is barren of opera composers of great genius. To listen to a modern opera is to realize it. People attempt to be unusual and end only in being grotesque. I fear the romantic world is finished—imagination no longer counts. The great thing today is to distort. People are afraid to express themselves.

"To reflect our age, opera of the future must be sketchy. We are impatient of anything but brevity. The favorite motto is 'Make it snappy!' Opera is not a pure form of music—it has to deal with human passions and everyday problems. The classics in any art are the result of contemplation. The most beautiful things require the deepest thought. We have no time to think today. We are too superficial to use our brains. If opera is to live, those who make it must delve deep down to find it in the truth. The concert will never go. It is very easy to keep the attention of people with short sketches of sincere emotional or intellectual expression in songs and the appeal of the human voice lives immortal in every heart.

". . . The public no longer cares for opera because opera is a pleasure of the mind, while everyone today makes an effort to drown the mind and seek excitement. What the public wishes is a new form of music which will express new tendencies and new desires of life. The question is whether opera can do this."

To her, a singer is just an instrument, which coincided exactly with her ideas of art; hence the Swendenborg theory that human beings are representations of ideal correspondences, channels through which the higher powers operate in streams of thought, suggested the key to the riddle. She wished to convey an inner peace to the people to whom she sang. This she could not do on the opera stage, which by custom and tradition is the prima donna's paradise and, as such, must dedicate its walls to the echoing of wild applause indicative of that approval which is the diva's due. But Galli-Curci's paradise was of a more ethereal kind. She felt that those who liked to hear her sing valued the gentle ease of her performance. This trend now blossomed forth in the doctrine of correspondences, which gave her the philosophic principle of art she had sought and thereby enabled her to turn that instinct into a concrete idea for use.

Those who compared the Galli-Curci voice of 1916 with that of 1928 found an improvement in *style of presentation*: "Through this," she says, "I think I have become a better artist and I think I have found a greater and more solid favor with the public. I have grounded myself firmly in the conception that my purpose in art is to transmit a soothing calmness and a harmony of soul."

In 1916 the voice was high and lovely; in 1926 it was sweeter and lower; in 1934 it became mellower and richer. As she developed style, she abandoned show. Her later programs testify to this. Year by year and one by one, she dropped those numbers that made for applause, and in their stead put numbers that made for esthetic happiness. Let the younger coloraturas sing pyrotechnics—she would sing the songs that speak to the heart and calm the soul.

Galli-Curci, Mus. Doc.

A signal and rare distinction fell to the lot of Galli-Curci late in 1929. On the day after her concert in Ripon, Wisconsin, Ripon College conferred on the diva the degree of Doctor of Music. In conferring the degree, College President Evans said: "Thomas Alva Edison—Madame Amelita Galli-Curci. These two names have, at this time, by a singular and significant coincidence of Providence, been indited to our minds, and have vitalized our thoughts into reverent esteem. These two names are spoken in all lands, they transcend the barriers and distinctions of race and territory and all lesser differences. They speak a universal language. Their voice has gone out through all the earth, and their fame unto the ends of it. They are alike ministers of the Creator in the service of two fundamental aspects of the human spirit. I refer to Science and Art . . . Madame Galli-Curci also is carrying the great messages of operas, arias and songs into the hearts of men. She, too, is a great, useful world citizen. She feeds the hungry hearts. She heals the wounded spirits. Man does not live by bread alone. The art by which this is done is quite indescribable. Certainly it is not in my power to describe, nor in my conceit to attempt to describe in terms of technic, that which we felt so deeply last night in terms of appreciation."

As a true Doctor of Music Galli-Curci began to move into a higher sphere, unseen by all save those gifted with uncommon perspicacity. Her method of announcing her matured state of mind may have been materialistic, but anything less potent might not have wrought the effect desired. Outspoken, direct, terse, amazing, bewildering—the Galli-Curci way—was her later proclamation concerning opera: "Very old-fashioned entertainment for today—pompous and slow." That set scribes to penning and tongues to wagging. But that was just the opening gun: "Opera is a back number—behind the times—dusty. An artist stagnates in the hallowed old back-stage precincts of the Metropolitan Opera House."

"The opera is not as high a style of music as the concert. The whole world, particularly Italy, is losing interest in opera. The public and the artists alike both feel that it is a little old-fashioned. The modern composers can never write anything to equal the older operatic compositions because such music is not in our temperament in this mechanical age. We have no time for contemplation or for thought. We have no silence. Creative work requires these things. We need fun, and newness is the zest of life. An artist must progress with her times and no beginner should go to the Metropolitan, for the Metropolitan is quite a thing apart. The general fate of all beginners, if they are so fortunate as to get 'Met' engagements, is to be discouraged and submerged for a long period in minor rôles. The better way is to gain fame in smaller fields and come to the 'Met' with a reputation already secured. Americans, for a time, thought they liked opera because they thought they had to accept it from the older countries. They listened so they would be well-educated, but they don't take to it. The people are right—the period for it is past. Now needle-work is an art which will persist as long as there are women. That we cannot say of opera."

Her views on opera were ridiculed. Leaders of opera cults questioned her statements as untenable, called her premises absurd, labled her a sorehead, asserted that her voice no longer responded to demands and had lost its appeal. They even asserted that the real motive was mercenary. That Galli-Curci continued to draw crowded houses and that opera continued to decline is all that need be said by way of a rebuttal.

Again we ask, Is opera doomed? We have seen the passing of opera companies everywhere in America and the closing of opera houses. We have been shown the futility of trying to maintain opera as a luxury and the impossibility of trying to give it economically— hence the collapse of grand opera. Galli-Curci was uttering an immortal truism when she said: "Opera, as we know it in the United States, was a commercial proposition, a materialistic form of entertainment; as such, it did not stand the test of time, therefore could not endure."

Said Lawrence Tibbett in an address at the Waldorf-Astoria, New York, on September 26, 1934: "At present, the American people in general are not interested in opera. Why should they be? They go to an opera house, and what happens? For several hours they listen to singing in a language of which they can understand little or nothing. They see things happening on the stage, but have only a vague idea of what it's all about, except that at odd moments the soprano kicks up a terrific row, the tenor waves his arms excitedly, and the baritone scowls at everyone indiscriminately. They look at scenery, lighting, and staging that would cause Ziegfeld to turn over in his grave. The operatic form as they know it does not intimately touch their inner sympathies. To bring opera really close to Americans, certain changes must be effected."

Opera Adieu!

In January, 1930, the announcement of Galli-Curci's retirement from opera at the end of her short season by consent of the Metropolitan, although the contract had another year to run, created an unexpected surprise. Her action, after a nine-year association with that organization, involved questions of policy, future welfare. The fact that she was abandoning opera for concert stimulated speculative opinions and comic conclusions. Our artist gave her reasons fully and clearly, but they were viewed as an attempt to be facetious, as a peevish fling at the "Met." With respect to her ideas concerning the decadence of opera, it is of interest to recall that Campanini, in 1919, was reported to have previsaged the demise of opera. "What on earth," said he, "is the use of clamoring for new operas when the days of grand opera are slowly but surely coming to an end— grand opera has no future."

Galli-Curci did not consider the opera with which she had been associated as the acme of achievement or the *summa summarum* of art endeavor. "The person who climbs to the top of the mountain and sees no other peak ahead to scale is a desolate figure for whom life holds no future, and I hope I may never see the time when there isn't another and higher peak ahead. Moreover, I was sick of the intrigues of the opera world. Other singers were fighting for my place at the 'Met.' They couldn't push me out of my star rôles, but they said I was so expensive I could not have supporting stars in my casts. I was partnered by lesser known singers. Then the orchestra was cheapened down. At last I saw I should have to descend to intrigue or give up my place. It was a choice between my loyalty and my fame, between security—working out my contract in New York —or chancing a series of concerts throughout the world. I gambled with fate—at a rather critical moment when my investments had disappeared in the financial slump. But I never regretted the choice or the risk."

Let Mr. Samuels testify. "Why save opera? Galli-Curci left the 'Met' because she felt opera a dying thing, and artists must realize that they are struggling with something heavy, obsolete, a form of art no longer meaningful. Galli-Curci is right when she says that radio cannot revive it—the talkies offer no panacea—it has been outmoded."

In an article, "Grand Opera Ludicrous but Lovely," in *Liberty*

Magazine for September 25, 1926, Galli-Curci sets forth her views thiswise: "If you really don't enjoy opera but are just a wee bit bored by it, don't write yourself down a lowbrow. If, after the opening chorus, you begin to count the exit lights, to study the arches of the ceiling or to stretch your legs and doze—don't get an inferiority complex and think that something is wrong. You're right! Grand opera combines two very great arts—the art of music and the art of drama—each one of which is complete in itself. Unite them and one must suffer. It is like breeding together two super-creatures of wholly different species. The result is an incongruous, hybrid growth neither horse nor ass, but mule. All the great operas are tragedies. Everyone dies in the end, and in their dying moments, they always sing. The normal person dies gasping, certainly not lilting arias, and an intelligent audience finds it hard to get the most from the music when it is accompanied by action that is not even plausible.

"Human reactions on the opera stage seem so piteously unnatural. The only place in opera where the acting can be logical is in the mad scenes, as in *Dinorah* and *Lucia*, where the heroine goes insane, where the music, too, becomes mad and nothing is expected to be reasonable. I presume that to most of the public all of our opera scenes seem quite mad. To know any one art at its finest, one must study that art alone, not in combination with another art that divides the interest. Drama is at its best in the theatre. Music is at its best in concert. If the two must be combined, you'll find it most reasonably done in the musical comedies which make no effort to be dignified and therefore are sincere. I love opera because I come from Italy, where opera was born. It is a great national thing there, like baseball in this country. America loves concert much better than opera, for unless opera is superbly done in America, it is absurd."

Passing of the Prima Donna

This attitude of one of the world's greatest coloraturas presaged the ultimate passing of the prima donna and of the primo tenore, and with their egress will also close the era of *bel canto*. The pre-Wagnerian school of opera was entirely vocal. The singers were the whole show. They had to be exceptional. The standard of vocal requirement was high—very high. Singing was technically better, tones smoother and purer, phrasing lovelier. In olden times singers really sang. They had to or take a hissing and a booing from the audience. Great singers were worshipped, lauded, placed upon a pedestal, almost sainted. Their names were household words and passed into musical history as legendary worthies. Horses were not good enough to haul a diva's carriage—her admirers themselves attended to that little service.

With the new order of opera came a new order of singers based on a new order of singing. An unromantic age succeeded to a romantic one. A many-starred era superseded a single-starred. The premier vocalist became one unit in a galaxy of similar units.

Last Performance

A farewell performance of *The Barber of Seville* on Friday evening, January 24, 1930, witnessed the end of a cycle, because it completed a phase of art endeavor with respect to Galli-Curci's Life of Song. Stern realization of this withdrawal from an established status and an honored position in the operatic world, even though in favor of a broader field of operation, would have been emotionally evident in her singing or feelingly expressed in her acting; also that, while the usual glamor of her performance and the usual finely-gauged vocal production were in evidence, there was in addition a highly sensitized coalescence between singer and auditors that put them wholly *en rapport* with each other. Following the "lesson scene," for which our artist had chosen the *Dinorah* "Shadow Song," the applause was so vociferous as to invite an encore, so she seated herself at the piano and sang "Home, Sweet Home," to her own accompaniment.

A farewell to opera! That is what she thought and wished. Now to be free, unfettered, unrestrained! Henceforth to sing when and where and how she pleased, to shout with joyous exultation *The World is Mine!* But wait—the unconscionable Norns willed otherwise. This farewell to opera was to be enacted far from home and terminate in an implacable catastrophe.

CYCLE OF
DISCERNMENT

1930-1934

"Success often proves dangerous
to a weak person. One must
know how to keep one's head."

—GALLI-CURCI

As Rosina, in Barber of Seville. *Farewell Metropolitan Appearance, 1930*

A Curious Fling at Art

NEW CYCLE for Galli-Curci was about to begin—a Cycle of Discernment through adventurous experiment. Hitherto her journey through the several cyclic periods, while not aloof from sorrow and misfortune, had avoided precarious pitfalls, but the supreme experience seemingly required of every life in order to balance and mellow it, now awaited her. The mental, physical and spiritual pain which she was called upon to endure was to be the more distressing because unexpected and unwarranted.

The path of art is never one entirely of roses. Wasps in human form attack the flowers, harassing their growth, often blighting their beauty while thorns of intrigue, scandal and dishonesty abound. No conscientious artist can escape the pricks entirely, many being able to show scars of battles with jealous rivals who work under cover in an effort to render impotent earnest effort and honest endeavor. Galli-Curci was not immune from such contagion. Her American and British successes had travelled across the continent of Europe and there created so great an interest as to be akin to a demand. Besieged by requests for appearances in continental music centers, Evans and Salter finally agreed to a tour embracing Germany, France, Austria, Hungary, Roumania and Czechoslovakia.

Galli-Curci made her second radio broadcast for the Victor Company February 7, 1930, just before sailing with her husband, her manager (Salter), and her flutist (Raymond Williams). With smiles and gladness, our artist bade America a short farewell that she might carry the message of her heartfelt song to sections of the European continent yet unvisited. This tour, extending to June, had been arranged by the foreign manager, Dr. DeKoos, who affirmed that the mid-eastern hemisphere was waiting eagerly to hear this famous singer and vouched for her triumphal march across the map of Europe's musicland. The specific points on the itinerary were those of cultural importance in Scandinavia, Holland, Germany, Belgium, France, Switzerland, Austria, Roumania, and Hungary, wherein she could test her plan and inaugurate her policy of proclaiming music's message direct rather than through the theatrical medium of opera. But this desire was thwarted, due to the insistence of the agent upon three appearances in opera in Budapest, which request was granted against her wishes and contrary to the judgment of her managers.

Disembarking at Plymouth, the concert rovers sped to Prague for a recital on February 17. As anticipated, the recital was a stupendous success, and our singer was tendered one of the most ardent ovations of her career by a house that could neither contain itself in fervent outbursts of acclamation nor hold all those who hoped to enter. By the unbiased opinion of auditors and press, Galli-Curci never sang more enchantingly, never roused more genuine enthusiasm. This circumstance, together with the excited interest displayed by the public and the overwhelming reception bestowed, ought to have augured well for the tour—but adversity crashed down unexpectedly to turn it into gall.

In confirmation of her success, the following cable was received in America from Prague February 17, 1930: "Amelita Galli-Curci opened her first tour of continental Europe here tonight in the great Lycerna Auditorium, which was filled to capacity. More than 1,000 standees joined the seated audience in a tremendous ovation for the diva. Fourteen encores in addition to numerous recalls were demanded by one of the most enthusiastic audiences ever assembled in this city."

Nevertheless, after the concert a dispatch was released conveying an opposite and erroneous report to the effect that the appearance was a failure, that the artist sang badly, that she was not as good as reputed, and that the fees demanded were far in excess of her value. This dispatch, said to have been instigated by another singer, was wholly unknown to Galli-Curci and Salter until the effect began to register in various ways.

All might have gone well and the episode been forgotten had Galli-Curci not caught cold en route to Bucharest (necessitating a long rail journey southward), which became more stubborn as the hours passed, refusing to respond to first-aid treatment. A laryngeal disorder followed which became so acute as to positively prohibit singing, and the concert in the Roumanian capital was cancelled, to the disappointment of the many who had purchased tickets, although somewhat appeased with the promise of a return appearance after the Budapest engagement. But that promise was destined never to be fulfilled. The party therefore retraced its route back to the Hungarian metropolis, which it found antagonistically minded and disinclined to grant Galli-Curci the customary courtesies due to any celebrated visitor.

In contrast to other appearances, Budapest had demanded operas instead of concerts. Galli-Curci's program therefore involved the singing of three rôles with which she had been successfully identified in the past—Violetta, Gilda and Rosina. Upon arrival, however, her throat was still unfit for use, so it was decided to send the singer to a sanitarium in the mountains outside the city for a recuperation; but the first performance day dawned with the lady unready vocally to undertake the task. The local manager, pleading a sold-out house, because of which cancellation was impossible, secured the singer's consent to appear with the understanding that her condition would be explained to the audience—which promise, however, was not carried out by the manager.

Under the circumstances, Galli-Curci performed surprisingly well. The auditors accepted her vocal offerings with apparent satisfaction and pleasure, although not apprised of her vocal ailment. The press, however, turned sour and vindictive, harping on the large sum of money paid to a rich singer when their own artists were hungry and many of their people committing suicide because of poverty. This journalistic attitude, according to Salter, only served to inflame the damaging reports sent out from Prague, which by then had penetrated into the territory to be covered by the tour. The unfortunate cold was the one thing needful to abet this calumnious propaganda, for Galli-Curci could not do justice to her art and thereby counteract the deceptive statements concerning it, inasmuch as the refractory vocal cords and infected throat persisted in rebellious resistance against even expert treatment.

Reports of her alleged vocal incompetence circulated throughout Central Europe, particularly in Austria and Germany, where not only were the fees criticized as exorbitant, but the singer discredited with attempting to cash in on a manufactured publicity about a mediocre talent. The Budapest papers, caught in the anti-Galli-Curci whirlpool, concocted erroneous accounts of her performances, even stating that in *Rigoletto* she had been hissed off the stage, whereas it was an unfortunate Italian tenor, suffering from nosebleed, who was obliged to retire. Aside from this, no anti-demonstration occurred—a fact attested by Salter, who sat throughout the entire performance noting carefully the public attitude and the singing of his charge.

The second night safely passed, artist and manager began to breathe normally once more; but again the enemy struck through further dispatches asserting that most of the audience had demanded their money back—grossly imaginative, since no money was refunded by the box-office. Some of those disparaging messages went so far as to say that there were numerous local singers better than she, willing to take the rôles at small remuneration.

A congestion of the throat meanwhile developed which, with the accentuated nerve and mental strain, made it imperative to cancel the third performance; whereupon Galli-Curci left for Vienna in hopes of being able to meet her future scheduled dates. The substitution of another Rosina proved an amusing contrast in that $8,500 of Galli-Curci tickets were refunded and the performance was given to a $53 house.

In Vienna, our artist was examined by the noted specialist Dr. Friedrich Hanzel, who gave out the statement that for Galli-Curci to sing within three or four weeks would be impossible, and advised a rest on the Riviera. Both Salter and Samuels agreed that to attempt a revamp of the schedule and combat the antipathetic prejudices in other cities, the better part of valor would be avoidance of further illness and excitement by returning to America forthwith. The Vienna concert was abandoned and the tour dates cancelled, enabling the party to catch a steamer for home on March 18. This provoked an aftermath equally distressing and absurd. Ignoring the physician's statement, papers continued to pervert and persecute, one journal printing a three-column headline: *Galli-Curci Scandal in Vienna*, with similar public-voiced invectives in Berlin, Amsterdam, Paris, and other points of the itinerary, distorting the truth with claims that she had sung in Vienna and that her concert was a notorious fiasco. Nothing could be gained by contending against such determined hostility for which, no doubt, the political situation at that time was responsible. There was resentment abroad toward American artists with great drawing power, who commanded large fees, a circumstance that was made the basis of the preliminary attack. That the public concurred in or abetted this policy was disproved in the large advance sales and in general interest everywhere manifested.

"I am sure," said Galli-Curci, " that my singing in Prague and Budapest was quite up to my usual standard—and yet what Americans accepted apparently was not good enough for them. Why?"

That *why* involves a quality character peculiar to certain countries—one based on both national and local prejudice and jealousy, both racially imbued. Galli-Curci's world-wide reputation was made principally in America and Britain. Europeans perhaps had purposely forgotten her Italian origin and her Italian training, covering her first twenty-seven years of life. Her successes, during the next fourteen years, her marriage to an American, her avowal of allegiance to the United States and her adoption of its customs, manners and thought, were evidence sufficient to set the stamp of Americanism on her which, at that time, Europe apparently was not ready to sanction and condone.

What a reception for a new cycle entrance! What a future to face if the new order was to be so ignominiously smitten! What a choice, if only to be ingloriously expunged! How was it possible to ward off the tidal-wave that rushed upon this "rich American singer coming

to take money from poor Europeans,"—overlooking the fact that
Galli-Curci took a tremendous financial risk, as most of her appearances were on a percentage basis and the scale of prices no
higher than that used by other artists of equal repute; yet Budapest
papers considered such fees excessive and censured the visitor "who
wanted their money." Some papers laid the blame upon the singer's
shoulders, charging her with being afraid to appear and accusing her
of having trumped up the cold pretext. Excuse it as we will on any
ground, the evidence condemns. That the intentially-aroused anti-
pathy proved a recoiling boomerang for Central Europe became
actual, since no subsequent opportunity was ever given to hear this
accomplished vocalist, acquaintance with whose art must now be
gained, if at all, from records and from books.

After so distressing an adventure, made more emphatic by its un-
righteous origin and more keen by its concluding forfeiture, a period
of retrievement was in order. Anyone unjustly charged and perse-
cuted becomes exceedingly conscious of the hurt and does not
quickly or easily dismiss it. How strange is life! To think that Galli-
Curci's last appearance in opera should have been amid such in-
glorious surroundings after the brilliant Metropolitan farewell. How
uncompromising is fate! To think that she was forced to make so
calamitous an exist, though with dignity and honor, in the very rôle
with which she first delighted an opera audience—Gilda—separated
by a twenty-four-year interval.

So to the Catskills and to a life of gardening, reading, golf, swimming, with practice and sweet forgetfulness. Another duty, long
deferred, was catching up with correspondence and business matters and wading through a multitude of published songs and manuscripts awaiting calm perusal. At home her favorite sport is golf.
"In playing it," she declares, "that little white ball for the moment
represents the world. To hit it properly has become the single,
solitary aim in this mortal life." To her everything has an inner significance—even a little white ball. "In golf, the mask of civilization
is dropped and the real self . . . stands boldly forth. Golf develops
the benignly human in us . . . it means a lot as training in mental
concentration. Golf is refreshing. If one lets out energy, it is con-

structive; to keep it in is destructive. I believe in silence—the silence of a Scotsman in golf."

During the intermission from concert work, Galli-Curci evolved a new philosophy, the *Philosophy of the Outward* or the *Worship of Beauty*, which she sets forth briefly thus:

> "Man must learn to fall in love outwardly. Yet we must not be impressed with things from the outside. Man is no longer satisfied with what he finds of humanity within four walls nor with what he finds in the four walls of a church. Modern music and painting have no beauty or truth because they deal with the outside—the big hurry, the machine, the dollar. They have nothing for the inside of man. Dollar civilization has to do with externalities—the inside of man is forgotten. Americans must learn to love to watch the rose open—to think of nature as something that lived hundreds of years ago—a prehistoric monster. Americans are like little children. Some day they will be glad to abandon the worship of the machine and the dollar and go back to nature. Some day the *Worship of Beauty* will be the religion of Americans. They must become aware that in nature lies all the truth and beauty in the world. God is in beautiful music, poetry, the sunset, the plant, the flower. Art that even reflects externals is not for us who live in a world of melody."

No pantheist is she, no iconoclast to upset beliefs, but a votary of Beauty freed from the materialistic touch of man.

And so the Summer passed, and with the Autumn began the preparation for a second British tour, fraught with curious conjectures as to the particular states of mind English critics would disclose and the particular states of mood English auditors would reveal. Philosophically as ever, Galli-Curci applied reason instead of speculation. Well she knew that audiences really constitute the prime factor in molding musical thought.

Off to England

Galli-Curci sailed from New York October 3, with Samuels, Salter and Williams, and on arrival at Southampton, proceeded at once to Newcastle for the opening concert, thence on an extended tour with London at the closing end, the middle of November. Any misgivings she or her companions may have had as to the kind of reception awaiting her, were immediately dissipated, for the receptions proved even more hospitably cordial than before.

An enterprising Birmingham gramophone merchant, on the occasion of Galli-Curci's visit, issued an artistic folder with colored portrait of our artist and listing her records under the caption "These Masterpieces of Vocal Art are ready for You!" Forty-four selections from her repertory, principally choice opera arias and song gems:

> "Why not retain the memory in your own home of the phenomenal vocal performance you heard last night? Encore! Last night you would have liked the great coloratura soprano to sing to you over and over again. Surely this was the most wonderful concert ever brought to Birmingham. Everyone wonders will she come again? She may—she may not, but her voice will always be available for your pleasurable entertainment. Galli-Curci can sing to you in your own home, entertain you whenever you wish. Her voice is yours to enjoy for the asking. Last night in public, tonight—take Galli-Curci home!"

Galli-Curci found England, Scotland and Ireland earnestly friendly, eagerly ready to receive her art. Seemingly, during her absence, music-lovers had learned to appreciate her, learned to love her, learned to value her. She became the accepted Queen Regent of the Kingdom of Song. So individualistic a person could hardly be mistaken for another, but as everyone appears to have a double, Galli-Curci found hers in a no less notable—the great Anna Pavlova, whom she met in Liverpool. The resemblance was so marked that, in a picture, they might be taken for sisters. Later, in London, where both were well known, the singer was indeed mistaken for the dancer. These two interpreters of two similar forms of art had another mutual relation—each a leader, each an adept, each a nonpareil, each a sovereign in her own sphere, while both possessed that singular grace and charm that grips and holds us enchanted in a world of wonderment.

Of this tour it is sufficient to note a duplication of the first, with swarming crowds and boisterous adulation and perhaps more circumspect reviews, those of London in particular. Singing to an audience of 9,000 in the Royal Albert Hall—her sixth in that huge auditorium—on November 16, Galli-Curci was accorded an ovation that will be ever memorable:

> "The crowd stormed the platform, men throwing hats in the air, and Galli-Curci was nearly lost amid flowers."—*Daily Sketch.*

> "So enthusiastic was the audience that she gave over a dozen encores. At the end there was a wildly enthusiastic scene, men and women stamping and shouting their applause."
> —*Daily Telegraph.*

> "Seven thousand women of all ages and types were spellbound . . . All sat bewitched for two hours by the golden voice of Galli-Curci, who never faced a more rapt audience."
> —*Daily Mail.*

And the provinces, too, responded:

> "It was easy to understand how Galli-Curci has won triumphs . . . for the magic of her glorious voice, the fascination of her singing, and the apparent ease with which she obtains her effects, are among the most impressive things the concert platform can offer."—Brighton *Standard.*

> "The most remarkable soprano of her day and generation."
> —Yorkshire *Evening News.*

> "She held her audience in the grip of varying emotions, excited by the charm with which she appeared to live the words and melody her voice was interpreting."
> —Bournemouth *Daily Express.*

> "As an executant of the bel canto method she stands on a pedestal alone."—Bournemouth *Times.*

> "Here was lyrical beauty of a golden voice, mellowed sweetness, melody unalloyed."—Manchester *Dispatch.*

> "Deservedly brought down the house by the sheer power of her art."—Newcastle *Chronicle and North Mail.*

> "The respect in which Galli-Curci towers above contemporaries lies in the amazing flexibility of her voice."
> —Dundee *Advertiser.*

"She is probably the greatest and most popular coloratura soprano who has graced the concert platform and the operatic stage for many years."—Belfast *News Letter*.

"She remains the finest coloratura singer of our age and generation."—Dublin *Irish Times*.

One of the most notable of her London appearances was that at Alexandria Palace, wherein Germans were interned during the war, and where, on this occasion, stood the largest audience recorded in the history of the building.

Another remembrance of this memorable tour—old *mal de mer* —set its clutches on our prima donna and that while crossing back from Ireland. Due to severe and unremitting gales, the boat cut up inconsiderate seaway capers that brought on illness followed by a chill. This made impossible the scheduled appearance at Middlebrought, but Galli-Curci recovered in time to sing her final concert at Reading before sailing December 9 for America.

An Expansive Year

1931. The most fully-expanded year of all, for it witnessed the full-blown stage of her career with the largest number of engagements constituting a sequence of ninety-one concerts extending into 1932. Galli-Curci began activities by contributing a syndicated article "Sports Make for World Peace" to the *Public Ledger* Syndicate, the purpose of which was to show that "everything we do is better done if we are physically fit." As mediums for this acquirement, she recommended golf, hiking, swimming, dancing, tennis, gardening, horseback riding. In Florida during a short vacation, she was of course the target for cameras and questioners. Asked for an elucidation of her operatic abdication, she replied: "I cannot stomach longer the ludicrous dramatic situations of opera—and the coloratura gets the worst of them. There are only five coloratura rôles and always they throw them back at you. It takes so long, so frightfully long, to get to the 'Mad Scene.' When you are twenty, you want to sing opera. When you are older, you learn. I love this concert work. I am my own boss. I come and go. I choose my own seasons. I believe the human voice is at its best when accompanied by the piano or a few string instruments. No one really sings in opera —you just make loud sounds. The orchestra drowns out the voice and the situation becomes a matter of quantity rather than quality. My preference is for the orchestra, which is the highest type of music art."

Ormond and John D. Rockefeller provided another situation early in January that publicity hounds took full advantage of, and later spread their pictures country-wide. When the oil magnate was introduced to Galli-Curci, he exclaimed: "Bless you, bless you! I have enjoyed hearing you sing so many times and I am very pleased to have the pleasure of knowing you. I found these violets and sweet peas at my plate this morning and they made me think of your voice." He had attended her concert the evening before, so presented our singer with the bouquet and added an inscribed photograph together with a famous Rockefeller dime.

Always front-page copy, sometimes commanding an entire page, as in the instance of the Columbia *Missourian*, which carried the overflow of Galli-Curci news onto the second page. Herein is a puzzling paradox. Do people flock to concert halls when others do and stay away when they no longer feel the urge of curiosity and turn to something else? Art is commercial, but, says Galli-Curci, "Selling the voice is a very different proposition from selling merchandise. The biggest factor is creating a listening market, holding that market, and extending it. The secret of such endeavor lies, of course, in the belief that one has something to give to the world, whether that something be a voice, an invention, business ability or literary skill, and naturally, behind the merit of the goods offered for sale, there must be the belief in their genuineness. That gift for entertainment must bring pleasure or profit or comfort to its ultimate consumer; otherwise, it will earn the reputation of being a cheat. But given something we know is genuine, that is fine and real, and given confidence in that thing, there is no limit to the happiness we can offer the world or to our own success."

"Did you ever consider what a singer would be without an audience?" she asks. "An audience is an integral part of a singer, for after satisfying himself that he has done his best, he wants everyone else to hear and be satisfied. An artist without that is not a complete person. Therefore when I speak of my audience, I am speaking of a part of myself, for so I consider them . . . Meeting my audiences personally is another thing I love—not the mere greetings from the platform, but the actual shaking hands with the people who have heard me. This happens most frequently on tour, in towns where people are starved for music and eager to know something at first hand of its personalities. People are still worshippers of individuality in spite of the tendency toward a standardization and mass action. Consequently, when some artist of whom they have heard comes to their town, they long to know that artist personally, even if only to the extent of shaking hands and begging an autograph. How they touch my heart! these wistful people who come behind the stage to press my hand and murmur a few words.

"I have come very close to many individuals of my audience. This is not a tiresome bore to me but a refreshment and a glory. How can an artist say sincerely that he loves the audiences which come to bask in his art, and then scorn the individual members who, after all, merely want to express a deep appreciation?"

Queer letters pour in upon public figures and famous artists and Galli-Curci had her share. Many filled with pathos, many requests for help, for autograph pictures, for appointments, auditions, advice and funds. To one and all she lent an interested ear, for she was ever a sympathetic human being. Many of the letters came from children ventilating their joy, in artless fashion, over her singing.

On February 8, 1931, Galli-Curci was greeted at Chicago by a massive audience on tiptoe with anticipation and responsive to her gifts. Said Eugene Stinson in the *News*, "This beloved creature holds a unique place in contemporary music. Almost every artist, and almost all art, represents that restless spirit in man which strives to offset unsatisfactory realities of life acknowledged. In her the strife is at an end, for a singularly pure artistic vision had looked through the appearances of experience and caught sight of something behind them. Her singing is both miraculously serene and miraculously affecting. It is so because it has caught hold of what art originally only aspires to and because what art commonly holds to be only ideal, is, in it, actually fulfilled.

"The great power of the human voice is that it is the testimony of one's convictions. Galli-Curci wields this power with a transporting beauty of tone, through whose silken translucency there shines a candor of soul as from another world. Curiously reassuring it is, yet too human to fail of intimacy with every heart that hears it. Somehow it wakens in the memory an echo of the relinquished innocence of youth which knows that life is promise and which dreams, as youth does, that this dream of youth is mysteriously realized."

South Africa

As the years roll by, come birthdays to be celebrated, so with the advent of November 18, a forty-second anniversary was observed *en famille* at Harvey Samuels' home, in Minneapolis. Following this event the concert season was resumed until January 30, 1932, on which auspicious day our trio of music couriers embarked for Capetown, South Africa, where the first concert was given on the 26th to the delectation of a tremendous audience, graced by the presence of Governor-General, the Earl of Clarendon and Countess Clarendon, Deputy-Premier General and Mrs. Smuts, Sir Lionel and Lady Phillips, Count Labia with members of the Italian Consulate, also many prominent musicians and persons of the Peninsula. As another tribute to Galli-Curci and her art, the Countess Labia gave an *At Home* at the Cape Town Royal Italian Legation attended by 200 guests. Of this first visit the Capetown *Times* said: "It is much to have a name that is world famous—it is even more, in a new country, amid unfamiliar surroundings and with an equally unfamiliar audience, to magnificently justify that name. Galli-Curci's first concert will remain as a notable event in the history of musical South Africa."

A new country, unfamiliar surroundings, unfamiliar audiences— yes, but only so territorially, surfacely, objectively. As our artist has often said, people are the same the world around if you can but reach their hearts, and here she found the response that confirmed her belief in a congeneric bond between her Anglo-Saxon disposition and her Italian birth. It was no surprise to her that this distant land should give her warm and hearty welcome for, after all, it was merely two big souls in an initial contact, two big hearts beating in unison—a country that responded to her art in the same way as did Australia.

A distinctive feature of this concert series was the excellence of the reviews, which displayed both musical understanding and keen discrimination, vocal knowledge and acquaintance with the literature of song. From Johannesburg came this *chef d'oeuvre* of repertorial art—a special paragraph in the *Star*, under the caption "Art of Accompaniment": "Contrasting moods and styles followed one another in quick succession, stressing the artistic adaptability of the great soprano. Galli-Curci's is a remarkably versatile brain. The widely differing qualities of an English folk-song and of an elaborate operatic aria present to her no problems either in significance or delivery. She is authoritative in an early 17th century Italian ditty as she is in the complex partsong of modern Germany. Then there is the singer's charming stage manner and graceful personality—big factors, truly, in the musical atmosphere that characterizes a Galli-Curci recital."

How neatly expressed is this same reviewer's tribute to Homer Samuels: "Like all master accompanists, Mr. Samuels has developed an ironbound specialization . . . As an accompanist, he is of vastly different stature. It is true that his wonderfully finished work in this capacity is apt to be overshadowed by the vocal achievements of the singer, but it is precisely such a standard of perfection in song delivery that makes possible the kind of accompaniment with which Mr. Samuels is identified . . . The singer does not lead and the accompanist does not follow, so that the listener gets the benefit of a complete fusion of ideas through a perfect ensemble. Such song deliveries are, in fact, models of an ideal co-operation between voice and instrument, each part independently controlled, but directed to a single and predetermined end. Every mood and color in the voice is fastidiously reflected by the piano, making possible a dynamic range and a degree of tempo inflection usually associated with a Kreisler. The audience last night was again roused to admiring enthusiasm."

To conclude his estimation of Galli-Curci, "C.A.O.D." wrote a special article which is worth a full quotation:

"The Essence of Great Art

"Having heard Galli-Curci at each one of her recitals, it is possible to assess her vocal endowments and her many musical graces with some confidence. Neither her technic of voice production nor the voice itself in its quality, range or power is the supreme factor in keeping her in the high place that she has maintained in the ranks of great singers. Unlike a great many with unusual vocal gifts, Galli-Curci's strength as an artist lies as much in her musical intelligence and in her extraordinary sensitiveness for beauty in those finer things of interpretation which seldom penetrate the consciousness of the ordinary concert singer.

"Probably no contemporary singer can be more scrupulously the artist in such illusive matters as phrasing, tempo and vocal color. Galli-Curci's effects are strictly within the duration of the notes as they are set down, and she neither lengthens nor shortens even a semiquaver rest by a hairbreadth. Then there is the precise beginning and polished ending of a Galli-Curci phrase. Behind all this undeviating exactness is the mind of a subtle interpreter, so that the delicately poised flight of those carefully measured, or rather sensed, phrases has always a fluent grace of movement.

"Beyond this is the problem of word and mood coloring, in which respect Galli-Curci is unapproached by any other singer heard in this country for a quarter of a century. Her vocal method is entirely opposed to strain or force, and the resulting technical freedom gives her command of a variety of color between her softest *pianissimo* and its relative *forte* as subtle as it is eloquent. This factor in her singing is tempered by that rarest of musical gifts—a sense of tempo inflection. Very few of the world's great artists, vocal or instrumental, can claim the gift of an inborn feeling for the intimate refinements in rhythm to the point of controlling a deeply felt rubato.

"These factors in singing are apt to escape the attention of the casual listener, but they constitute the difference between performance and interpretation—between fine singing and great art."

Mutual Esteem

In return for the gracious hospitality tendered her visit, Galli-Curci was glad to contribute her services on behalf of the musicians and the symphony orchestra fund, appearing with the City Orchestra at City Hall during luncheon hour, which some 2,000 attended —many city typists and clerks who gladly sacrificed their sandwiches and tea to hear a voice that had thrilled a world. It was an audience such as this artist had never faced before—a heterogeneous multitude but nevertheless awed and captivated. There was a lame man who had limped down from the hospital and, from a rear seat, listened intently though obviously in pain. There was a man, deaf in one ear, who adopted a reclining position across two seats and made an ear-trumpet of his hands. Another in overalls stumbled awkwardly into the hall to associate with the curiously motley crowd. Here is a finely-chiseled phrase from the Sunday News (Bulaways): "One does not criticize a voice like this. One is grateful for it."

These points were noted by those who heard Galli-Curci for the first time in person: (a) gramophone records tend to flatter; (b) Galli-Curci is likely to be remembered by posterity for her superb control and technic; (c) her platform deportment is charming and makes her better than her most brilliant record. Why waste words on peccadillos. "One does not critisize a voice like this!"

At Johannesburg the third concert was subjected to several little touches of delicacy that always serve to put an audience at ease and lift the tension from formality. On this occasion a young man occupying a platform seat behind the singer, after she had turned about to sing directly to this group, became the hero of the hour by retrieving a pearl which had fallen from an ear-ring and, with well-timed adroitness, presented it to the owner. Occupying middle-aisle seats, a girl in pink with an elderly woman in green, created something of a diversion by rising to applaud every time the artist left the stage.

At the final concert in Capetown (April 25, 1932), there was an interruption that might have been taken for a tribute or otherwise. With the singer, flutist and pianist set for the rendition of the

"Pretty Mocking Bird," suddenly there was a sound of revelry from a military band outside the hall breezing merrily away, unconscious of the interruption but accepted by those inside as a serenade. Galli-Curci smiled, saluted, and waited. The opposition finally blew itself out and moved off, leaving the atmosphere free for the voice of the mockingbird to fill. Finally up the Zambesi River with crocodiles disporting alongside. The natives, photographed with Galli-Curci, evinced no interest in posing with a famous singer until they had been paid a fee to have their nudity registered on the little movie camera. Monkeys were more appreciative and quite sophisticated. On a little island in the river, where a picnic was held, hundreds of tiny simians jumped out of the trees and joined the party, so tame that the boldest came up close and took the proffered biscuits, which they nibbled at in great contentment.

This quotation is from an article in the Natal Mercury of March 24, 1932, entitled "From Music Teacher to Prima Donna": "Audiences today, I find, are often extraordinarily sympathetic and appreciative. What the artist likes to feel when performing is that the Spirit of Music is with the audience. A musical audience brings out the very best in a singer. It is my experience that one cannot help responding to the wave of sympathy from an audience that so engulfs one that one's own voice seems an impersonal thing. One's body has become the vehicle from which the spiritual ecstasy of the entire audience is being poured forth. By singing you open the heart, let in joy, and find solace and content. Everybody ought to sing."

Australia Again

Came May, and with it a long sea journey through the Indian Ocean to Melbourne, which the party reached on May 26, to renew acquaintances holding over from the previous visit and to gain new friends—not a repetition of former happenings and triumphs, but a continuation of them with the same deep affection for herself and the same fair estimate for her art.

Among other places visited was Hobart, capital of Tasmania. That a singer should wish to chance it in so small a community would seem inadvisable, but Galli-Curci knew her clientele, and as the smaller American cities gave her audiences of most creditable size, so did the smaller places of the Commonwealth.

Not to be entirely cut off from home, in early May there appeared in America a *Public Ledger* syndicate article, "True Happiness; A Definition": "Happiness is getting what one looks for as the greatest thing to have or do in life." But this definition has a corollary. "It would not be well or wise if all had the same ideal and goal—that would only cause a huge blockade. Fortunate that there are so many notions as just what constitutes true happiness. Yet the fascination of the world lies in this amazing variety of ideas which spur on ambition to achieve. As time passes most of us progress in our ideals of what makes happiness. The trivial is no longer desirable. We reach for bigger things. *My greatest joy is to sing!*" So she evolved a creed which sustained her through her entire career: "Happiness is making a living by doing what you want to do best."

The Hobart *Mercury* gave its readers of June 29 this information: "It is not difficult to understand why the famous singer should enjoy this unbounded popularity. She has also gained, through an increased sense of style, a refinement far beyond what was shown before, and a dignity beyond measure." From Perth comes this tidbit of July 10: "Time has not frayed the flutenotes nor dimmed the matchless artistry of Galli-Curci," and this of July 11: "The liquid music of her voice is as beguiling as ever." Brisbane adds her tribute thus in the *Daily Standard* of July 29: "Those who remembered the charm of Galli-Curci during the year since she last visited Brisbane fell anew under her spell. The great soprano employs her voice with an artistry that amazes and enchants," and the *Sunday Mail* of the 31st added: "The fact that she left the vast audience clamoring for more was a tribute to her artistry."

Even in such a practically unknown place as Toowoomba in Queensland there was an atmosphere of musical discrimination: "Galli-Curci will leave a lasting impression of her personal magnetism and charm. She is absolutely fascinating. One does not give voice production a thought when listening to the notes of a bird; so it is with Madame."

Rockhampton on the coast above Brisbane is where they called Galli-Curci's recital "A Feast of Art," and Mackay, a little place still farther north, said, on August 8 in the *Daily Mercury,* that "the irresistible appeal of Galli-Curci's marvelous voice . . . captured completely all hearts until, at times, the applause rose and surged through the auditorium like the roaring of waves of the sea." Maryborough gave our singer a similar reception. Then to New Zealand where at Wellington, Christ Church, Aukland, Hawke's Bay, Waikato, Dunedin, Nelson, Timaru all record the same brilliant successes.

The evidence is too voluminous to reproduce, but most persuasive as to the elegance, the charm and the appeal of Galli-Curci's art so decisively reflected in her popularity. Whether in America, Great Britain, Australia, South Africa, New Zealand, China, Japan, the Philippines, Hawaii—the verdict is the same—multitudes flocking to hear her, demonstrations seldom witnessed. The eighty-seven concerts of this tour strengthened her position of priority among living vocalists and established her right to the oft-voiced title *Queen of Song.*

One place there was where Galli-Curci's voice produced an opposite effect. Two members of an expedition exploring the northwestern coast of Australia were lying at anchor in a small schooner when they were visited by a canoe full of natives. After a coaxing invitation, the darkskinned aborigines were induced to come aboard where they were given sweets and tea. To amuse them further, a Galli-Curci record of Lucia's aria was placed on the gramophone and, at the first sound of the voice, the natives jumped up in alarm, made a concerted rush to the boat's side—men, women, children and dogs disappearing into the water and swimming frantically away to escape what they must have supposed to have been the devil in a woman's form concealed in the box.

Concluding her engagements in October, after nine months away from home, our three musicians set their faces once more toward America aboard the steamer "Monterey," which conveyed them to Los Angeles where they disembarked November 8. After a tour of 40,000 miles around the globe, a lengthy respite covering the winter and most of 1933 was the chief desideratum of the globe-trotters. At "Sul Monte" we will leave our diva and her husband to their thoughts and activities until the call of early winter summoned them again to the concert stage. After four home appearances, the little company again put forth to sea, this time England bound in bleak December.

Again in England!

Galli-Curci found her world so big that she had to make foreign tours continually, though sometimes unable to visit her favorite countries but once in several years. On January 21, 1934, 5,000 people gathered again in the Royal Albert Hall in spite of a fog—a fine, black fog that settled down on London so densely that it penetrated the auditorium where the audience could see the singer only dimly through the haze. "Her white figure on the platform," read the cable, "seemed like an ethereal being and her bell-like voice served to heighten the illusion," and the recital passed into history as another Galli-Curci triumph. And now comes the rub—the rub of adverse comment that every artist in time must face and complacently endure.

Some London papers, which previously had praised, now looked for flaws and found them, for she herself always disclaimed perfection, and on this occasion again declared: "All my defects are original and I know that I have only the audience to please." The critics and their views interested her not, but unfortunately they are factors in careers of art and useful as evidences of the diversity of opinion and of the frailty of human judgment.

The provinces, however, disagreed. Birmingham, Torquay, Bournemouth, Nottingham accorded her great acclaim while a Preston scribe noted that "she is singing better today than ever she has done," and from Brighton, "The remarkable evenness and purity of her voice was strikingly evidenced."

In the prewar days debuts were made in Europe in order to secure the prestige necessary to a successful American approach. Nordica, Eames, Bispham and Farrar made Metropolitan opera debuts via

European houses. Things changed after the war. Garden, Ponselle and Galli-Curci were famous in America before singing in London, which city, according to the English writer Percy Colson, sometimes reverses the New York verdict, with disastrous results to the popularity and earnings of the artist in question after he or she returns to the United States.

While in England, Galli-Curci contributed an article to the Birmingham *Mail*, dated January 30, 1934. Its title was "Songs People Want and Why," the gist of which reads as follows:

"In this prosaic life of today when stark, staring facts are served up for breakfast, dinner and tea, many people delude themselves into thinking that they have grown out of that time-worn hallucination called Love. They tell us that it is a back number and belongs to a decade of Victorianism; that nowadays we are more sensible, more broadminded, and see beyond mere romance. In my experience, I have found Beauty and Love to be inseparable, and I believe that a love of beauty will conquer almost any difficulty.

"Eminent scientists and clever psychologists may have explained away many so-called fallacies, but they will never persuade me that love is old-fashioned, for I am incurably romantic. Besides which, I believe, for many reasons, that nothing else in the world can ever be regarded as a substitute for love, which is as old as the hills and will endure for all time.

"I believe in love because none of these people who profess today that love is out of date can convince me that they have found a satisfactory substitute. I see no happiness in their faces and they give the lie to their conviction by a restless striving to cram every inch of the day with feverish activity.

"Sensation is the only substitute they impress me with having found, and that is a poor garment which will soon wear thin. If I question them as to their friendships, they hurriedly reply that one can be a good pal without being in love. But do they realize that love is the seed of all friendship? I believe myself that friendship is the very highest sphere to which one can attain and that love is the stepping-stone to this height.

"Had I not believed in this, I would never have become a prima donna, for I should have succumbed long ago to morbid questionings as to the futility of existence. Life is like that. You cannot do anything worth while if you are hating and fearing. You have only to look back into the history of mankind to find

that love was the spur behind all the greatest deeds and achievements. The most mundane deeds can be accomplished, even
made thrilling, if love is their inspiration.

"I have proved this so, time and again, by the immediate
response which love songs call from my audiences. They are not
afraid then to stamp and shout for what they want—those
beautiful songs of love, which rose from the hearts of simple
folk, a decade or so ago, who were not too proud to show all
the world their sincerest feeling."

The Last Lap

Leaving Aberdeen, Scotland, March 6, Galli-Curci and her associates arrived in New York on the 15th. As she was scheduled to sing
in Los Angeles on the 20th, there was but a single day at her dis-
posal to attend to the numerous details demanding attention; nevertheless with scarcely a moment to rest, she consented to give a radio
audition at the National Broadcasting Company studios, which
resulted in an engagement for June on a new commercial hour, the
sponsors wishing to have this artist for a special purpose, the broadcast to be made from Chicago. On the 16th the trio entrained for
California and on the 20th gave their concert on scheduled time.
This constituted a record journey—from Aberdeen to Los Angeles,
approximately 6,000 miles, half water, in fourteen days, with two
days intermission. Instead of being fatigued or out of voice, Galli-
Curci sang with her accustomed spirit and artistry, according to the
coast records.

Ending her season at Omaha, a short visit was made to Minneapolis, then back to "Sul Monte" until time to go to Chicago for
the broadcast on the "Contented Hour" June 18, her first appearance before the microphone in over four years and her third in all.
She was brought to Chicago to sing the "Cradle Song" by Brahms,
which had been chosen by listeners to this hour as the most popular
of lullabies to be sung by the most popular of singers. In addition
to the "Wiegenlied," Galli-Curci gave a delightful rendition of
Arditi's "Parla" waltz.

Her custom of taking four months off during the summer whenever possible was forfeited in 1934 because of her having to sail for
South America to begin another world tour, the contract for which

she brought back from England and which was deemed a proper adjunct to this notable career, inasmuch as its itinerary embraced new points of contact—points that had been asking a visit from the artist whose fame and art had become known everywhere.

CYCLE OF
ADVERSITY

1934-1936

"All who aspire to be great
artists must have moments of
concentration."

—GALLI-CURCI

Southward to South America

N JULY 28, Galli-Curci with Homer Samuels, pianist, and Raymond Williams, flutist, sailed out of New York harbor aboard the "Northern Prince," not to return to the United States until the spring of 1935. Arriving in Montevideo, the little company of artists appeared in the 1915 haunts of the former opera prima donna, but now a platform singer—in song programs rather than in operatic enactments. Concerts were given in Río, São Paulo, Montevideo, Rosario, Cordoba, and Buenos Aires—a total of ten—which carried them to the end of September.

Having completed the South American schedule of concerts, the trio sailed for South Africa, arriving at Capetown October 10, where former successes were duplicated and new triumphs won. Booked for seven concerts, they were destined to remain until the following February because of an unprecedented demand for appearances, which rose to fifty-nine in fifty-five cities with repeats in Johanesburg, Durbin, and Lowrenco Marquis (Portuguese East Africa). The people simply would not let Galli-Curci go, strongfully aware that this would be the final chance to hear their favorite. It is significant that much of the uninterrupted continuity of this happy march was through new territory with scant music privileges, yet all eagerly heard the singer whom they had come to adore through glamorous recordings.

It is noteworthy, too, that these fifty-nine concerts were crowded together into a period of four months, beginning October 12 in Capetown and ending February 11 in Durbin, the evening before embarking for India. This made an average of a concert every second

With brother-in-law, Gennaro Curci, coaching her for her Chicago return in La Boheme, *1935, Los Angeles*

Last photograph before her final public appearance, 1935-1936

day, on one occasion (November 20) two recitals in two different places. A twenty-eight-day sea journey brought the party to Calcutta on March 8, 1935, where two days later the first of three concerts in five days was given.

In Spectacular India

No doubt there are many who look upon India, Siam, Indo-China, Malaya, and Java as sluggish, inert territories mired in a bog of traditional ignorance and superstition, but those who have visited them are conscious of an obverse side. Galli-Curci went there, not as merchant nor diplomat, but as messenger of art, hence was able to form a liberal conception of this land of pomp and pageantry where princes ride on elephants, where palace gardens gleam, jewels flash, sabers clank, alabaster temples enchant, and where the ancient spell of the Orient grips you as nowhere else. One enters India enchanted, but leaves it bewildered.

India, ancient battle-ground of innumerable invaders and hordes of conquerors, is saturated with historical romance—Kashmir, Lahore, Delhi, Amristar, Bombay, Allahabad, Lucknow, Agra, Benares, Madras, Calcutta—names of intriguing charm. India the land of poetry, fable—the land of mosques, palaces, temples, idols, mausoleums, of rajputs, fastnesses and squalid sublimity, of fascinating emporiums, of fantastic dress and queer customs, of clever fakirs, great rivers, mountain barriers, of impenetrable superstition and colossal legends, of alluring myths and monstrous deities—a mighty continent, much of it shut in from occidental influence and progress, yet renowned as the seat of occult philosophic systems, of Sanscrit literature, of distinctive temple architecture and of hoary archeology. Only the princes, the native regiments, the men and women of high castes, meet upon a pseudo-equality with Britishers.

The opaqueness of the veil that separates the natives and their rulers quickly dawns upon the visitor. If audiences could be drawn upon from the former, steeped in traditional folk-lore, religious fanaticism, venerable intellectuality and the wisdom of ancient saints and sages, it would mean one thing; but when drawn almost exclusively from Hindoos, Parsees and English, it means quite another thing.

It is the women, however, who attract the most attention and lend a unique glamour to any formal gathering. Their grace, dress, jewels, bearing, culture and speech are proverbial, while such brilliancy is set off by a fringe of turban-headed gentlemen and the glittering array of military uniforms, all of which provide a stimulating surprise for any artist for the first time facing such an audience. Yet everywhere Galli-Curci found capacity houses drawn, of course, from the social and educated ranks.

The prime query is, how can an artist unite such a complexity of thought and training even among upper-strata groups? The answer is this—geographic type differences of audiences, while racially, culturally or characteristically at variance, possess in common one outstanding trait, i.e., an innate feeling for song and a naturally sympathetic response to music. All peoples, whether in the higher or lower stage of civilization, are creators of musical sounds, be they artistic or crudely made. The one universal medium of emotional appeal is that of song, hence one can charm an audience anywhere effectively with ear-caressing tones.

The glamorous quality of the Galli-Curci voice alone was ever sufficient to enchant her auditors while its soothing timbre, which so glowingly invested it, always put her en rapport with souls attuned to cosmic impulses, while the witchery of her smile, the charm of her personality, the ingratiating excellence of her art, left her invulnerable to criticism, unless one chose to cavil. Thus may we account for the marked success of and the spontaneous tributes bestowed at these parting concerts in the Orient despite the fact that they were sung amid distressing circumstances.

The introduction to India via Calcutta afforded our artist an opportunity to gain acquaintance with the prevailing audience type. She was not a little surprised that her programs were not only approved but accepted joyfully—even the opera arias and the foreign-language groups. The auditors had become acquainted with most of the singer's repertory as phonographically recorded and had learned to comprehend occidental music at concerts by other visiting artists.

A journey of 600 miles brought the party to New Delhi, the imperial capital of India since 1931, for a single concert, after which a three-day intermission enabled the trio to journey leisurely another 400 miles to Rawalpindi, chief city of the Punjab, near the Indus River.

Thrilling Climax

The story now rushes to a thrilling climax. On March 20, our artist awoke with a pronounced irritation of the throat that alarmed her. It so happened that in the lobby of the hotel, Samuels met an American tourist who introduced herself as a patient of his brother, Harvey. Homer was suffering from a new form of throat distress, due probably to the highly infectious dust which prevails during the dry season along the frontier of Northwest India. In the course of the conversation, it developed that Dr. Arnold H. Kegel of Los Angeles was, at that time, investigating the causes and effects of epidemic goiter in the district, with headquarters at Srinigar in Kashmir, the most propagable region for this malady.

Dr. Kegel was notified of the singer's plight by telegram embodying a request for an appointment, which was arranged to take place at Rawalpindi. The examination showed a marked irritation of the nose and throat, which condition was made decidedly worse because of the goiter, from which she had been suffering for several years, and which had, by now, grown larger. It was pushing on the trachea, narrowing the passageway of the tubular organ to fifty per cent of its normal diameter. Temporary relief was obtained by local treatment and Galli-Curci was advised not to hazard further exposure to dust particles and to limit her traveling in that territory to a minimum. Accordingly the party returned to Lahore for a recital which was given on March 22. This ancient town served merely as a starting point for the southward journey, for speed was the order of the day. A government mail plane was chartered to fly them over the dust area along the Buluchistan border to Karachi, 600 miles away, where another concert was scheduled for the 25th.

A most unusual incident of this flight occurred en route. When the plane came down in some unfamiliar spot for luncheon, the occupants were greeted by a horde of natives. On arrival at Karachi, thousands of dusky individuals were waiting for the singer and gave her a welcome greeting with vigorous handclapping.

But time still pressed. Therefore, after a hurried departure and a thousand-mile sea journey along the coast, the travelers reached Bombay, the principal gateway to India. With its million people— Europeans, Mahrattas, Parsees, Arabs, Afghans, Sikhs, Tibetans, Cingalese, Bagdad Jews, and a Japanese colony—Bombay is a paradise of interest for the visitor.

Here our artist had three of the most glorious receptions of her song career. Apparently she was in the best of voice and won impetuous ovations, according to a review appearing in the *Evening News of India*, April 3, 1935, which is quite unusual. After passing through so harrowing a mental and physical ordeal and facing uncertainty as to her ability to continue her curtailed schedule, it was little short of miraculous that Galli-Curci could not only sing well but was able to submerge her nervous tension during this series of receptions. Evidently neither audiences nor critics had any idea of the goiter trouble. Such a display of heroic fortitude and courageous mastery of self is not often recorded in the annals of vocal art.

Audiences differed from those of Lahore and Delhi, inasmuch as they were composed of a goodly number of Parsees and Hindoos with gorgeously gowned women, who never appear in public places except on special occasions and thereby lend a fascinating touch to such gatherings. This in contrast to the other two places which contributed audiences mostly English. But the Bombay recitals were graced with personalities of varied distinction, including potentates with entourages. Each of the three programs was different in scope, the most favored numbers being arias from standard operas.

One outstanding incident of this visit was a banquet to which the artists were invited, at the close of which one of the officials whispered to Mr. Samuels that he was privileged to smoke although the Parsees might not do so; for to them fire is hallowed, and the holy flame burns continuously in the homes of this ancient sect.

By a prearrangement with Dr. Kegel, Galli-Curci was to meet the surgeon in Calcutta, so whatever plans had been made for other appearances in India and Ceylon were abandoned. The quartet moved from Calcutta to Rangoon, where two recitals were given on April 9 and 10. Dr. Kegel's motive in thus accompanying the artist was to afford him an opportunity to study her vocalization under varying circumstances—climatic conditions and altitudes, periods of nervous tension and relaxation, and from different distances in the auditoriums in which she sang. Before and after each concert, a careful examination of the vocal chords and larynx was made to determine the cause for changes and differences in the various voice ranges.

These observations were most important in that it was discovered that, in phonation, the most difficult passage was in the vowels from A to E, due to inability to raise the larynx, as it was bound down tightly by the goiter. While Dr. Kegel was making his diagnosis, the others were experiencing new enjoyment in Burma—land of extraordinary charm where, on the road to Mandalay, "the flying fishes play, and the dawn comes up like thunder outer China 'crost the bay." Gay Burmese girls, with smiles and flower-decked hair, swished in rustling silks and flopping sandals, while Buddhist monks sat in saffron robes.

Rangoon, the capital, is modernistic, so the Galli-Curci audiences were predominantly English, hence constituting a well-dressed assemblage of modish men and finely-clothed women. Penang, the next stop, on the Prince of Wales Island in the Malacca Strait, was visited for a single concert, then it was back to the mainland for a recital at Kuala Lumpur, which gives the impression of English cultural grafting perhaps more than at any other point on the peninsula, where both sexes observe dress formalities just as they would do in London.

A pair of concerts in Singapore—that island of conglomerate masses which a hundred years ago was only a desolate jungle and which, at this time, was a picturesquely onward-moving city. At this point Dr. Kegel left the party, going into China, the others proceeding to Java, agreeing to meet again at Tokyo about the middle of June. The schedule called for three concerts in Batavia, two in Samarang, and one in Bandong, with a farewell in Batavia, and occupied the time between April 28 and May 15.

Concluding the Java tour, the party returned to Singapore, from whence they sailed to Japan, arriving in time for the opening concert on June 2 at Kobe. This was followed up with one in Kyoto, two in Osaka, and two in Tokyo, the last taking place on the 12th. Dr. Kegel had already arranged for an examination at the University Hospital, where the X-ray disclosed startling conditions. The trachea was fifty per cent compressed; the larynx was displaced one and one-half inches to the left, tilting to a fifteen-degree angle; the esophagus was a whole inch out of line. As a result, tones instead of being projected upward, were forced against the muscular walls of the throat. Doctors told the singer that the obstruction would have to be removed in order to obviate serious future consequences, and that not to have it done would certainly compel retirement.

An amusing incident occurred in Kyoto indicative of Japanese keenness. When there in 1928, Galli-Curci and her husband had bought several souvenirs from a local dealer in art objects. With true American inquisitiveness, the couple revisited the shop, where they were cordially greeted by the owner, who quickly recalled their previous visit, even remembered what they had purchased. In Tokyo, they were accorded the same hearty receptions as before, Prince and Princess Chichibu attending both events, one being delayed because the Premier, oblivious to the lateness of the hour, had called at the hotel for an autographed picture of the singer for his Emperor.

After each concert there was a rush backstage for Galli-Curci signatures, for the Japanese have a pronounced penchant for collecting autographs of famous persons. The same types of programs that had won approval and applause throughout the entire tour served also to entertain the Nipponese, everyone, however, concluding with a response to an insistent call for "Home, Sweet Home."

Came June 13, with the party sailing for California, arriving June 28 after a world tour covering 35,000 miles, occupying eleven months during which seventy-eight cities were visited and ninety-eight concerts given, without a postponement or a cancellation. That probably constitutes a record, particularly when one considers the tremendous mental and physical handicap the singer was under.

A Momentous Decision

For fifteen years Galli-Curci had been combatting a throat tumor, but kept on until there was insufficient room for proper breath passage to insure full tone production, while the tones themselves retained their natural loveliness; only by potent will-power did she secure enough volume to get them across to her audiences.

It would not have been possible for her to have continued to sing under such conditions; either she must retire or submit to an operation. Retire? Appalling word! No, not if modern surgical skill could keep her from it, so certain did she feel that there remained in art something to be accomplished ere she affixed a concluding *finis* to her Life of Song. Therefore, after a hurried conference, an immediate operation was decreed and the artist, her husband, and her surgeon moved on to Chicago, where the operation was performed in the Heurotin Hospital on August 10.

The diva was calm and cheerful as she entered the operating room. Only a local anesthetic was applied so that the patient might test her vocal organs during the work, thereby enabling the surgeons to note the successive steps as they progressed and thus secure the proper muscular tension as the larynx was adjusted into place. The gentle coughs and "ohs" emitted and the final fragment of a passage from the *Barber of Seville* brought smiles of satisfaction from the doctors, which transmitted confidence to the courageous woman on the table during that tense hour and ten minutes. The "potato" when removed weighed six and one-half ounces and measured four and one-half inches by two and one-half inches.

An anatomical artist stationed nearby sketched the various stages of the operation for later study. Dr. Kegel would hazard no comment on the outcome, but indicated that the voice quality would be unimpaired. He thought that the removal had corrected a seventy-five percent deviation of the trachea and that the remaining correction would be expected to occur gradually over a period of time. "Galli-Curci," declared the surgeon, "will have only to adjust her voice to the fifty per cent increase in air volume she will now have. It might be six to eight months before she can sing in an opera house, but anyone who knows her will power will agree that whatever she wants to accomplish, she will accomplish. We are banking heavily on the artist's grit to aid her voice to come back. Single notes and simple scales will adjust the disturbed throat muscles before more difficult exercises begin. That will be after all danger of lesions has been passed."

Among the hundreds of letters, cards and telegrams Galli-Curci received while in the hospital was one huge card, 9 x 15 inches, from fifty-six Boy Scouts wishing her a speedy recovery, while newspapers phoned daily to ascertain her condition.

As soon as the singer was able to speak she said: "I do not think it will be so difficult to learn to sing again. My vocal chords are not impaired. There is no soreness. All I want to do is rest and baby my voice along . . . It is full again, unbridled after years of struggle. The result of the operation is just short of marvelous. My voice is like a young colt—I will have to restrain it."

"Although I had orders to keep madam very quiet," said her nurse, "I caught her singing early in the morning." "Yes," smiled the diva, "and it was the first time anyone had ever told me to stop singing."

A week later Galli-Curci left Chicago for her new home in California, with some months of hard work ahead in order to accustom herself to the increased volume of air available and to the new positions of the throat organs.

It was not long before she felt that new vocal strength. "My voice wants to rise to new heights. I am astonished at the facility with which the tones come forth and at its strength. My voice is coming back in a thrilling way—it is richer, more brilliant, and absolutely lyric and dramatic. I am almost intoxicated with its volume, and yet I love to mother it so I can give it out in the climaxes. That has been a considerable work; to mother the insistent flow of my voice. At last, I can express my emotions. At last, I can realize all my artistic intentions."

CYCLE OF
SUSPENSE

1936-1938

"There is no such thing as a
cold audience—it is what you
make it."

—GALLI-CURCI

At her Los Angeles home, 1938

A California Home

"I HAVE lived in many countries of the world," said Galli-Curci, "but I think California is the most beautiful. My Westwood Hills home, outside of Los Angeles, has a sweeping view. On one side the university spires are an inspiration of knowledge; on the other side the sunset—for I have built my home to face the sunset." Prophetic? Perhaps to face nature's sunset while facing, too, the ultimate sunset of a brilliant and colorful career. In contrast to "Sul Monte" in the Catskills, which was sold in July, 1937, the new home is white stucco. A handsome wrought iron gate from Venice leads into a spacious garden. Antiques dot the living rooms. Orange, lime and olive trees contribute shade and beauty, while roses, hibiscus, camelias, and magnolias give fragrance to the air and charm to the eye.

And so a year sped by, during which time it appeared that not only had the voice been saved, but that it was again ready for service.

Her former brother-in-law, Gennaro Curci, was teaching in Los Angeles and to him Galli-Curci went for consultation. He found the throat in such excellent condition and the voice of such volume as to suggest dramatic possibilities. Thereupon she began work on the roles of Tosca and Aida, which she had already learned during the recovery period.

A Vocal Mirage

In the summer of 1936, Salter went to Hollywood to hear the "new" voice and to discuss with the artist the practicability of stepping out again into public activity; and in order to ascertain its precise status, arranged a test in the Philharmonic Auditorium, where the artist sang several dramatic arias in such a manner as to beguile herself, her husband, her coach, and her manager into believing that the operation had turned a lyric-coloratura voice seemingly into a more potential one.

After this test it was decided, as soon as warrantable, to launch her forth upon this newly-uncovered vocal highway. The occasion for the launching came sooner than expected, for Paul Longone, manager of the Chicago Civic Opera Company, induced Salter to agree to an operatic appearance in Chicago, which Galli-Curci was willing to do, both for sentimental reasons and for an opportunity to give her "new" voice the critical test of a stage performance.

Salter returned to New York via Chicago, where he closed the contract for one appearance, albeit Longone asked for an option on others, depending on the outcome of the first, a proposal her manager discreetly declined. Which opera should be used for her re-entry was the mooted question. Galli-Curci wanted either *Tosca* or *Butterfly*. Longone argued for a lyric role, so the matter was left in abeyance for the time being.

GALLI-CURCI TO SING AGAIN!

That was the message flashed by the Associated Press from Chicago on September 11 and confirmed by the diva's managers in New York. Though the announcement *per se* was surprising, that she would sing again in opera was truly amazing in view of her previous declaration that opera was not only an outmoded form of musical art but that she was through with it forever.

So early in November our singer and Samuels journeyed eastward to Chicago, where they met Evans and Salter. Then began an official conference out of which emerged two decisions: the date was changed from the 18th to the 24th in order to avoid interjecting this special performance between two regular evenings, each featuring a Metropolitan Opera star; and as there was no time to prepare either *Tosca* or *Butterfly*, *La Bohème* was chosen, despite the fact that Galli-Curci had not sung the role since her early New York days. Other handicaps loomed as possible embarrassments: she had not participated in an operatic performance in America since her

Metropolitan farewell in 1930; she was a stranger in the new opera house, and to Longone's singers, orchestra and stage direction; she had not been in costume or faced flashing footlights for years, and to crown these discomforts of mind and body, she was told that there would be no rehearsal—only time to run through the principal arias during a rehearsal of another opera. Under the circumstances, a halt upon the brink of chance, rather than an attempt to leap the chasm, would have been the wiser move.

Came the night of November 24. When she made her entrance Galli-Curci was greeted so vociferously for seven minutes by the enthusiastic audience as to completely overwhelm her. For the first time in her thirty-year career, she succumbed to an emotional agitation that upset her mental equilibrium and vocal poise. That rousing welcome proved too much for her tensioned nerves, so when the hubbub had ceased and the audience had settled back to hear the opening strains of "Mi chiamano Mimi," no full-voiced tones floated across the orchestra pit to greet that hushed expectancy. Galli-Curci was experiencing "stage fright."

The complete cast for this performance was:

Mimi	Amelita Galli-Curci
Rodolfo	Armand Tokatyan
Marcello	Giacomo Rimini
Colline	Nino Ruisi
Schaunard	George Cehanovsky
Musetta	Lola Fletcher
Alcindoro } Benoit }	Vittorio Trevisan
Parpignol	Giuseppe Cavadore
Sergeant	Teodor Lovich

The conductor was Roberto Moranzoni.

If the accounts of the performance are any criterion, the objective was not attained, while hope for an operatic return was, in consequence, dispelled. Galli-Curci had sung the rôle before and the music, which lay in the loveliest part of her vocal register, offered no technical difficulties. Her inability to qualify on this occasion can be attributed perhaps to a too-early start and the strain incidental to

a return to the scene of her first triumphal debut, before a sympathetic audience.

The artist's previous activities had been guided so unerringly and
with such masterly care and forethought, such a *faux pas* as this can
be viewed only as a too-hasty desire to reinstate her in the public
limelight, whereas a calm and rational re-entry unquestionably
would have been the normal and the better way. Perhaps the kindest
explanation would be to class it as an adventure in line with the
modern age of rush. We live in a world of experimental thrusts,
most of them sincere, all of them intensive, converging into a
forward push to gain, if possible, new outlets in which energy might
assert itself. But this sort of blind adventuring leads to uncertainty,
prominently evidenced in the sphere of art. Any full-developed and
well-seasoned form of self-expression must *ipso facto* be permeated
with one's own individuality and personality, and when linked to
the emotional and spiritual, constitute a complete unity, thereby
precluding any radical divergence.

Since childhood, Galli-Curci's art had been an inherent entity—
an essential part of her being. She and it could hardly be other than
inseparable, for her whole career had been molded along a definite
line of artistic endeavor. It would appear, then, that her natural
instincts would have rebelled against any such drastic alteration of
the metier in which she had been assiduously engaged for thirty
years. But she caught a glimpse of a mirage that beckoned her onward, alluringly.

Certain fixities are immutable. Certain grooves claim us at birth.
In these we remain if we accept them and follow their courses.
Galli-Curci spent her entire life in the groove of lyric song and in
that groove won renown. She never ventured into extraneous fields;
she never altered her style, never changed her method, never experi-
mented. Why then hazard a renascence merely because the throat
passage gave more space for breath emission and tone volume?
Nevertheless, the fact remains that the world was witness to a most
unusual and heroic effort to rehabilitate a suspended activity occasioned by an unfortunate physical ailment. All who adored this
artist in her prime must admire the courageous woman whose

greatest joy is to sing, and none would withhold from her one iota of that joy in the remaining years of her singing life.

The ordeal over, Galli-Curci banished from her thought all remembrance of the joyless incident and turned her face toward a happier horizon. She read no comments upon her performance, voiced no regrets, blamed none. Too much lay ahead to fuss about an injudicious step, yet she gained by the experience. She would shun opera for the time being and devote her energies to re-establishing her status on the concert stage, still laboring under the belief that her voice had changed; for, said she: "I can now state definitely that my new voice is as close to perfection as I had ever hoped it would be. It is dramatic and lyric now, whereas before it was coloratura. My voice is not simply improved, it is a new voice. I have richness, color I never had before. I am going to sing a whole new repertoire. I was condemned to craftsmanship. I had to think too much about details of technic. Now I can sing. I can express emotion, drama. I was more nervous over that appearance than when I made my original debut in Italy at seventeen. Then I was blessed with ignorance and it was no more momentous than going to one's first dance. Even my Chicago debut in 1916 did not seem half so exciting as this new debut. I was so nervous that it took some time to feel that my face wasn't actually frozen. But now that is all gone and I feel that my voice has more power, more depth than it ever had and I feel more full of energy and vitality than before."

Here is irony of a very high degree. "There were no rave notices when the great Galli-Curci sang at the Chicago Civic Opera the other week in what some writers said was her 'comeback.' The critics were gentle—but not too enthusiastic. There was more enthusiasm here about a puppet act at Loew's State . . . This unheralded act stopped practically every show and the applause was thunderous. This was chiefly because of the leading lady puppet. Every time she sang the audience went wild. The ironic tag is that the voice behind the puppet was a Galli-Curci recording made many years ago; while the star in the flesh was being greeted coldly in Chicago, her voice on the disc pulsating through the animated puppet, was scoring a tremendous success." (New York *Journal*, December 9, 1936.)

Further Experiments

Discs of the "new" voice were sent to Detroit, and on the evidence thus presented, Galli-Curci was engaged for the Ford Sunday Evening Hour broadcast of December 13. Whether she had lost her golden voice—as some seemed to think—or whether she could still charm more thousands—as others seemed to think—the public would decide. Certainly those who listened in heard excellent singing in "Il Bacio," "La Paloma," and "Les Filles de Cadix," but "Un Bel di Vedremo" was manifestly labored.

Again opinions differed, but there were no such impromptu explosions in the press as at Chicago. The artist, however, was pleased with the result, and José Iturbi, guest conductor of the evening, who had never heard her sing, said: "She sang beautifully. She is an artist."

There is real mystery in this attempt to prove herself still a quality singer. With everything to lose and nothing to add to the fame which her earlier years had won—years when she had nothing to lose but everything to gain—she braved the danger of a questionable experiment in an attempt to satisfy an inherent yearning to regain her prestige and re-win the admiration of a mighty populace eager for her return to vocal greatness.

But here's the answer. At forty-seven, Galli-Curci did not propose to spend her remaining years in inactive contemplation. Guided and inspired by a philosophy that sustained her unfailingly, the future held hope for continued artistic and spiritual uplift.

In New York, where she came for the Christmas holidays, rejuvenated and looking almost as young as she did in the 20's, Galli-Curci appeared quite as lovely and vivacious as of yore. There was no dejection in her attitude, no sorrow or regret in either speech or countenance.

While the future is ever uncertain, with respect to this artist we know that she was primed to sing at least another season. Suddenly she discovered that her voice was not a "new" voice, but the same voice, only expanded, enlarged, unfastened—a voice more accessible to her singing urge, hitherto suppressed. "I am not a dramatic or a lyric soprano," she declared. "I am a coloratura and I shall use some favorite florid arias on my programs." She kept her word, for on her recitals appeared such numbers as the "Romeo et Juliette" waltz, "Hamlet" mad scene, "Parla" waltz, and the like.

After the Albany concert on April 10, 1937, she gave out in an interview the following statement: "I'm studying just as hard as I ever did. I practice long hours each day. It's just like being a schoolgirl again and I love it. When I feel as I do now when I sing, I know my voice is like it was in the old days. I feel comfortable and my whole body vibrates during a song."

Leaving New York, Galli-Curci gave several more recitals en route westward, then went to her California home for the summer. In the fall, she and Samuels began a concert tour of the Pacific Coast which extended from Los Angeles to Victoria. In these appearances the singer found that she could still please with her song, as disclosed in the following critical excerpts:

> "The famed diva was brilliant testimony to the surgical skill which has restored to its limpid, volatile beauty the clarity, range and delicacy of her famed coloratura voice."
> —Los Angeles *Examiner*.

> "She sang gorgeously; her tones were tender, caressing, true as a precision instrument."—Seattle *Post-Intelligencer*.

> "As great today as when she was at the zenith of her fame. Amazed everyone by the beauty, flexibility and strength of her voice."—Victoria *Daily Colonist*.

> "Delights audience in recital on comeback tour. It was the same Galli-Curci."—Winnipeg *Free Press*.

> "Her singing revealed new depths and a fervor and warmth which were most appealing. Voice took on the color and warm nuances of the past."—Los Angeles *Times*.

> "The great diva's entertaining powers were as charmingly naive as ever. She was the exquisite, immaculate artiste."
> —Los Angeles *Evening Herald and Examiner*.

> "Scores turned away as the 'Standing Room Only' signs were hung out. Quality of her voice was as great as ever."
> —Wadena *Pioneer Journal*.

With such a verdict, the pathway loomed alluringly, the prospects encouragingly. Galli-Curci's managers therefore made the following announcement in the early part of 1938:

"GALLI-CURCI

"with her elegance, charm and universal appeal
is singing again.

"Music lovers everywhere have welcomed joyously the return of this incomparable diva this season to the concert stages of America. The press in both large and small cities covered by her tour have devoted columns to her amazing recovery.

"Once again . . . Galli-Curci's potent charm is electrically gripping audiences and charging them with vivifying currents. Her dazzling platform presence, buoyancy and intriguing surge of rhythm—are thrilling all who hear her exquisite voice, and inspiring listeners—from orchestra seats to topmost balcony."

But, alas! while the spirit was willing, the throat was weak, so the 1938-39 season was inactive, the singer's physician counselling her to avoid cold climates. The dates that had been booked were cancelled, forecasting the coda to her Life of Song.

The Final Cycle

by WILLIAM SEWARD
Director, Operatic Archives

ALLI-CURCI expressed no regrets at the sudden termination of her career. The Chicago *Boheme* had brought her to the brink of disaster and only her professionalism had seen her through a performance some feared she might not be able to finish. Her colleagues were old friends from the Metropolitan (Armano Tokatyan and George Cehanovsky) and the Chicago Opera Companies (Giacomo Rimini and Vittorio Trevisan).

Trevisan, the great basso-buffo of the Chicago Company from the days of Campanini, had taught Galli-Curci her roles in *Crispino e la Comare*, *Linda di Chamounix*, and *Don Pasquale*. She had a special affection for his daughter Olga, who, forty years later, related the events of that night:

"I went into Amelita's dressing room and she said, 'Is this Olga, the one who likes to sing?' And she seemed to remember me from way back, which thrilled me to no end. So we kissed and walked to the wings of the stage. I have never heard such an ovation as when she knocked and opened the door for Mimi's entrance. It just gave me cold chills! Hysteria swept through the theatre and onto the stage. There was yelling and screaming and stamping of feet. The music couldn't continue for fifteen minutes. Their 'Beloved' had come back.

"She was overcome and in tears. Mimi's first words, 'Scusi. Di grazia, me s'e spento il lume,' were understandably shaky. Then Tokatyan sang his aria and she started 'Mi chiamano Mimi." And

239

when she finished it the entire audience exhaled at once, 'Ahhh. . . !'
It was a sound that said, 'This isn't our goddess anymore!' And the
chill of death went down my back.

"In the Second Act she was a little better and she would come
off the stage at intervals and say, 'Oh Olga, what a bore! All of this
will soon be over. . . .'—making jokes—which wasn't at all like her.
There were a couple of times I thought, during the Third Act, that
she would not be able to finish because the orchestration is so heavy.
But she was a pro; she looked adorable, and acted and phrased
beautifully. She did the best she could. The public gave her a tremendous ovation but you could see that she was putting up a front.
Perhaps she thought, 'This is the first time I'm singing after that
terrible operation.'

"She went to Detroit next; then she sang some concerts and
retired. She was too intelligent a person to put herself through that.
She had a perfect instrument and when she saw that that instrument could no longer respond to what she expected from it, she
stopped, which I think was wise.

"Galli-Curci was more than a singer. She was an artist. She could
make an audience laugh or cry; she could move them with that
voice of hers. It was her love of humanity that allowed her to play
not only on her vocal chords, but on human emotion."

Galli-Curci was 54 years old. She had never forced her voice into
musical areas not intended by nature and it had survived the test
of time with little deterioration. Following her concert tour she said,
"I did not have fun with my voice so I don't know how the public
can either. It is a very simple and honest way to face it. I don't have
to sing for my ego."

The following years passed quickly for Galli-Curci and her husband (Homer Samuels). Their Westwood (Los Angeles, California) home was a gathering place for aspiring young singers who
coached with Homer. One of them, Florence George, a beautiful
and talented soprano, seemed destined for a fine career and Galli-
Curci herself took an active part in her lessons. Following her success with the San Francisco Opera, Miss George fell in love with a
successful businessman and that ended her vocal aspirations.

Relieved of the responsibility of their career, the Samuels were frequently seen at the theatre, and Amelita for the first time in her life seemed to enjoy social activity. It was a period of transition, of gradually re-directing that enormous physical drive into new realms of activity. Galli-Curci was an artist. She had the soul of an artist, so when she could no longer sing she found new tools with which to express herself. "After all," she said, "we don't play with the same toys all of our lives!"

At the end of the Second World War, the Samuels found their one-time suburban home surrounded by a rapidly expanding Los Angeles. The increasing air pollution noticeably affected Homer's asthmatic condition and they were advised to leave the city for a more congenial environment.

Near the Mexican border (in Rancho Santa Fe) they found a large tract of land and, in 1949, built there the home of their love. It was a typical Italian farmhouse with its white stucco walls and red tile roof. The rolling California hills and the eucalyptus trees gave the setting an Old World charm. For twenty years they had roamed the world together as musical nomads and to fight for their privacy; now they guarded it jealously. Visitors were discouraged; so the guest room was seldom used.

The north side of the house was all window, and the large studio with its twenty-foot raftered ceiling afforded a magnificent view. Galli-Curci became an accomplished painter and her still lifes and landscapes filled the room. "What a gift and recreation you enjoy," Geraldine Farrar wrote to her, "to be able to paint—such another type of release into beauty and illusion." The piano was stacked with the music of Chopin, Schumann, and Mozart—her favorite composer above all others.

Friends were chosen carefully and rarely were the old days discussed. "I don't want to plague tomorrow by looking back to yesterday!" As students of the world's philosophies, she and Homer read a great deal, and among the books were the writings of Paramahansa Yogananda. They became acquainted and Galli-Curci was proud of this friendship. "He was a very simple man with a great soul— extremely kind and cultured—and with it all he was very practical. He did a lot of good!"

Daisetz Suzuki was another writer who fascinated her, especially

his book on Zen and Japanese Culture. "I am reading it with great
interest—a little at a time—because you cannot assimilate so much
wisdom in a hurry! The illustrations are intriguing. They say so
much with very simple means and they are very forceful in their
simplicity. The Orientals stay close to nature with the exquisite
drawings and sincere interpretations from the artist—minimum of
effort with maximum of effect. Of course that minimum has cost a
lot of thought to the artist, but that's why it does not harass the
onlooker who drinks in only the beauty of the artistic work! And
that is the technique that hides technique! Thank the Lord! Simplicity, sincerity, serenity—that is my creed! And by serenity I mean
order, not apathy!"

By the early 1950's, Homer's health was rapidly deteriorating and
Galli-Curci invited some old friends and musical colleagues to her
home in an attempt to keep her husband bright and cheerful. The
duo pianists, Bartlett and Robinson, and the conductor, Sokoloff,
were among those who were warmly received.

Homer Samuels was the great love of Galli-Curci's life. "He was
more than my husband; he was my beloved, my musical companion,
and, best of all, my friend!" When he died in 1956 she was grief
stricken, but "not depressed because I feel my sweet Homer always
near to me. I am sure there is no separation, and the thought that
he can take a free breath after six long years of struggle fills me with
joy!"

Kathryn Brown, an intimate friend from Chicago, came to
Rancho Santa Fe to provide the solace and companionship that
Galli-Curci needed during this difficult period of her life. Their
reunion was a happy one and she rapidly became the trusted confidante of Galli-Curci's final years. Kathryn was one of the few with
whom Galli-Curci would discuss the past, as well as the future, so
when RCA wrote to the singer in 1957 offering terms for the re-
issuing of her recordings, Kathryn urged her to accept.

The first LP recital was an attractive collection of operatic arias,
and songs with Homer accompanying on the piano. A new generation of record collectors, to whom Galli-Curci was little more than
an exotic name in reference books, became acquainted with her art.

She pointed with pride to the pile of letters on her desk: "I thought at first I could answer with a short note of thanks, but so many keep coming that I stopped in desperation and sent to all God's blessing in spirit. . . . It should reach them! I am deeply touched by so much love!"

Following the success of the first LP, the author arranged with Chet Crumpacker at RCA a recital that would be devoted entirely to the composers Bellini and Donizetti, since it was in their music that Galli-Curci was unequalled. He readily accepted these suggestions and wrote the singer for authorization. "These records are my 'pets'," she replied, "and I would hope they help vocal students to re-orient themselves toward a saner outlook on the art of bel canto!"

The coincidental appearance of the second disc with the first American release of Joan Sutherland's provided some interesting notices. Irving Kolodin wrote in the *Saturday Review*: "Insofar as one can make comparisons derived from recording techniques some forty years apart, Miss Sutherland's sound indeed has some of the airiness, limpidity and sweetness of Galli-Curci's. This still leaves ample areas of individuality for the older singer—grace, lightness, suppleness in ornament—which still surpass anything heard since her time. This is the most absorbing collection of Galli-Curci that has ever come to attention: An infinitely more flattering tribute to her art than the oft heard 'Lo! here the gentle lark' and 'Shadow Song,' which have been issued and re-issued. Amid all the brilliance are such extra-dazzling gems as the d-flat at the end of 'Ah! non credea mirarti' which is less sung than exhaled, and the shakes in Lucia's Mad Scene which remain the last real trills sung by such a vocalist."

In the fall of 1961, while the Australian soprano was singing for the first time in California, Galli-Curci wrote: "I have met Sutherland and her talented husband. They were both very kind to come and pay me a visit after I sent to Joan a warm and sincere telegram of congratulations following her triumph here. We had a cup of tea together at my home and I found them delightfully human, simple and charming, and dedicated to the career very conscientiously—a rare approach to art in these days! I have the record you sent me of her *Lucia* and was very much impressed with her flawless technique. Perfect technique should never be in the way to arrest that marvelous natural flow coming from the 'Great Source'. If we can pass it along in its purity and freshness it would be quite an accomplishment! It would produce those two captivating qualities—spontaneity and originality."

Ever since she was a little girl Joan Sutherland had loved the records of Galli-Curci. For her, Amelita was *The* Golden Age Coloratura. When she invited Sutherland and her husband to come and visit her, they could hardly get there fast enough. "She was the most enchanting little lady I ever met in my life," Sutherland recalls, "so full of vitality and personality—and so warm. So often one's idol does not meet one's expectations when the time comes. But we can in all honesty say Lita surpassed our dreams. With her, we spent some of the most pleasant hours of our lives—hours we can never forget."

For more than a year Galli-Curci had been plagued by a persistent cough due to a worsening asthmatic condition. Her doctors advised her to forsake rural life for an urban location where medical facilities were more readily available. On a quiet hill overlooking the city of La Jolla and the mighty Pacific, Galli-Curci built, in 1962, a new home similar in design to the one at Rancho Santa Fe. Like its predecessor, it was filled with those priceless works of art that she and Homer had collected on their world tours. Dominating the living room was Henrique Medina's life size portrait of Galli-Curci as Rosina in the *Barber of Seville*. It is so alive she seems ready to speak. The portrait now hangs in the Metropolitan Opera House in New York.

The adjoining studio was graced by the piano which she played daily, spending hours over the intricate fingerings of Bach and Mozart. On the wall hung a Liszt manuscript of "Uber allen Wipfeln ist Ruh" and letters written by Rossini and Mozart. On her easel, at the time of her death, was a picture of a desert scene she deliberately left unfinished. She felt this picture was her last work of art and constantly changed the periphery—a little here, a little there—but never disturbing the illusion of sand, sky and shadows, with their effect of limitless distance. Some places had been retouched so often that the paint was a quarter of an inch thick. She seemed to have an intuition that her life interest would end with the laying down of the brush.

In the fall of 1962, when Galli-Curci sought only rest and peace of mind, Tito Schipa, a colleague from the past, disturbed her new surroundings. The famous tenor of the 1920's was making his ill-advised farewell concert tour of the United States. They hadn't seen each other for years. Mutual friends told him where she was living and Schipa arrived, unannounced, at her door. That cycle of her life was finished and she had no intention of discussing the "old days" with their aims and ambitions. His plans for opening a school in California were fine, provided he didn't expect support from her. In the end he returned to New York and died in poverty.

Galli-Curci wanted to show her gratitude to America, the country that had given her fame and success. She established a foundation that would provide scholarships for musicians and scholars, and she planned to donate a quarter of a million dollars to the Bishop's School in La Jolla for a Concert and Arts Auditorium. The school reminded her of the one she attended in Milan as a child, and its motto—'Simplicity, Sincerity, Serenity'—had been her creed throughout life. "I wish to express my gratitude to this wonderful country which responded so generously to my performances and which is now my home."

Shortly before her death on the 26th of November, 1963, she wrote: "I am learning to make peace with my handicaps. I read a lot; I still have much to learn and I enjoy fully this final, fascinating cycle of my life that prepares me for the exodus—The Great Adventure!"

At La Jolla, Calif., August, 1963

A Conversation with Amelita Galli-Curci
by WILLIAM SEWARD

N THE 26th of November, 1963, eight days after celebrating her eighty-first birthday, Amelita Galli-Curci quietly passed away in her home in La Jolla, California. In a recent letter she had told me of the pleasure she took in living in this new house that overlooked the mighty Pacific and afforded a view of spectacular sunsets and moonlit nights.

Galli-Curci retired from the operatic arena in 1937, and the ensuing years were spent delving into occult philosophy (one of her rare literary exercises is an introduction to a book of Hindu meditations), painting in oils, playing the piano music of Mozart, and enjoying fully "the final, fascinating cycle of life that prepares one for the exodus—The Great Adventure!"

The attitude Galli-Curci adopted in the last years of her life has occasioned a good deal of comment. How could she, the most celebrated singer of her day, abandon the world that had given her overwhelming success? In her own words of explanation, we find both the warmth and the charm of her personality: "I thank the Lord for the many benefits given me, but the greatest luxury I have found here among the trees of California—the reward of quiet hours with plenty of time to think! The qualities to value in life are summed up in the phrase 'Simplicity, Sincerity, and Serenity,' and long ago I adopted it as my motto. It is unwise to plague tomorrow with backward glances to yesterday—you cannot play with the same toys all of your life!"

The following conversation is a departure from Galli-Curci's custom of not talking about herself or her career, but it was her hope that these observations would "help the vocal student to re-orient himself toward a saner outlook on the art of bel canto."

William Seward: It is said that Pietro Mascagni discovered your voice. How did this come about?
Galli-Curci: Mascagni came often to our house during my child-hood and would play with my brothers and me for hours at a time. He adored children, and was a bit of a child himself! What an original type he was, with a great aureole of bushy hair falling over his artistic and interesting face—a face that reflected every idea and stormy thought that came into its owner's mind. He was a magnifi-cent talker, and often under the power of his own beautiful phrases he would be moved to devastating rages or tears.

I remember the day he spoke to me of my voice, because that was the day I brought home from the conservatory the gold medal for piano. I was very young and much too excited to notice that Mas-cagni listened more attentively when I started to sing than he had been doing while I played. "Well, Maestro," I asked when I had finished, "are you pleased?" He took my hand and looked into my eyes. "Lita," he said, "as a pianist you will have a fine career, but as a singer you will have a great one!" At these words, the sun of my ambition climbed straight up and stood hot in the sky. Thoughts that I had scarcely dared to permit myself before began surging through my head.

Always, always I had wanted to sing. Even while I had worked at my piano studies I had sung the melodies of the Chopin etudes and the Mozart sonatas. I was irritated at the lack of a true legato, a smooth, unbroken line of melody, on the piano, so I strove to supply it with my voice. I always wanted to master the science of song. In the beginning, I received no encouragement from my parents—but neither was there opposition.

My teacher was common sense and a determination that turned into obstinacy once my mind was made up. How I worked! Cau-tiously, anxiously, hopefully! But fortune had given me two great gifts—health and a voice. So I worked and learned. And by this process what one learns one knows! Not too many singers can say that. When I sang, I knew exactly what muscles were being used, and in what condition they were. If I began a long, high trill I knew exactly what was happening in my throat, to my tongue, to my lips, to the muscles of my face.

W. S.: Then you were a self-taught singer?

G.-C.: When I took up the study of singing, I decided to rely upon myself, and, if I was to have defects, then they would at least be my own and not those given me by a teacher. Don't misunderstand me. I do not mean that there are not good teachers, for there are. I simply did not choose that way for myself. I had read about the technique of singing, but I spent little time on the exercises of Concone, Rossini, or Garcia because for me it would have been a waste of time. I had a natural gift for coloratura, for swift, clear and rapid passage work. This much-sought-after ease in staccato singing in the high register was always easy for me. I did not require musical knowledge—I had that from ten years of piano study at the conservatory. But I needed special drill. I knew what my weak spots were. So why spend many precious hours on technical studies that would only occasionally touch those portions of the voice that needed special attention?

W. S.: What were your weak spots? What did you find difficult?

G.-C.: I found sustained legato singing far more difficult than the coloratura fireworks. For a perfectly smooth legato one must work very hard. None of the great singers who were on the stage when I began my career slid or scooped their tones. You must be sure of intonation, so sure that you do not have to give it a thought. The sound must float from the lips on your breath. It should be a con-centrated tone, rather dark in quality. To produce this covered tone the throat must be kept completely open, with just the right mixture of bright and dark vowel quality. This beautiful covered voice car-ries much farther than a voice that is too shrill. It is so very expres-sive, and it certainly has a lovely quality of pathos. To me, it is the ideal tone and is the only kind of singing that really deserves the name.

W. S.: Do you think that a singer is born, or made?

G.-C.: Well, first the singer has to be born, *then* he has to be made! It has long been my very decided conviction that only long, hard years of unremitting work can make an artist. Singers are unquestionably born with certain throat formations and certain mental and emotional endowments, and these form the basis on which to build, with labor and persistence, a superstructure that in the end will bring success.

In my case, even in the beginning I seemed to comprehend that no shortened roadways lead one to high places. I approached my singing studies with humility. Nature had imposed upon me none of those vocal faults that fetter so many. I sang easily, without much physical effort, and though my voice did not have a great deal of power, the tones were pure and the volume came with maturity.

W. S.: Generally speaking, singing comes much easier, does it not, for those who speak a Romance language—because of the looseness of the jaw and the fullness of the vowels?

G.-C.: This is of course partly true. From birth the vowels are emitted from a perfectly open throat, and so the obstacles with which many singers from other lands have to struggle are avoided. I often used to wonder why teachers did not instruct their pupils to read aloud sonorous sonnets and prose which gives to the vowels a very beautiful quality. I feel certain that this cultivation of vowel beauty would be as valuable for many students as time spent on so-called vocal exercises which do not develop the vowel sense.

W. S.: Do you remember studying the role of Gilda for your debut in *Rigoletto*?

G.-C.: For nearly a year I lost myself in the pages of my *Rigoletto* score, trying to become the Gilda I fancied Verdi meant she should be. Then dawned the day I took the first irrevocable step of my career. Fearful that in my home city I might be like the prophet in his own land, I sought a place where I was not known. With my mother I journeyed (from Milano) to Trani. There, with my *Rigoletto* score tucked under my arm, I arrived at the threshold of my career! I might speak more of that debut, but it doesn't really matter. I had gone a considerable distance in the first year of my vocal journey, but still I was aware of that endless vista that stretched out of sight before my young eyes and of that artistic journey which remained to be traversed.

W. S.: Today it is often very difficult for even the young singer of quality to achieve engagements. Was it so in Italy at the time of your debut?

G.-C.: Real talent has always faced a struggle. But let me say to the young girl who goes away to make an operatic career: Take your mother with you! She is your only perfectly safe confidante in this world, and she is the only human being who has your interests at heart all the time and before all else.

W. S.: Although I know that you do not teach young singers as a rule, may I ask what your advice would be on the development of the voice?

G.-C.: Today I think that the vocal student is apt to spend entirely too much time on lessons studying mere songs, and often very poor songs. Songs contribute a great deal to the beauty of life and of course serve to keep the family interested in the vocal progress of the student. But they should not be allowed to supplant the real vocal food upon which the voice must be nourished for years. Songs are comfortable for the teacher who does not care, but they are bad for the pupil!

W. S.: Then you recommend the study of operatic scores?

G.-C.: The average soprano voice will develop wonderfully by the study of the operas of Bellini, Mozart, and Puccini. These are regarded with apprehension by the ignorant, but as a matter of fact they are much easier on the voice than are many songs—that is, of course, when the songs are sung properly. But you must remember that these composers, Bellini, Mozart, and the like, really understood the voice, and their music has the salubrious effect of freeing the voice and at the same time exercising and strengthening it. One hour of *Sonnambula*, *Giovanni* or *Norma* is worth five hours of ordinary songs.

W. S.: How important is technique?

G.-C.: I have no elaborate plea to make for technique. I do not mean that a singer can be a success in opera or on the concert platform without it. But I will say that technique alone, without the deep love for music that only nature can give, will not make a great career.

In singing you must learn to breathe, to articulate the song, to keep the vocal mechanism in prime condition through practice. But what good is the most beautiful voice in the world if it belongs to a being without a heart? The vocal student must be able to imagine a beautiful tone—and then produce it! Without this imagination there is nothing! In fact, if one had to choose between the two, it would be better to have less technique and more imagination, for the latter lends its life, spirit, and feeling to music. There are, of course, many factors that go to make the musical mind—sense of pitch, rhythm, timbre, time, volume, and the control of all these—but imagination must come first, imagination and a great sensitiveness to color.

W. S.: A difficult problem for many young singers today is the proper placement of the voice. How should the tone be produced?

G.-C.: When I first heard of "tone placement" I tried that. But not for long! Having only one voice to lose, I decided that such things were not for me. Nowadays when students are told by a teacher that he wants to "place" their voices, these aspirants should know enough to stay from him. The voice belongs outside the face, on the lips, and not in your chest or the top of your head! Just as soon as you try to keep the voice in some part of your body the sound becomes forced and ugly, tight and stiff—the freshness is gone! The tone must be supported on the breath and travel out of the body on it. The tone should leave the body as easily and as beautifully as the air one exhales. The voice is never placed, but rather uses the whole head as its sounding board. You remember, Mr. Seward, that little Hindu prayer bell you gave me? The delicate vibrations fill its whole being when it chimes. So the head should vibrate with the sensation of the singer's tone—a beautiful, round, healthy tone.

W. S.: Your way of singing produced a very clear attack when the voice struck a note. The great teacher Garcia called this "the neat stroke of the glottis." Can you explain in laymen's terms what is meant by this?

G.-C.: To avoid physiological explanations, this "neat stroke of the glottis" can best be described as the effect achieved by saying the word "crisp" or "curt." There has been a great cry in recent years against this "stroke of the glottis." But I have noticed that singers who have set their faces so sternly against it remain before the public only a very short time before losing their voices. Others have, by nature, the unconscious ability to sing this way, and never know exactly how the attack is achieved, so they refer to it as the "ping" attack.

W. S.: How did you develop the dramatic interpretation of operatic character?

G.-C.: As I studied, I felt my voice growing firmer, my art surer. But I was not satisfied with my dramatic interpretations, so I sought advice from Boetta Valvassura, a famous actress of the time.

"You can do what you wish," she declared after she had tested my dramatic resources, "because you have the feeling here"—tapping her left side—"and enough here," putting a forefinger to her brow.

Her enthusiasm was intense, and her great art moved me often to tears. So from Valvassura I learned how to express emotion in acting, and I sought to apply to my roles all that she taught me. Presently, the public commenced to notice my acting as well as my singing.

From Valvassura I learned to ennoble things as much as possible. From her I learned the safer, the wiser path of idealization of character. So in fashioning my interpretations I never gave in to what one might call the naturalistic school of acting, but always idealized wherever possible. I felt that it was much more important to dwell on the thought behind the action rather than the simple aspects of the physical action itself. One careless gesture can ruin a whole performance, regardless of how "realistic" it might be, and, when the audience leaves the theater, it is that ugly stage business that remains in its mind, not the beauty of the voice it has heard! The singer must paint with the voice, must color the emotion with the tone he produces. This painting of the characterization with the voice is the secret of all singing.

But lest you think I do not believe in verity, when I first was to sing Mimi and Violetta, I went to a physician to learn the correct use of the hands, the quick, almost jerky gestures and incessant fidgeting that are characteristic of the consumptive. The doctor impressed upon me that in the last stages of tuberculosis there is no cough, only a terrible stabbing pain in the lungs. So in the last acts of *Traviata* and *Boheme* I did not cough, but clutched my chest as if to tear out the pain.

W. S.: A few moments ago you were talking about coloring tones. Was your concern for color in tone matched by your reaction to color in everyday life?

G.-C.: One of my very first recollections of childhood is ecstasy over color. The color of the sky, and those incomparable blue heavens stretching out over distant mountains, still fill me with rapture. A bright piece of Florentine glass, or a flower in the woods, or a length of golden silk—by the bright and shining I was enthralled. So it was a natural thing, when I became a singer, to put this love of color into my voice. I was a better artist because of it, and it grounded more firmly my conception of art's purpose: that through the color of beauty we can transmit a soothing calmness and a harmony of soul.

W. S.: In addition to a beautiful voice, what other gifts are necessary for a successful career?

G.-C.: The greatest gift to the singer—to any performing artist—is the gift of simplicity: simplicity of character, of vision, of sympathy, of poise with the rest of the world. We must learn to look the other man straight in the eye, with friendliness, not suspicion, with sympathy for him and faith in what he is. This is the only way for the artist to look at life—at the things, people and impressions that life give him. There are no intellectual dangers or complications to this kind of outlook, no radical disturbances. During my public career I set aside at least one hour every day in which it was possible for me to be entirely alone. The spirit can only be refreshed by private conference—it stimulates and strengthens one who is made to be constantly active. And it is in these quiet hours that we learn the simplicity of understanding that brings about simplicity in art.

W. S.: Lately we have had some very tempestuous prima donnas in our opera houses. Were you ever one of these?

G.-C.: I had plenty of that vital energy sometimes called temper, or temperament. But there was nothing morose or sullen about it. I exploded at things I considered to be injustices, and then all was sunny again. Artists must remember one very important thing: to be practical!

The great career is built alone, in solitude and discouragement. One must weep in tears and sweat blood for it!

W. S.: What do you think is the most important element in art?

G.-C.: Art must always be beautiful. The artist's realization of beauty transmutes itself to the voice, without question. Beauty must be emphasized in the performing life of the artist, just as it is in the performing life of Nature.

Galli-Curci Performances with the Metropolitan Opera

1921 – 1922 Season

11-14-21 TRAVIATA: Gigli, DeLuca, Moranzoni
11-17-21 LUCIA: Gigli, Danise, Mardones, Papi
11-23-21 TRAVIATA: Gigli, Danise, Moranzoni
11-26-21 RIGOLETTO: Chamlee, DeLuca, Rothier, Papi
11-27-21 Caruso Memorial Concert: Galli-Curci sang Ave Maria (Gounod)
12-2-21 LUCIA: Gigli, Danise, Martino, Papi
2-2-22 TRAVIATA: Gigli, DeLuca, Moranzoni
2-6-22 BARBER OF SEVILLE: Chamlee, DeLuca, Mardones, Papi
2-10-22 RIGOLETTO: Chamlee, DeLuca, Rothier, Papi
2-18-22 BARBER OF SEVILLE: Harrold, DeLuca, Mardones, Papi
2-19-22 Caruso Foundation Concert: Polonaise (Mignon)
2-22-22 RIGOLETTO: Gigli, DeLuca, Rothier, Papi
2-24-22 LUCIA: Gigli, DeLuca, Mardones, Papi

1921 – 1922 Tour

11-29-21 (Philadelphia) LUCIA: Martinelli, Danise, Mardones, Papi
1-31-22 (Brooklyn) BARBER OF SEVILLE: Harrold, Ruffo, Didur, Papi
2-14-22 (Philadelphia) TRAVIATA: Gigli, DeLuca, Moranzoni
4-28-22 (Atlanta) TRAVIATA: Gigli, DeLuca, Moranzoni

1922 – 1923 Season

1-24-23 LUCIA: Martinelli, Danise, Mardones, Papi
1-26-23 RIGOLETTO: Lauri-Volpi, DeLuca, Rothier, Moranzoni
1-29-23 BARBER OF SEVILLE: Chamlee, Ruffo, Didur, Papi
2-3-23 TRAVIATA: Lauri-Volpi, Danise, Moranzoni
2-8-23 BARBER OF SEVILLE: Lauri-Volpi, Ruffo, Didur, Papi
2-15-23 RIGOLETTO: Lauri-Volpi, DeLuca, Rothier, Moranzoni
2-19-23 LUCIA: Gigli, DeLuca, Rothier, Papi
2-23-23 BOHEME: Chamlee, DeLuca, Mardones, Papi

1922 – 1923 Tour

2-6-23 (Philadelphia) RIGOLETTO: Chamlee, Danise, Mardones, Bamboschek
2-13-23 (Brooklyn) LUCIA: Chamlee, DeLuca, Mardones, Papi
4-25-23 (Atlanta) LUCIA: Gigli, DeLuca, Mardones, Papi

1923 – 1924 Season

1-16-24 BARBER OF SEVILLE: Chamlee, DeLuca, Mardones, Papi
1-19-24 LUCIA: Martinelli, DeLuca, Mardones, Papi
1-21-24 COQ D'OR: Didur, Diaz, Bamboschek
1-24-24 TRAVIATA: Chamlee, DeLuca, Moranzoni

2–1–24 COQ D'OR: Didur, Diaz, Bamboschek
2–3–24 Concert: LUCIA: Mad Scene, Bamboschek (conductor)
2–7–24 RIGOLETTO: Lauri-Volpi, DeLuca, Papi
2–11–24 ROMEO AND JULIET: Johnson, DeLuca, Hasselmans
2–15–24 COQ D'OR: Didur, Diaz, Bamboschek

1923 – 1924 Tour

1–29–24 (Brooklyn) RIGOLETTO: Chamlee, DeLuca, Mardones, Papi
2–5–24 (Philadelphia) LUCIA: Harrold, DeLuca, Mardones, Bamboschek

1924 – 1925 Season

1–12–25 BARBER OF SEVILLE: Errolle, Ruffo, Didur, Papi
1–16–25 RIGOLETTO: Fleta, DeLuca, Mardones, Serafin
1–22–25 DINORAH: Tokatyan, DeLuca, Papi
1–24–25 LUCIA: Gigli, DeLuca, Mardones, Papi
1–28–25 RIGOLETTO: Fleta, Ballester, Mardones, Serafin
1–30–25 DINORAH: Tokatyan, DeLuca, Papi
2–5–25 COQ D'OR: Didur, Diaz, Bamboschek
2–8–25 Concert: Polonaise (Mignon), Home, Sweet Home
2–13–25 TRAVIATA: Lauri-Volpi, DeLuca, Serafin
2–17–25 LUCIA: Gigli, DeLuca, Mardones, Papi

1924 – 1925 Tour

2–3–25 (Philadelphia) DINORAH: Tokatyan, DeLuca, Papi
2–10–25 (Brooklyn) LUCIA: Lauri-Volpi, Danise, Mardones, Papi

1925 – 1926 Season

1–15–26 TRAVIATA: Chamlee, DeLuca, Serafin
1–18–26 BARBER OF SEVILLE: Chamlee, DeLuca, Mardones, Papi
1–22–26 LUCIA: Martinelli, DeLuca, Mardones, Papi
1–30–26 RIGOLETTO: Chamlee, DeLuca, Mardones, Serafin
2–3–26 LUCIA: Chamlee, DeLuca, Mardones, Papi
2–5–26 ROMEO AND JULIET: Johnson, DeLuca, Hasselmans
2–7–26 Concert: DINORAH: Ombra leggiera
2–9–26 TRAVIATA: Lauri-Volpi, DeLuca, Serafin
2–11–26 BARBER OF SEVILLE: Chamlee, DeLuca, Mardones, Papi

1925 – 1926 Tour

1–12–26 (Philadelphia) BARBER OF SEVILLE: Tokatyan, Danise, Mardones, Papi
1–26–26 (Brooklyn) BARBER OF SEVILLE: Tokatyan, DeLuca, Mardones, Papi
5–3–26 (Cleveland) RIGOLETTO: Lauri-Volpi, DeLuca, Didur, Serafin

1926 – 1927 Season

1–5–27 TRAVIATTA: Gigli, DeLuca, Serafin
1–10–27 BARBER OF SEVILLE: Chamlee, DeLuca, Pinza, Bellezza
1–13–27 RIGOLETTO: Gigli, Basiola, Rothier, Serafin
1–21–27 LUCIA: Tokatyan, Danise, Rothier, Bellezza
1–23–27 Concert: DINORAH: Ombra leggiera
1–27–27 BARBER OF SEVILLE: Chamlee, Basiola, Pinza, Bellezza
1–31–27 TRAVIATA: Chamlee, Danise, Serafin
2–5–27 RIGOLETTO: Chamlee, DeLuca, Pinza, Bellezza

1926 – 1927 Tour

1-18-27 (Philadelphia) RIGOLETTO: Lauri-Volpi, Danise, Didur, Bellezza
1-25-27 (Brooklyn) RIGOLETTO: Lauri-Volpi, Danise, Rothier, Bellezza
4-20-27 (Baltimore) RIGOLETTO: Gigli, DeLuca, Pinza, Bellezza
4-22-27 (Washington) TRAVIATA: Gigli, DeLuca, Serafin
4-25-27 (Atlanta) TRAVIATA: Gigli, Tibbett, Serafin
5-4-27 (Cleveland) TRAVIATA: Gigli, Tibbett, Serafin

1927 – 1928 Season

1-2-28 BARBER OF SEVILLE: Chamlee, Ruffo, Rinza, Bellezza
1-6-28 LUCIA: Martinelli, DeLuca, Pinza, Bellezza
1-9-28 RIGOLETTO: Lauri-Volpi, DeLuca, Didur, Bellezza
1-13-28 TRAVIATA: Lauri-Volpi, DeLuca, Serafin
1-19-28 BARBER OF SEVILLE: Chamlee, Ruffo, Rothier, Bellezza
1-22-28 Concert: DINORAH: Ombra leggiera
1-28-28 TRAVIATA: Chamlee, DeLuca, Serafin
2-3-28 BARBER OF SEVILLE: Chamlee, Ruffo, Rothier, Bellezza

1927 – 1928 Tour

1-17-28 (Brooklyn) LUCIA: Martinelli, DeLuca, Pinza, Bellezza
1-31-28 (Philadelphia) BARBER OF SEVILLE: Tokatyan, DeLuca, Pinza, Bellezza
4-24-28 (Atlanta) BARBER OF SEVILLE: Tokatyan, DeLuca, Pinza, Bellezza
5-3-28 (Cleveland) RIGOLETTO: Gigli, DeLuca, Rothier, Bellezza

1928 – 1929 Season

1-7-28 BARBER OF SEVILLE: Tokatyan, Ruffo, Pinza, Bellezza
1-11-28 LUCIA: Jagel, Danise, Pinza, Bamboschek
1-18-28 BARBER OF SEVILLE: Tokatyan, Ruffo, Rothier, Bellezza
1-23-28 RIGOLETTO: Lauri-Volpi, DeLuca, Rothier, Bamboschek
1-25-28 TRAVIATA: Lauri-Volpi, Basiola, Serafin
1-27-28 Concert: DINORAH: Ombra leggiera, Dein blaues Auge (Brahms), Die Forelle (Schubert), La Paloma (Yradier), Clavelitos (Valverde)
2-2-28 LUCIA: Jagel, DeLuca, Rothier, Bamboschek

1928 – 1929 Tour

1-15-29 (Brooklyn) TRAVIATA: Lauri-Volpi, DeLuca, Bamboschek
1-29-29 (Philadelphia) BARBER OF SEVILLE: Tokatyan, Ruffo, Pinza, Bamboschek

1929 – 1930 Season

12-26-28 BARBER OF SEVILLE: Tokatyan, DeLuca, Pinza, Bellezza
12-31-28 RIGOLETTO: Gigli, Danise, Rothier, Bellezza
1-12-29 Concert: Romance (Debussy), Die Forelle (Schubert), Das Veilchen (Mozart), La Paloma (Yradier)
1-18-29 ROMEO AND JULIET: Johnson, Tibbett, Rothier, Hasselmans
1-24-29 BARBER OF SEVILLE: Tokatyan, DeLuca, Pinza, Bellezza

1929 – 1930 Tour

1-7-30 (Philadelphia) LUCIA: Martinelli, Danise, Pasero, Bellezza
1-14-30 (Brooklyn) BARBER OF SEVILLE: Tokatyan, Danise, Pinza, Bellezza

Galli-Curci Performances with the Chicago Opera

1916 – 1917 Season

11–18–16 RIGOLETTO: Nadal, Rimini, Arimondi, Sturani
11–21–16 LUCIA: Nadal, Polese, Arimondi, Sturani
11–29–16 RIGOLETTO: Nadal, Rimini, Arimondi, Sturani
12–1–16 TRAVIATA: Crimi, Rimini, Sturani
12–4–16 LUCIA: Nadal, Polese, Arimondi, Sturani
12–13–16 RIGOLETTO: Nadal, Rimini, Arimondi, Sturani
12–15–16 ROMEO AND JULIET: Muratore, Maguenat, Journet, Charlier
12–21–16 TRAVIATA: Nadal, Polese, Sturani
12–23–16 ROMEO AND JULIET: Muratore, Maguenat, Journet, Charlier
12–27–16 LUCIA: Nadal, Polese, Arimondi, Sturani
1–1–17 BARBER OF SEVILLE: Nadal, Rimini, Trevisan, Campanini
1–3–17 ROMEO AND JULIET: Muratore, Maguenat, Journet, Charlier
1–7–17 LUCIA: Nadal, Polese, Arimondi, Sturani
1–9–17 RIGOLETTO: Nadal, Rimini, Arimondi, Sturani
1–11–17 ROMEO AND JULIET: Muratore, Maguenat, Journet, Charlier
1–14–17 BARBER OF SEVILLE: Nadal, Rimini, Trevisan, Campanini
1–19–17 Grand Gala: Galli-Curci sang LUCIA: Mad Scene with Arimondi, Sturani (conductor)
1–21–17 Benefit for Victims of War: ROMEO AND JULIET: Balcony Scene with Muratore

1917 – 1918 Season

11–13–17 LUCIA: Crimi, Rimini, Arimondi, Sturani
11–16–17 DINORAH: Dua, Rimini, Campanini
11–18–17 ROMEO AND JULIET: Muratore, Maguenat, Huberdeau, Campanini
11–21–17 DINORAH: Dua, Rimini, Campanini
11–25–17 RIGOLETTO: Nadal, Stracciari, Arimondi, Sturani
11–27–17 ROMEO AND JULIET: Muratore, Maguenat, Huberdeau, Charlier
11–29–17 RIGOLETTO: Nadal, Stracciari, Arimondi, Sturani
12–2–17 TRAVIATA: Nadal, Stracciari, Sturani
12–3–17 ROMEO AND JULIET: Muratore, Maguenat, Huberdeau, Charlier
12–8–17 DINORAH: Dua, Rimini, Conti
12–12–17 ROMEO AND JULIET: Muratore, Maguenat, Huberdeau, Charlier
12–16–17 BARBER OF SEVILLE: Nadal, Rimini, Trevisan, Sturani
12–19–17 TRAVIATA: Nadal, Stracciari, Sturani
12–21–17 LAKME: Muratore, Baklanoff, Charlier
12–24–17 DINORAH: Dua, Rimini, Conti
12–27–17 TRAVIATA: Nadal, Stracciari, Sturani
12–31–17 LAKME: Muratore, Baklanoff, Charlier
1–8–17 DINORAH: Dua, Rimini, Conti
1–13–18 BOHEME: Crimi, Rimini, Huberdeau, Sturani

261

1917 – 1918 Chicago Tour
New York Performances Given in the Lexington Theatre

1-28-18   DINORAH: Dua, Rimini, Huberdeau, Campanini
1-31-18   LUCIA: Nadal, Rimini, Arimondi, Sturani
2-6-18   BARBER OF SEVILLE: Nadal, Rimini, Trevisan, Sturani
2-9-18   RIGOLETTO: Nadal, Stracciari, Arimondi, Sturani
2-11-18   ROMEO AND JULIET: Muratore, Maguenat, Huberdeau, Campanini
2-13-18   BARBER OF SEVILLE: Nadal, Rimini, Trevisan, Sturani
2-15-18   TRAVIATA: Nadal, Stracciari, Sturani

1918 – 1919 Season

11-18-18   TRAVIATA: Ciccolini, Stracciari, Polacco
11-23-18   LUCIA: Dolci, Stracciari, Arimondi, Campanini
11-28-18   LINDA: Lamont, Stracciari, Lazzari, Trevisan, Sturani
12-1-18   BOHEME: McCormack, Rimini, Huberdeau, Polacco
12-3-18   BARBER OF SEVILLE: Carpi, Stracciari, Trevisan, Campanini
12-11-18   TRAVIATA: Ciccolini, Stracciari, Polacco
12-13-18   LINDA: Lamont, Stracciari, Lazzari, Trevisan, Sturani
12-16-18   BARBER OF SEVILLE: Ciccolini, Stracciari, Trevisan, Campanini
12-21-18   LINDA: Lamont, Stracciari, Lazzari, Trevisan, Sturani
12-25-18   CRISPINO E LA COMARE: Stracciari, Trevisan, Arimondi, Campanini
12-27-18   LUCIA: Lamont, Rimini, Arimondi, Campanini
12-28-18   Special Performance: HAMLET: Act IV
12-31-18   DINORAH: Dua, Rimini, Lazzari, Campanini

1918 – 1919 Tour

2-4-19   LINDA: Lamont, Stracciari, Lazzari, Trevisan, Sturani
2-7-19   LUCIA: Dolci, Rimini, Arimondi, Campanini
2-12-19   BARBER OF SEVILLE: Carpi, Stracciari, Trevisan, Campanini
2-15-19   TRAVIATA: Dolci, Stracciari, Polacco
2-17-19   CRISPINO: Stracciari, Trevisan, Arimondi, Campanini
2-20-19   DINORAH: Dua, Rimini, Lazzari, Campanini
2-26-19   TRAVIATA: Dolci, Stracciari, Polacco
3-1-19   LUCIA: Dolci, Rimini, Arimondi, Campanini

1919 – 1920 Season

12-4-19   RIGOLETTO: Schipa, Galeffi, Cotreuil, Marinuzzi
12-7-19   LUCIA: Dolci, Rimini, Arimondi, de Angelis
12-9-19   TRAVIATA: Dolci, Galeffi, de Angelis
12-13-19   BARBER OF SEVILLE: Schipa, Galeffi, Trevisan, Marinuzzi
12-15-19   RIGOLETTO: Schipa, Galeffi, Arimondi, Marinuzzi
12-17-19   SONNAMBULA: Schipa, Lazzari, de Angelis
12-23-19   SONNAMBULA: Schipa, Lazzari, de Angelis
12-25-19   LUCIA: Dolci, Rimini, Arimondi, de Angelis
12-27-19   DON PASQUALE: Schipa, Trevisan, Rimini, Marinuzzi
12-29-19   SONNAMBULA: Schipa, Lazzari, de Angelis
12-31-19   DON PASQUALE: Schipa, Trevisan, Rimini, Marinuzzi and DINORAH: Act II, Scene 1

1919 – 1920 Tour
New York Performances Given in the Lexington Theatre

2-10-20 LUCIA: Bonci, Rimini, Arimondi, de Angelis
2-14-20 DON PASQUALE: Schipa, Trevisan, Rimini, Marinuzzi
2-18-20 DINORAH: Dua, Rimini, Lazzari, Marinuzzi
2-20-20 RIGOLETTO: Schipa, Ruffo, Arimondi, Marinuzzi
2-24-20 BARBER OF SEVILLE: Schipa, Galeffi, Trevisan, Marinuzzi
2-26-20 TRAVIATA: Schipa, Galeffi, de Angelis

1920 – 1921 Season

12-1-20 LUCIA: Schipa, Rimini, Lazzari, Cimini
12-4-20 SONNAMBULA: Schipa, Lazzari, Cimini
12-7-20 BARBER OF SEVILLE: Schipa, Galeffi, Trevisan, Marinuzzi
12-12-20 ROMEO AND JULIET: Hislop, Defrere, Cotreuil, Morin
12-16-20 LINDA: Lamont, Rimini, Trevisan, Lazzari, Cimini
12-18-20 LAKME: Schipa, Baklanoff, Morin
12-20-20 TRAVIATA: Schipa, Galeffi, Smallens
12-22-20 ROMEO AND JULIET: Hislop, Defrere, Cotreuil, Morin
12-26-20 BOHEME: Bonci, Rimini, Lazzari, Cimini
12-28-20 LAKME: Schipa, Baklanoff, Morin
12-30-20 LUCIA: Bonci, Rimini, Lazzari, Cimini

1920 – 1921 Tour
New York Performances Given in the Lexington Theatre

2-5-21 SONNAMBULA: Schipa, Rimini, Trevisan, Cimini
2-9-21 ROMEO AND JULIET: Muratore, Defrere, Cotreuil, Morin
2-11-21 BARBER OF SEVILLE: Schipa, Galeffi, Trevisan, Marinuzzi
2-15-21 LAKME: Schipa, Baklanoff, Morin
2-19-21 TRAVIATA: Schipa, Galeffi, Smallens
2-22-21 ROMEO AND JULIET: Muratore, Defrere, Cotreuil, Morin
2-24-21 BOHEME: Bonci, Rimini, Lazzari, Cimini
2-26-21 RIGOLETTO: Schipa, Galeffi, Lazzari, Cimini
3-2-21 TRAVIATA: Schipa, Galeffi, Smallens

1921 – 1922 Season

12-20-21 TRAVIATA: Schipa, Schwarz, Polacco
12-24-21 LUCIA: Schipa, Rimini, Lazzari, Cimini
12-29-21 BARBER OF SEVILLE: Schipa, Ballester, Trevisan, Lazzari, Ferrari
1-1-22 RIGOLETTO: Lamont, Schwarz, Lazzari, Polacco
1-3-22 ROMEO AND JULIET: Muratore, Maguenat, Payan, Grovlez
1-7-22 MADAMA BUTTERFLY: Johnson, Baklanoff, Polacco
1-9-22 BOHEME: Pattiera, Rimini, Lazzari, Ferrari
1-11-22 LAKME: Schipa, Maguenat, Baklanoff, Grovlez
1-17-22 MADAMA BUTTERFLY: Johnson, Baklanoff, Polacco
1-20-22 TRAVIATA: Schipa, Schwarz, Polacco

1922 – 1923 Season

12-15-22 LUCIA: Schipa, Rimini, Lazzari, Cimini
12-21-22 MADAMA BUTTERFLY: Crimi, Rimini, Panizza
12-24-22 TRAVIATA: Schipa, Rimini, Polacco
12-26-22 BOHEME: Minghetti, Rimini, Lazzari, Panizza

12–29–22 MANON: Schipa, Defrere, Cotreuil, Hageman
 1–1–23   TRAVIATA: Schipa, Rimini, Polacco
 1–3–23   BARBER OF SEVILLE: Schipa, Rimini, Trevisan, Lazzari, Cimini
 1–7–23   RIGOLETTO: Schipa, Formichi, Lazzari, Panizza
 1–9–23   MANON: Schipa, Defrere, Cotreuil, Hageman
 1–13–23 TRAVIATA: Schipa, Rimini, Polacco

1923 – 1924 Season

12–3–23   LAKME: Errolle, Baklanoff, Panizza
12–7–23   DINORAH: Mojica, Rimini, Lazzari, Panizza
12–12–23 TRAVIATA: Schipa, Rimini, Polacco
12–16–23 LAKME: Schipa, Baklanoff, Panizza
12–18–23 DINORAH: Mojica, Rimini, Lazzari, Panizza
12–21–23 BARBER OF SEVILLE: Schipa, Rimini, Trevisan, Arimondi, Panizza
12–23–23 LUCIA: Schipa, Gandolfi, Lazzari, Cimini
12–27–23 TRAVIATA: Schipa, Rimini, Polacco
12–29–23 DINORAH: Mojica, Rimini, Lazzari, Panizza
 1–4–24   ROMEO AND JULIET: Hackett, Defrere, Cotreuil, Polacco

1936 Season

11–24–36 BOHEME: Tokatyan, Rimini, Cehanovsky, Trevisan, Moranzoni

Discography

Discography

Title	Matrix	Date Recorded	Victor s/s	Victor d/s	HMV s/s	HMV d/s
1 Abide With Me (Monk)	B–28463	12/22/25		1194	3–3061	DB–864
2 Air & Variations (Proch)	C–20663	9/13/17	74557	6134	2–053133	DB–265
3 Air & Variations (Proch)	CVE–20663	5/12/27		6784	2–053309	DB–1144
BARBIERE DI SIVIGLIA (Rossini)						
4 Una voce poco fa	C–20045	6/15/17	74541	6130	2–053142	DB–261
5 Una voce poco fa	CVE–20045	12/15/27		7110	42–663	DB–1355
6 Senti, senti (with Tibbett)	BVE–35446	5/7/26	—UNPUBLISHED—			
BOHEME: (Puccini)						
7 Mi chiamano Mimi	C–26888	9/21/22	—UNPUBLISHED—			
8 Cantata con stromenti (Scarlatti)	CVE–47428	9/5/28		7658	42–1043	DB–1516
9 Capinera (Benedict)	B–21961	6/11/18	64792	629	7–53029	DA–217
10 Capinera (Benedict)	BVE–21961	9/19/27		1338	7–53130	DA–1002
11 Carme (Neapolitan Folk Song)	BVE–45148	5/16/28	—UNPUBLISHED—			
12 Caro mio bene (Giordani)	B–20041	6/14/17	64723	629	7–53030	DA–217
13 Clavelitos (Valverde)	B–24176	6/21/20	64904	635	7–63005	DA–215
14 Clavelitos (Valverde)	BVE–46387	12/12/28		1449	40–1451	DA–1095
15 Comin' thru the Rye (Old Scotch Air)	BVE–46391	12/13/28	—UNPUBLISHED—			
COPPELIA: (Delibes)						
16 Waltze	B–30285	9/6/24		1068		
COQ D'OR: (Rimsky-Korsakov)						
17 Hymne au soleil	B–25549	9/8/21	66069	631	7–33053	DA–219
18 Crepuscule (Massenet)	B–21972	6/10/18	64807	632	7–33021	DA–212
19 Danza (Rossimi)	BVE–59731	3/28/30	—UNPUBLISHED—			
DINORAH: (Meyerbeer)						
20 Si carina	C–3091	6/17/24		6469	2–053230	DB–798
21 Ombra leggiera	C–20047	6/15/17	74532	6129	2–053134	DB–260
22 Ombra leggiera:						
(Part I)	BVE–34246	12/28/25		1174	7–53100	DB–817
(Part II)	BVE–34247	12/29/25			7–53099	

Title	Matrix	Date Recorded	Victor s/s	Victor d/s	HMV s/s	HMV d/s
DON CESAR DE BAZAN: (Massenet)						
23 Sevillana	B–28465	9/13/23		1018	7–33064	DA–611
DON PASQUALE: (Donizetti)						
24 Quel guardo	C–23169	9/23/19	74599	6128	2–053161	DB–259
25 Tormani a dir che m'ami (with Schipa)	B–26890	9/18/24		3034		
26 Tormani a dir che m'ami (with Schipa)	BVE–26890	9/6/28		1755 & 3056	40–2899	DA–1161
27 Dreamin' Time (Strickland)	BVE–34248	12/28/25		1144		
28 Echo Song (Bishop)	C–25548	9/8/21	74743	6127	03785	DB–258
29 Echo Song (Bishop)	CVE–25548	9/6/30	—UNPUBLISHED—			
30 Estrellita (Ponce)	B–30290	9/19/24		1097		
31 Estrellita (Ponce)	BVE–46387	12/12/28		1449	40–1367	DA–1095
ETOILE DU NORD: (Meyerbeer)						
32 La, la, la air cheri	CVE–36624	9/5/30		7655	42–1041	DB–1477
33 Veille sur eux toujours	C–26887	9/20/22	6357	74784	2–033089	DB–597
FAUST: (Gounod)						
34 Jewel Song	C–20670	9/14/19	—UNPUBLISHED—			
35 Filles de Cadiz (Delibes)	B–23134	9/4/19	64885	632	7–33030	DA–212
36 Filles de Cadiz (Delibes)	BVE–23134	3/31/30		1524	40–2895	DA–1164
37 Die Forelle (Shubert)	BVE–63627	9/5/30	—UNPUBLISHED—			
38 Gypsy & the Bird (Benedict)	BVE–38034	5/12/27		1267	3–3215	DA–928
HAMLET: (Thomas)						
39 Mad Scene: (Part I)	CVE–34232	12/28/25		6562	2–053256	DB–927
(Part II)	CVE–34233	12/28/25			2–053257	
40 Home, sweet home (Moore)	C–19149	1/31/17	74511	6123	03571	DB–602
41 Home, sweet home (Moore)	CVE–19149	5/13/27	—UNPUBLISHED—			
42 Home, sweet home (Moore)	BVE–45149	5/16/28		1355	3–3350	DA–1011
HIJAS DEL ZEBEDEO: (Chapi)						
43 Carcelaras	BVE–35445	5/7/26		1167	7–63035	DA–805
.44 I cannot sing the old songs (Barnard)	B–25551	9/7/21	—UNPUBLISHED—			
45 Jurame (Grever)	BVE–47429	9/5/28	—UNPUBLISHED—			
LAKME: (Delibes)						
46 Bell Song	C–18595	3/5/17	74510	6132	2–053130	DB–263
47 Lead Kindly Light	B–28468	6/18/24	—UNPUBLISHED—			
48 Lead Kindly Light	BVE–28468	12/22/25		1194	3–3134	DA–864

Title	Matrix	Date Recorded	Victor s/s	Victor d/s	HMV s/s	HMV d/s
LINDA DI CHAMOUNIX: (Donizetti)						
49 O luce di quest'anima	C–26889	9/22/22	74812	6357	2–053211	DB–597
50 Little Birdies (Buzzi-Peccia)	B–20040	6/14/17	64723	629	7–53030	DA–217
51 Little Dorry (Sappielli)	B–20662	9/12/17	64749		2–3324	
52 Little prayer for me (Russell)	B–30282	6/16/24	—UNPUBLISHED—			
53 Lo! Here the gentle lark (Bishop)	C–23131	9/4/19	74608	6127	03728	DB–258
54 Lo! Here the gentle lark (Bishop)	CVE–23131	12/15/27		6924	03952	DB–1278
55 Long, long ago (Bayly)	BVE–45151	5/17/28		1566		
56 Love's old sweet song (Molloy)	B–24179	6/1/23		998		
57 Love's old sweet song (Molloy)	BVE–45150	5/17/28		1412		DA–1056
LUCIA DI LAMERMOOR: (Donizetti)						
58 Verrano a te (with Schipa)	C–30910	9/17/24		8067	2–054152	DB–811
59 Verrano a te (with Schipa)	CVE–30910	9/7/28	—UNPUBLISHED—			
60 Sextette (with Caruso; Egener; de Luca; Journet; Bada)	C–19133	1/25/17	95100	10000	2–054066	DQ–100
61 Sextette (with Gigli; Homer; Pinza; de Luca; Bada)	CVE–41232	12/12/27		10012	2–054209	DQ–102
62 Il dolce suono	C–18587	2/1/17	74509	6129	2–053128	DB–620
63 Il dolce suono	CVE–18587	5/6/26	—UNPUBLISHED—			
64 Spargi d'amaro pianto	C–26595	7/11/22	—UNPUBLISHED—			
65 Spargi d'amaro pianto	B–26595	9/21/22	66125	634	7–53056	DA–214
66 Spargi d'amaro pianto	CVE–26595	5/7/26	—UNPUBLISHED—			
MADAMA BUTTERFLY: (Puccini)						
67 Un bel di	C–26598	9/20/22	74786	6130	2–053208	DB–261
MLLE. MODISTE: (Herbert)						
68 Kiss me again	B–28472	9/13/23		959		
69 Mah Lindy Lou (Strickland)	B–30281	6/17/24		1047		
MANON: (Massenet)						
70 Obeissons	B–28467	9/13/23		1018	7–33–65	DA–611
MANON LESCAUT: (Auber)						
71 L'Eclat de rire	B–19338	3/5/17	64609	635	7–33017	DA–215
MARTHA: (Moore-Flotow)						
72 Last rose of summer	C–20042	9/9/21	74536	6123	03652	DB–602
73 Last rose of summer	CVE–20042	5/13/27	—UNPUBLISHED—			

Title	Matrix	Date Recorded	Victor s/s	Victor d/s	HMV s/s	HMV d/s
74 Last rose of summer	BVE–45152	5/17/28		1355	3–3351	DA–1011
75 Memory Lane (Conrad)	B–30904	9/18/24		1047		
76 Messaggero Amoroso (Chopin-Buzzi-Pecia)	B–23132	9/3/19	64991	633	7–53051	DA–213
MIGNON: (Thomas)						
77 Io son Titania	C–22615	9/4/19	74653	6133	2–053186	DE–264
78 Io son Titania	CVE–22615	12/12/28		7110	42–689	DB–1355
79 My old Kentucky home (Foster)	BVE–46388	12/12/28		1412	40–744	DA–1056
80 No quiero casarme (Spanish folk song)	BVE–47429	9/5/28	—UNPUBLISHED—			
81 No te vayas, te lo pido (arranged by Guervos)	B–30286	6/18/24		1097		
NOZZE DI FIGARO: (Mozart)						
82 Non so piu	B–20661	9/12/17	64748	634	7–53023	DA–214
83 Ol' Car'lina (Cooke)	B–25550	9/7/21	66014	628	2–3629	DA–328
84 Old folks at home (Foster)	B–26594	7/12/22	66092	628	2–3695	DA–328
85 Old folks at home (Foster)	BVE–63628	9/5/30		1566		
ORANGE BLOSSOMS: (Herbert)						
86 A kiss in the dark	B–28464	9/13/23		959		
87 Parla! (Arditi)	BVE–38036	5/12/27		1267	7–53122	DA–928
88 Paloma (Yradier)	BVE–45147	5/16/28		1338	7–63089	DA–1002
89 Partida (Alvarez)	C–18586	10/30/16	74500	6134	2–063006	DB–0265
PECHEURS DE PERLES: (Bizet)						
90 Comme autrefois	C–25553	9/9/21	74718	6124	2–033086	DB–255
PEER GYNT: (Grieg)						
91 Solveig's Song	C–19339	3/5/17	74522	6132	2–033059	DB–263
92 Solveig's Song	CVE–19339	3/16/28		6924	2–033142	DB–1278
PERLE DU BRESIL: (David)						
93 Charmant oiseau	C–20664	9/14/17	74552	6124	2–033086	DB–255
94 Pretty Mocking Bird (Bishop)	C–30283	6/18/24		6469	03840	DB–798
PHILEMON ET BAUCIS: (Gounod)						
95 O, riante Nature	CVE–58128	3/28/30		7658	42–1042	DB–1516
PURITANI: (Bellini)						
96 Son vergin vezzosa	C–28466	9/11/23		6432	2–053214	DB–641
97 Qui la voce	C–20669	9/14/17	74558		2–053137	DB–259
98 Qui la voce	C–20669	6/22/20		6128		
RIGOLETTO: (Verdi)						
99 Veglia o donna (with de Luca)	BVE–41236	12/16/27		3051	7–54049	DA–1028

Title	Matrix	Date Recorded	Victor s/s	Victor d/s	HMV s/s	HMV d/s
100 E il sol dell'anima (with Schipa)	B–30909	9/17/24		3034		
101 E il sol dell'anima (with Schipa)	BVE–30909	9/7/28		1755 & 3056	40–2900	DB–1161
102 Caro nome	C–18596	2/2/17	74499	6126	2–053126	DB–257
103 Caro nome	CVE–18596	5/13/27		7655	42–1039	DB–1477
104 Tutte le feste	C–28470	9/12/23		6432	2–053217	DB–641
105 Piangi fanciulla (with de Luca)	B–21973	6/11/18	87567	3027	7–54011	
106 Piangi fanciulla (with de Luca)	BVE–41237	12/16/27		3051	7–54048	DA–1028
107 Si vendetta (with Tibbett)	BVE–35447	5/7/26	—UNPUBLISHED—			
108 Quartet (with Caruso; Perini; de Luca)	C–19132	1/26/17	95100	10000	2–054066	DQ–100
109 Quartet (with Gigli; Homer; de Luca)	CVE–41233	12/12/27		10012	2–054210	DQ–102
110 Lassu in ciel (with de Luca)	C–21973	6/11/18	—UNPUBLISHED—			
ROMEO & JULIETTE: (Gounod)						
111 Waltz	C–19148	1/31/17	74512	6133	2–033058	DB–264
112 Waltz	CVE–19148	12/13/28	—UNPUBLISHED—			
113 Russian nightingale (Alabieff)	BVE–40221	12/13/27		1449	40–1367	DA–1095
SADKO: (Rimsky-Korsakov)						
114 Song of India	B–26596	9/21/22	66136	631	7–33059	DA–219
115 Song of India	BVE–26596	3/26/30		1524	40–2896	DA–1164
116 Sandmannchen (Brahms)	BVE–63629	9/6/30	—UNPUBLISHED—			
117 Schnelglockchen (Schumann)	BVE–63629	9/6/30	—UNPUBLISHED—			
SEMIRAMIDE: (Rossini)						
118 Bel raggio	C–30905	9/16/24				VB–5
119 Serenade (Pierne)	B–30284	6/17/24		1068		
120 Serenata (Tosti)	BVE–34251	5/6/26		1167	7–53098	DA–805
121 Silver threads among the gold (Danks)	B–28471	9/12/23		998		
122 Sometime (Fiorito)	BVE–34235	12/24/25		1144		
SONNAMBULA: (Bellini)						
123 Come per me	C–24177	6/22/20	74644	6125	2–053198	DB–256
124 Sovra il sen	B–23170	9/23/19	64918	633	7–53050	DA–213
125 Son geloso (with Schipa)	C–27994	6/1/23		8067	2–054151	DB–811
126 Ah, non credea	C–20048	6/15/17	74538	6125	2–053135	DB–256
127 Ah, non giunge	C–30906	9/16/24				VB–5
128 Swanee River (Foster)	BVE–63628	9/5/30	—UNPUBLISHED—			

Title	*Matrix*	Date *Recorded*	Victor *s/s*	*d/s*	HMV *s/s*	*d/s*
TOREADOR: (Adam)						
129 Ah! vous dirai-je maman	C–25552	9/8/21	74734	6131	2–033087	DB–262
TRAVIATA: (Verdi)						
130 Un di felice	B–30907	9/17/24		3038	7–54034	DA–711
131 Un di felice	BVE–30907	9/6/28		1754	40–2396	DA–1133
132 Ah fors'e lui	C–22613	3/7/19	74594	6126	2–053183	DB–257
133 Sempre libera	B–22614	3/7/19	64820	627	7–53047	DA–216
134 Dite alla giovine (with de Luca)	C–21974	6/11/18	89134	8025	2–054099	DB–174
135 Dite alla giovine (with de Luca)	CVE–41235	12/16/27		8089	2–054213	DB–1165
136 Imponete (with de Luca)	C–21976	6/11/18	89133	8025	2–054089	DB–174
137 Imponete (with de Luca)	CVE–41234	12/16/27		8089	2–054212	DB–1165
138 Addio del passato	B–24178	6/21/20	64945	627	7–53044	DA–216
139 Parigi o cara (with Schipa)	B–30908	9/17/24		3038	7–54035	DA–711
140 Parigi o cara (with Schipa)	BVE–30908	9/7/28		1754	40–2396	DA–1133
TROVATORE: (Verdi)						
141 Tacea la notte	C–28469	9/12/23			2–053234	DB–813
142 Tacea la notte	CVE–28469	12/29/25		7652		DB–1474
143 D'Amor sull' ali rosee	C–30297	9/16/24			2–053233	DB–813
144 D'Amor sull' ali rosee	CVE–30297	12/29/25		7652		DB–1474
145 Villanelle (dell'Acqua)	C–24175	6/21/20	74639	6131	2–033081	DB–262
146 When Chloris sleeps	B–23133	9/3/19	64929	630	2–3549	DA–218
147 Waldeinsamkeit (Reger)	BVE–63627	9/5/30	—UNPUBLISHED—			
ZEMIRE ET AZOR: (Gretry)						
148 La fauvette	CVE–40220	12/13/27		6784	2–033129	DB–1144

CODE:

     s/s single-sided disc
     d/s double-sided disc
       B Victor Acoustic 10″ disc
   BVE Victor Electric 10″ disc
       C Victor Acoustic 12″ disc
   CVE Victor Electric 12″ disc

LP Collections of Galli-Curci

RCA CAMDEN—CAL 410   The Art of Galli-Curci   Vol. I
   No.'s: 2, 72, 132, 133, 138, 111, 90, 53, 42, 21, 79, 9, 102

              CAL 525   The Art of Galli-Curci   Vol. II   Bellini/Donizetti
   No.'s: 123, 124, 125, 126, 96, 98, 58, 62, 65, 49, 24, 25

RCA VICTROLA—VIC 1518   Galli-Curci   Golden Age Coloratura
   No.'s: 129, 82, 4, 118, 97, 127, 71, 46, 32, 77, 93, 70

OPERATIC ARCHIVES—Limited Editions
   The Fabulous Amelita Galli-Curci
   OPA 1009—Vol. I
   No.'s: 8, 148, 32, 54, 87, 3, 19, 120, 88, 43, 14, 31, 79, 85, 57, 55, 42
   OPA 1025/26—Vol. II
   No.'s: 99, 100, 102, 104, 105, 110, 141, 143, 129, 82, 4, 118, 97, 127, 71, 46, 32, 93, 39, 22, 12, 18, 51, 76, 87, 38, 115, 92, 1
   OPA 1041/42—Vol. III
   No.'s: 130, 132, 133, 134, 136, 138, 139, 29, 5, 59, 26, 95, 78, 52, 50, 94, 16, 119, 145, 81, 30, 13, 89, 45, 80, 15, 74, 122, 27, 48, 113, 36, 10

Index

Index